ULTIMATE
FANTASTIC FOUR

CROSSOVER

writer: **MARK MILLAR**
pencils: **GREG LAND**
inks: **MATT RYAN**
colors: **JUSTIN PONSOR** WITH Laura Martin
letters: **CHRIS ELIOPOULOS**
assistant editor: **NICOLE BOOSE**
associate editor: **JOHN BARBER**
editor: **RALPH MACCHIO**

collection editor: **JENNIFER GRÜNWALD**
assistant editor: **MICHAEL SHORT**
senior editor, special projects: **JEFF YOUNGQUIST**
vice president of sales: **DAVID GABRIEL**
production: **JERRON QUALITY COLOR & LORETTA KROL**
creative director: **TOM MARVELLI**

editor in chief: **JOE QUESADA**
publisher: **DAN BUCKLEY**

Previously:

Reed Richards, handpicked to join the Baxter Building think tank of young geniuses, spent his youth developing a teleport system that transported solid matter into a parallel universe called the N-Zone. Its first full-scale test was witnessed by Reed, fellow think tank members Sue Storm, Sue's younger brother Johnny, and Reed's childhood friend Ben Grimm.

There was an accident. The quartet's genetic structures were scrambled and recombined in fantastically strange ways. Reed's body stretches and flows like water. Ben looks like a thing carved from desert rock. Sue can become invisible. Johnny generates flame. The team's existence recently became public knowledge.

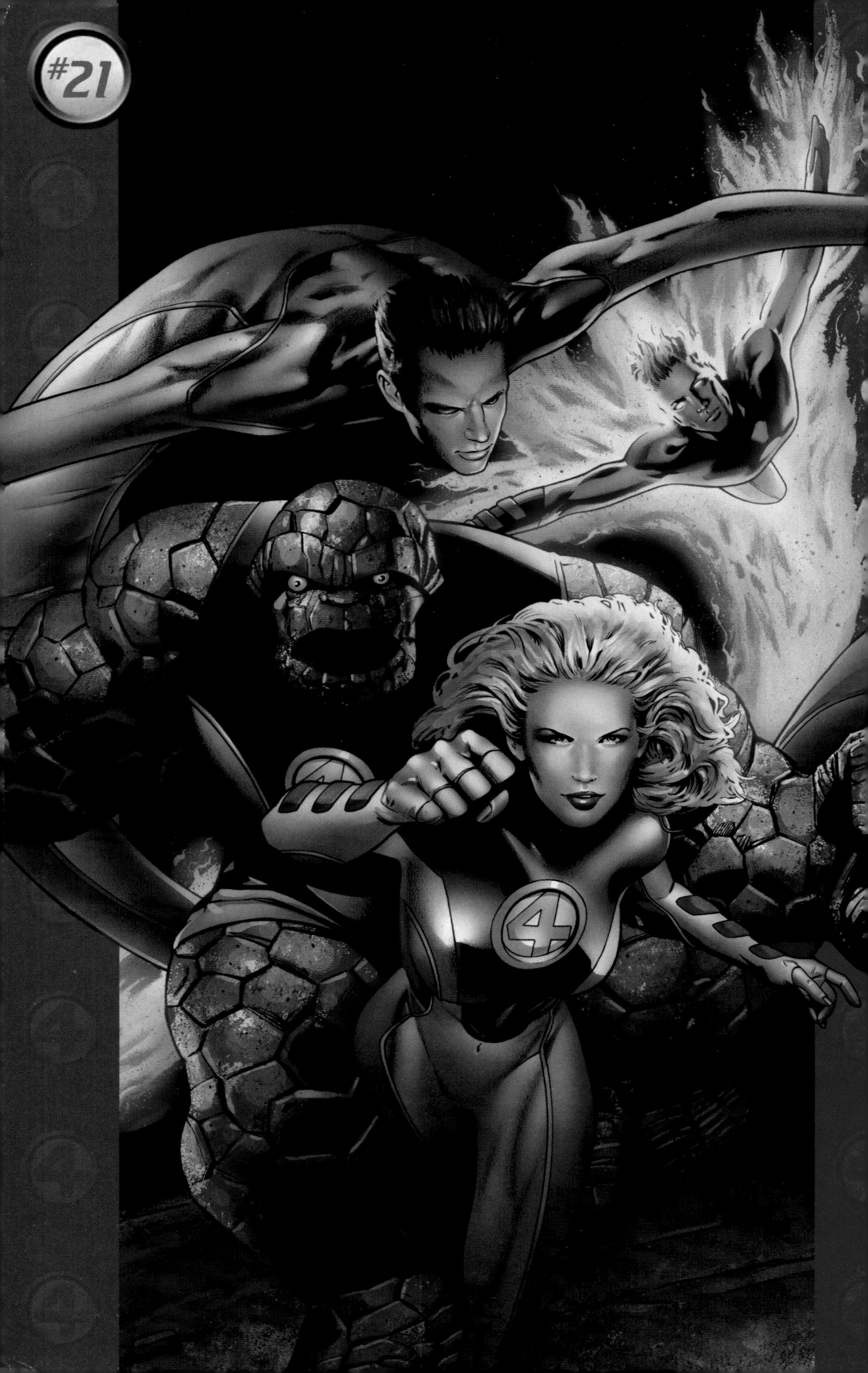
#21

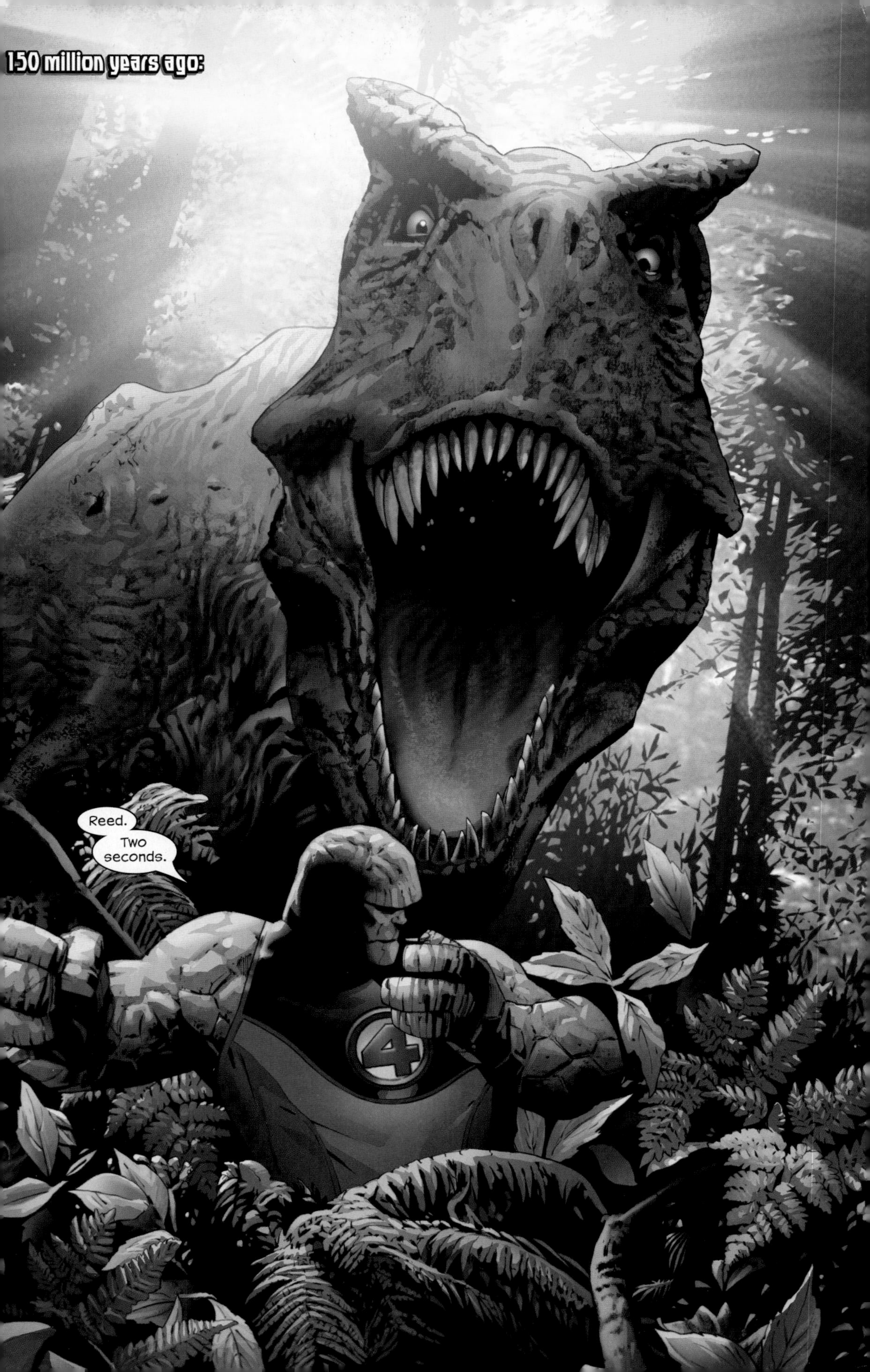
150 million years ago:
Reed.
Two seconds.

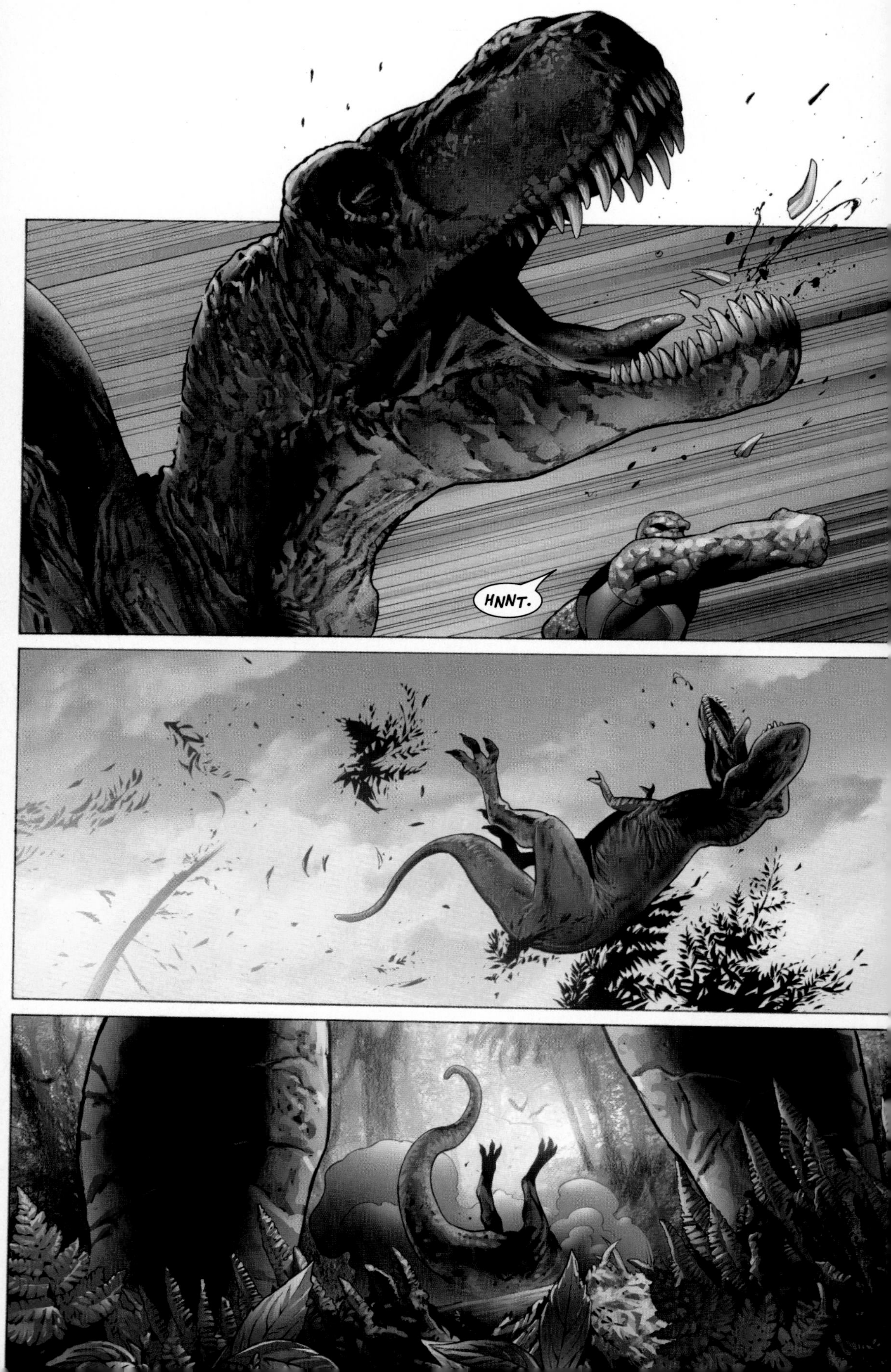
HNNT.

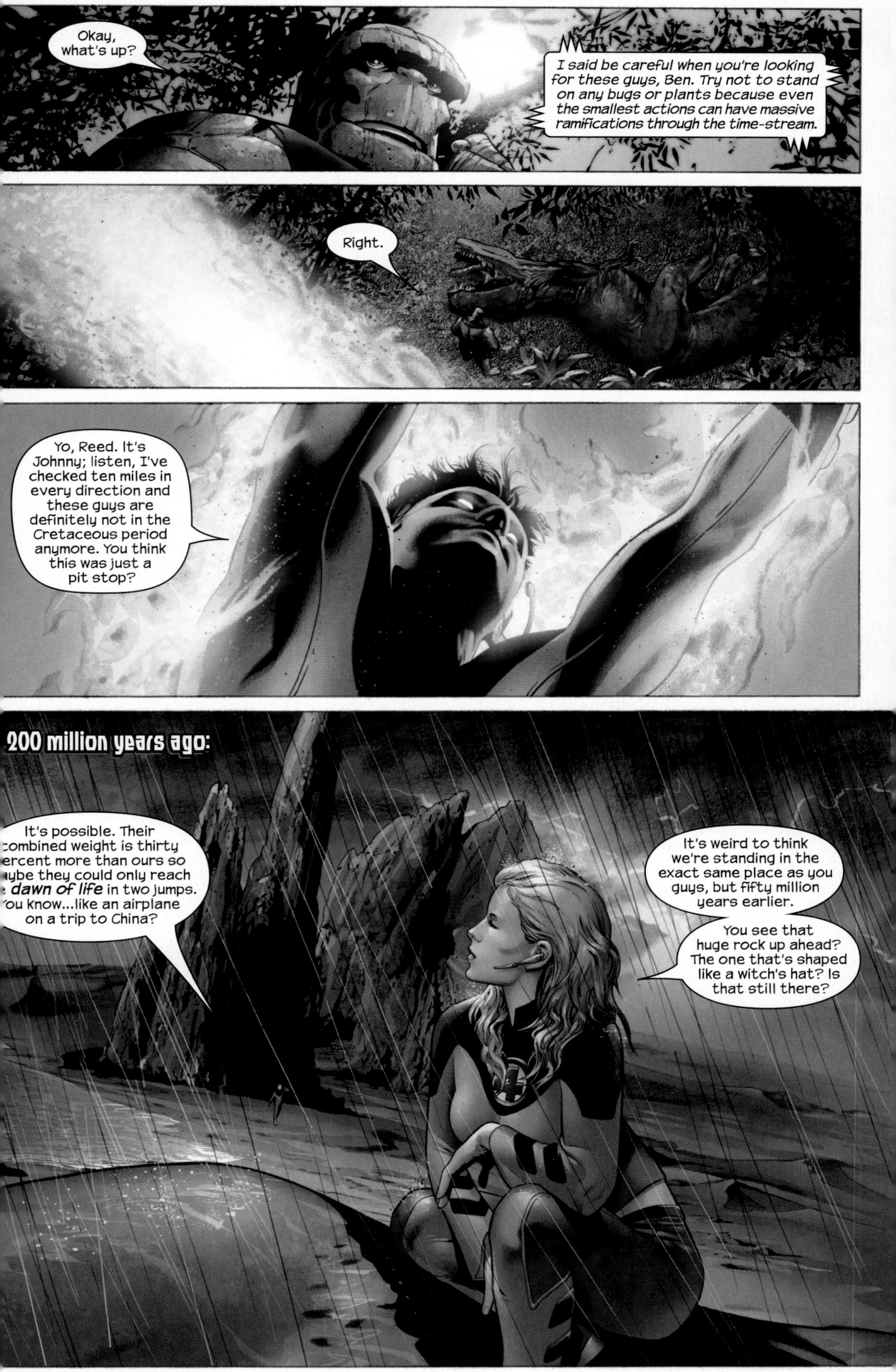
Okay, what's up?
I said be careful when you're looking for these guys, Ben. Try not to stand on any bugs or plants because even the smallest actions can have massive ramifications through the time-stream.
Right.
Yo, Reed. It's Johnny; listen, I've checked ten miles in every direction and these guys are definitely not in the Cretaceous period anymore. You think this was just a pit stop?
200 million years ago:
It's possible. Their combined weight is thirty ercent more than ours so aybe they could only reach dawn of life in two jumps. ou know...like an airplane on a trip to China?
It's weird to think we're standing in the exact same place as you guys, but fifty million years earlier.
You see that huge rock up ahead? The one that's shaped like a witch's hat? Is that still there?

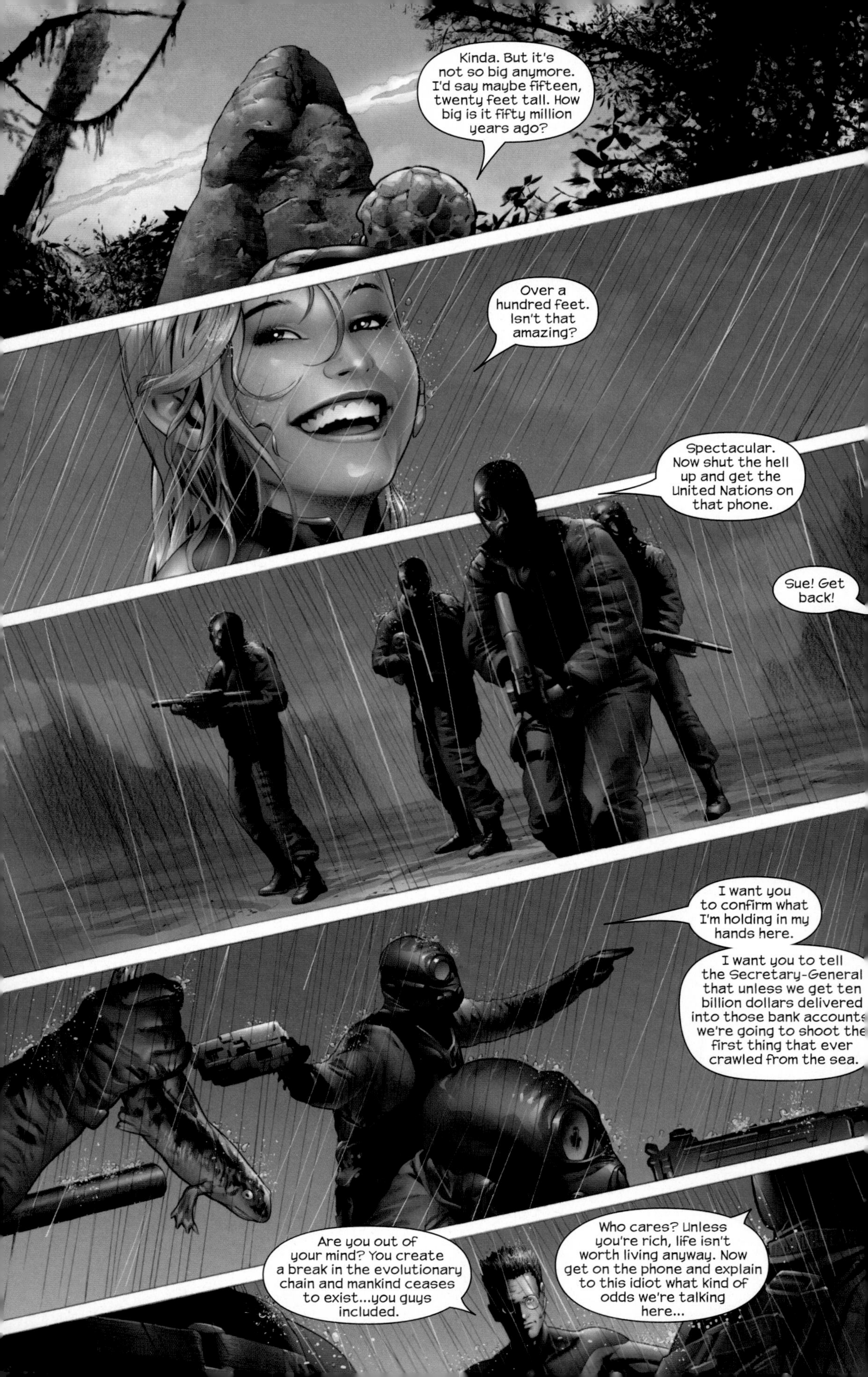
Kinda. But it's not so big anymore. I'd say maybe fifteen, twenty feet tall. How big is it fifty million years ago?
Over a hundred feet. Isn't that amazing?
Spectacular. Now shut the hell up and get the United Nations on that phone.
Sue! Get back!
I want you to confirm what I'm holding in my hands here.
I want you to tell the Secretary-General that unless we get ten billion dollars delivered into those bank accounts we're going to shoot the first thing that ever crawled from the sea.
Are you out of your mind? You create a break in the evolutionary chain and mankind ceases to exist...you guys included.
Who cares? Unless you're rich, life isn't worth living anyway. Now get on the phone and explain to this idiot what kind of odds we're talking here...

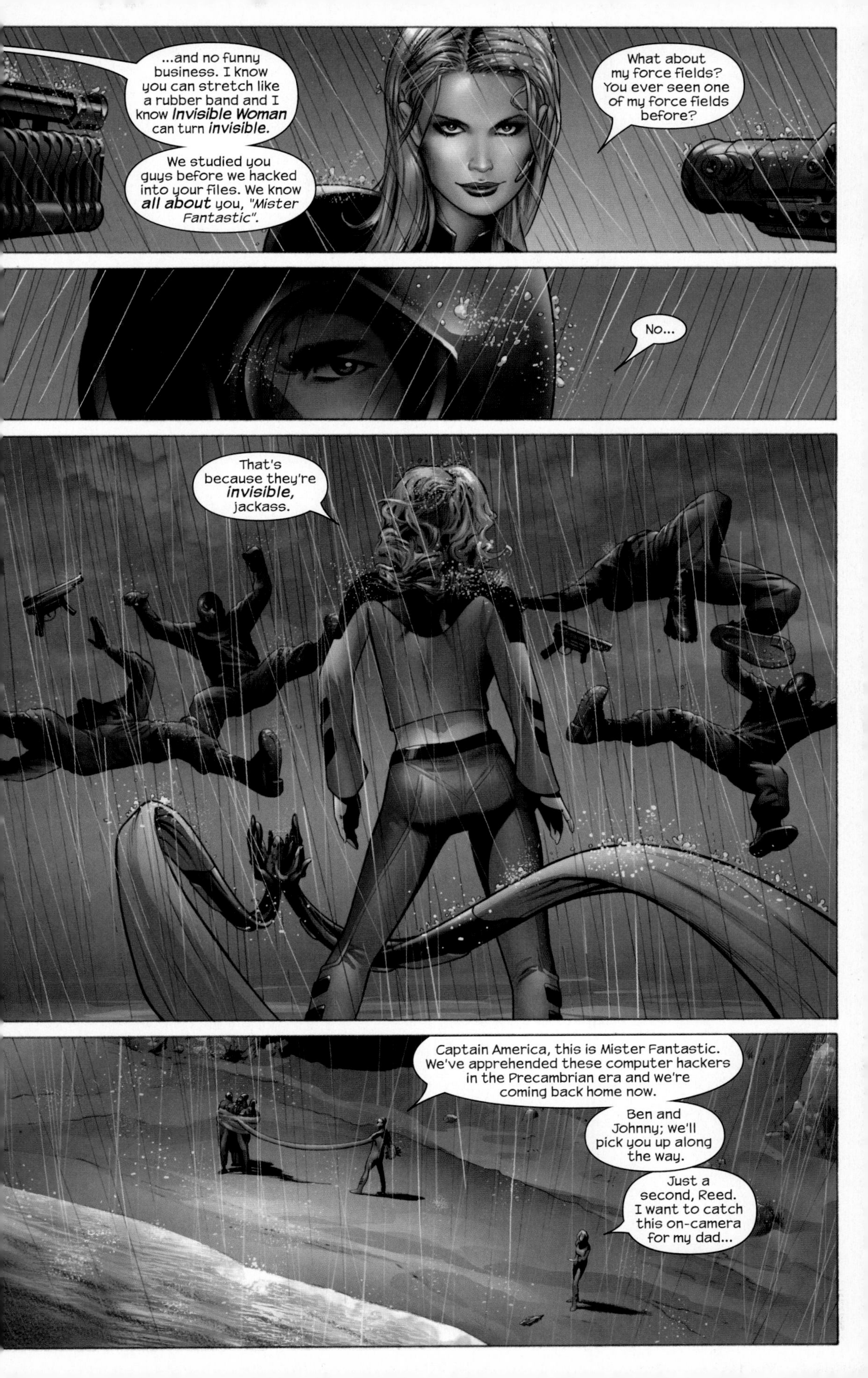

...and no funny business. I know you can stretch like a rubber band and I know *Invisible Woman* can turn *invisible.*
We studied you guys before we hacked into your files. We know ***all about*** you, "Mister Fantastic".
What about my force fields? You ever seen one of my force fields before?
No...
That's because they're *invisible,* jackass.
Captain America, this is Mister Fantastic. We've apprehended these computer hackers in the Precambrian era and we're coming back home now.
Ben and Johnny; we'll pick you up along the way.
Just a second, Reed. I want to catch this on-camera for my dad...

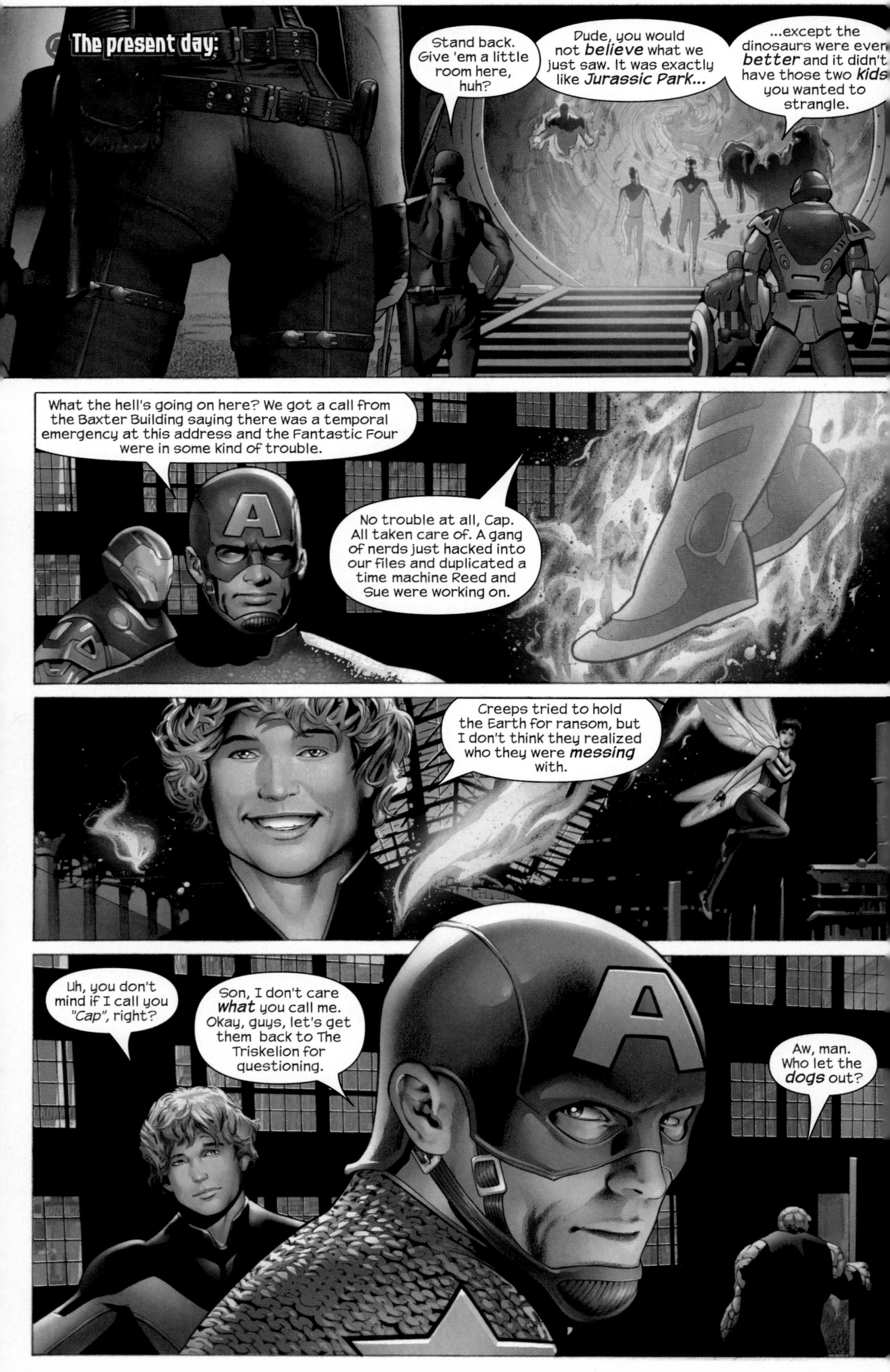
The present day:
Stand back. Give 'em a little room here, huh?
Dude, you would not *believe* what we just saw. It was exactly like *Jurassic Park...*
...except the dinosaurs were even *better* and it didn't have those two *kids* you wanted to strangle.
What the hell's going on here? We got a call from the Baxter Building saying there was a temporal emergency at this address and the Fantastic Four were in some kind of trouble.
No trouble at all, Cap. All taken care of. A gang of nerds just hacked into our files and duplicated a time machine Reed and Sue were working on.
Creeps tried to hold the Earth for ransom, but I don't think they realized who they were *messing* with.
Uh, you don't mind if I call you *"Cap"*, right?
Son, I don't care *what* you call me. Okay, guys, let's get them back to The Triskelion for questioning.
Aw, man. Who let the *dogs* out?

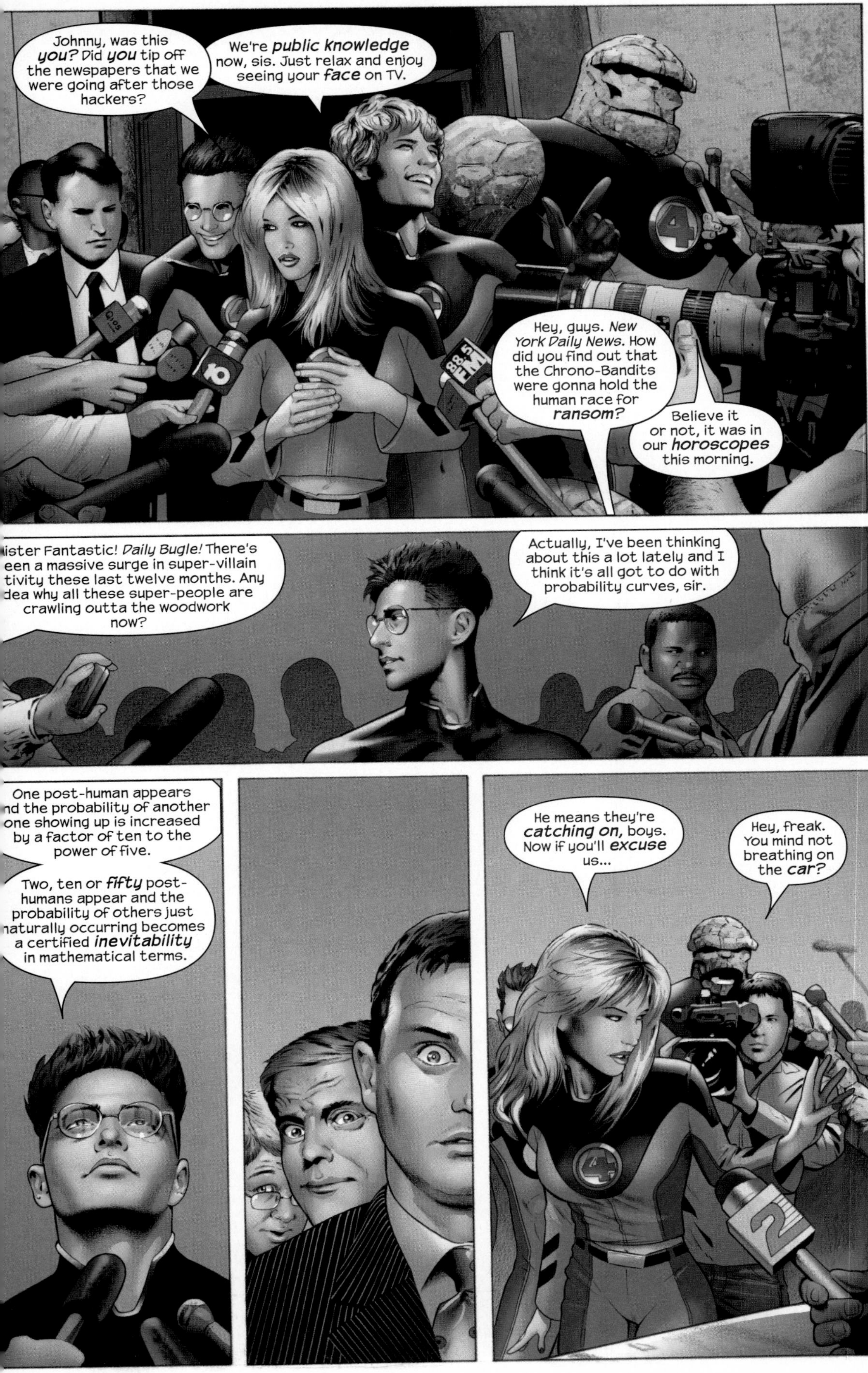
Johnny, was this *you?* Did *you* tip off the newspapers that we were going after those hackers?
We're *public knowledge* now, sis. Just relax and enjoy seeing your *face* on TV.
Hey, guys. *New York Daily News.* How did you find out that the Chrono-Bandits were gonna hold the human race for *ransom?*
Believe it or not, it was in our *horoscopes* this morning.
ister Fantastic! *Daily Bugle!* There's een a massive surge in super-villain tivity these last twelve months. Any dea why all these super-people are crawling outta the woodwork now?
Actually, I've been thinking about this a lot lately and I think it's all got to do with probability curves, sir.
One post-human appears nd the probability of another one showing up is increased by a factor of ten to the power of five.
Two, ten or *fifty* post-humans appear and the probability of others just naturally occurring becomes a certified *inevitability* in mathematical terms.
He means they're *catching on,* boys. Now if you'll *excuse* us...
Hey, freak. You mind not breathing on the *car?*

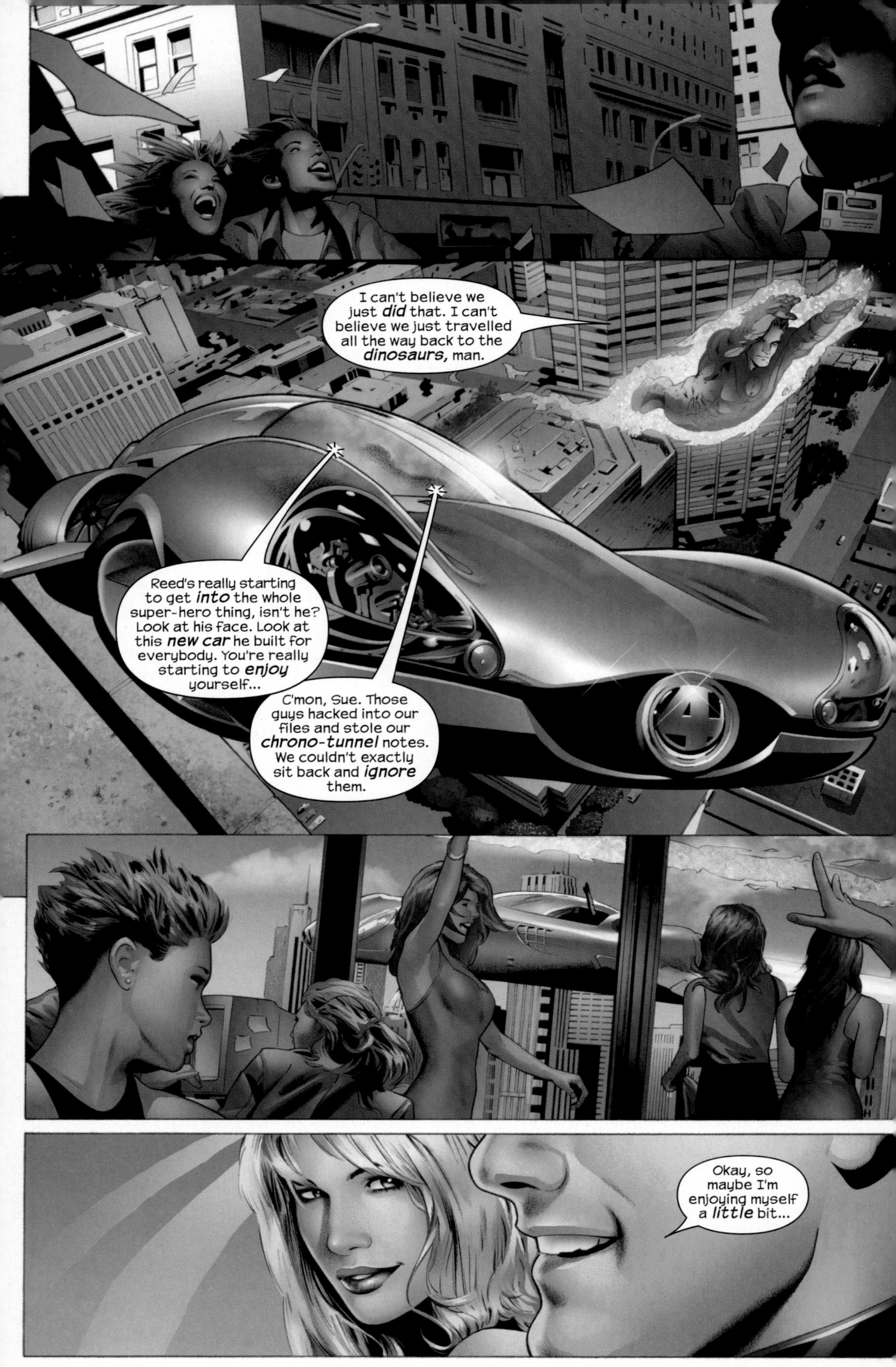
I can't believe we just *did* that. I can't believe we just travelled all the way back to the *dinosaurs,* man.
Reed's really starting to get *into* the whole super-hero thing, isn't he? Look at his face. Look at this *new car* he built for everybody. You're really starting to *enjoy* yourself...
C'mon, Sue. Those guys hacked into our files and stole our *chrono-tunnel* notes. We couldn't exactly sit back and *ignore* them.
Okay, so maybe I'm enjoying myself a *little* bit...

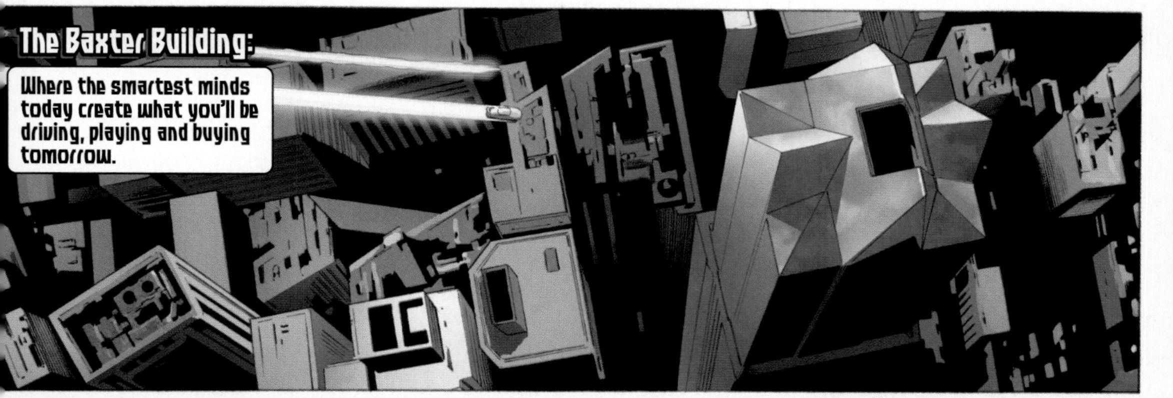
The Baxter Building:
Where the smartest minds today create what you'll be driving, playing and buying tomorrow.

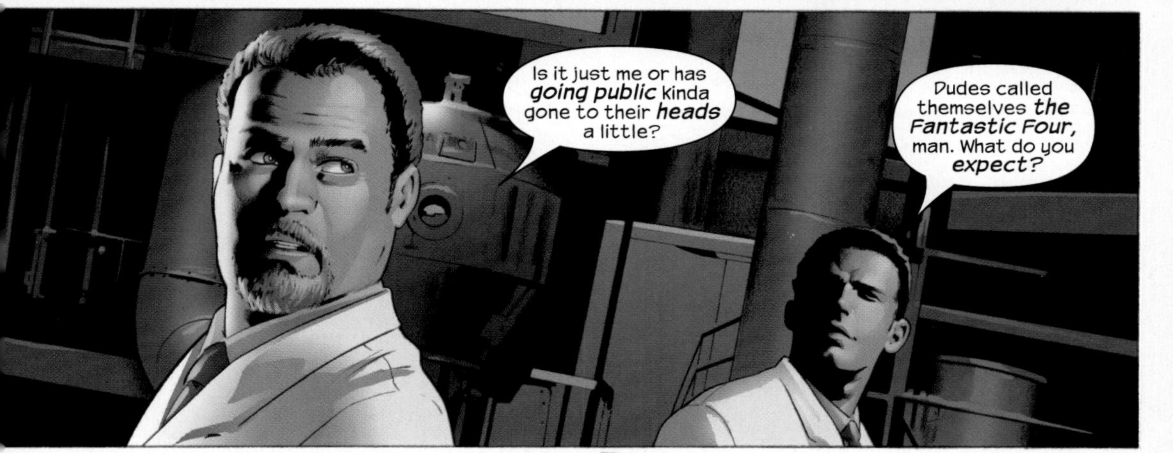
Is it just me or has going public kinda gone to their heads a little?
Dudes called themselves the Fantastic Four, man. What do you expect?

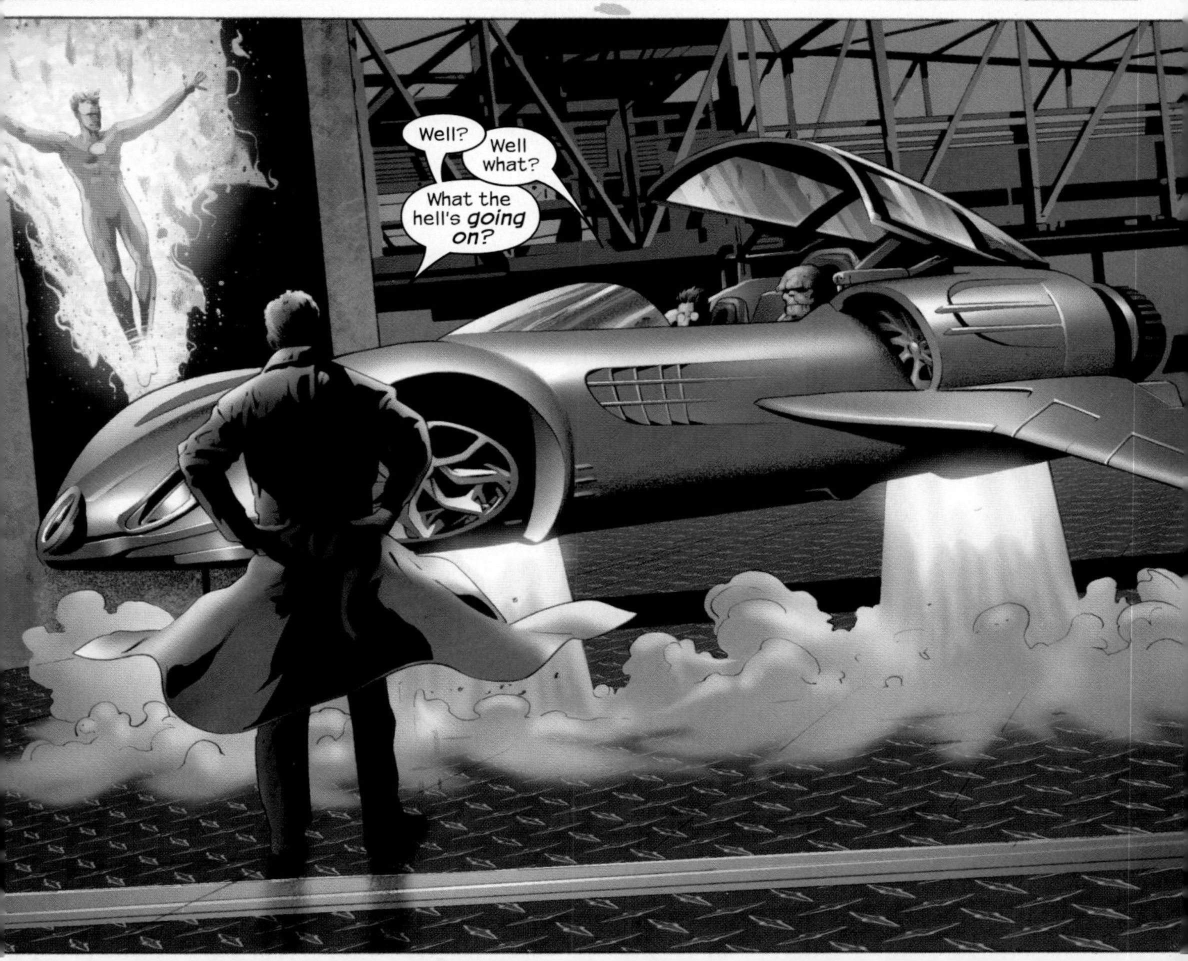
Well?
Well what?
What the hell's going on?

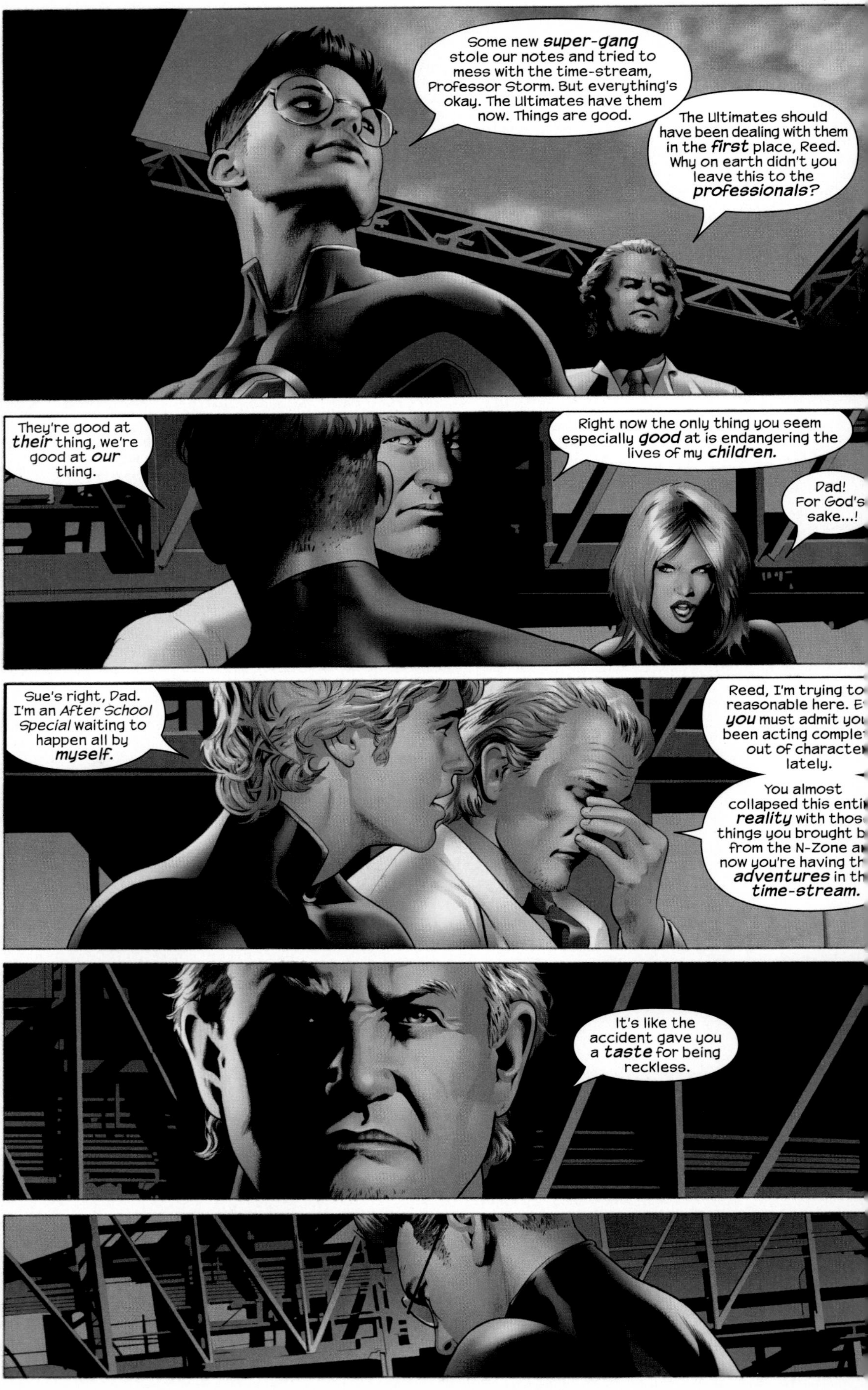
Some new *super-gang* stole our notes and tried to mess with the time-stream, Professor Storm. But everything's okay. The Ultimates have them now. Things are good.
The Ultimates should have been dealing with them in the *first* place, Reed. Why on earth didn't you leave this to the *professionals*?
They're good at *their* thing, we're good at *our* thing.
Right now the only thing you seem especially *good* at is endangering the lives of my *children*.
Dad! For God's sake...!
Sue's right, Dad. I'm an *After School Special* waiting to happen all by *myself*.
Reed, I'm trying to reasonable here. E *you* must admit you been acting complet out of characte lately.
You almost collapsed this enti *reality* with thos things you brought b from the N-Zone a now you're having th *adventures* in th *time-stream*.
It's like the accident gave you a *taste* for being reckless.

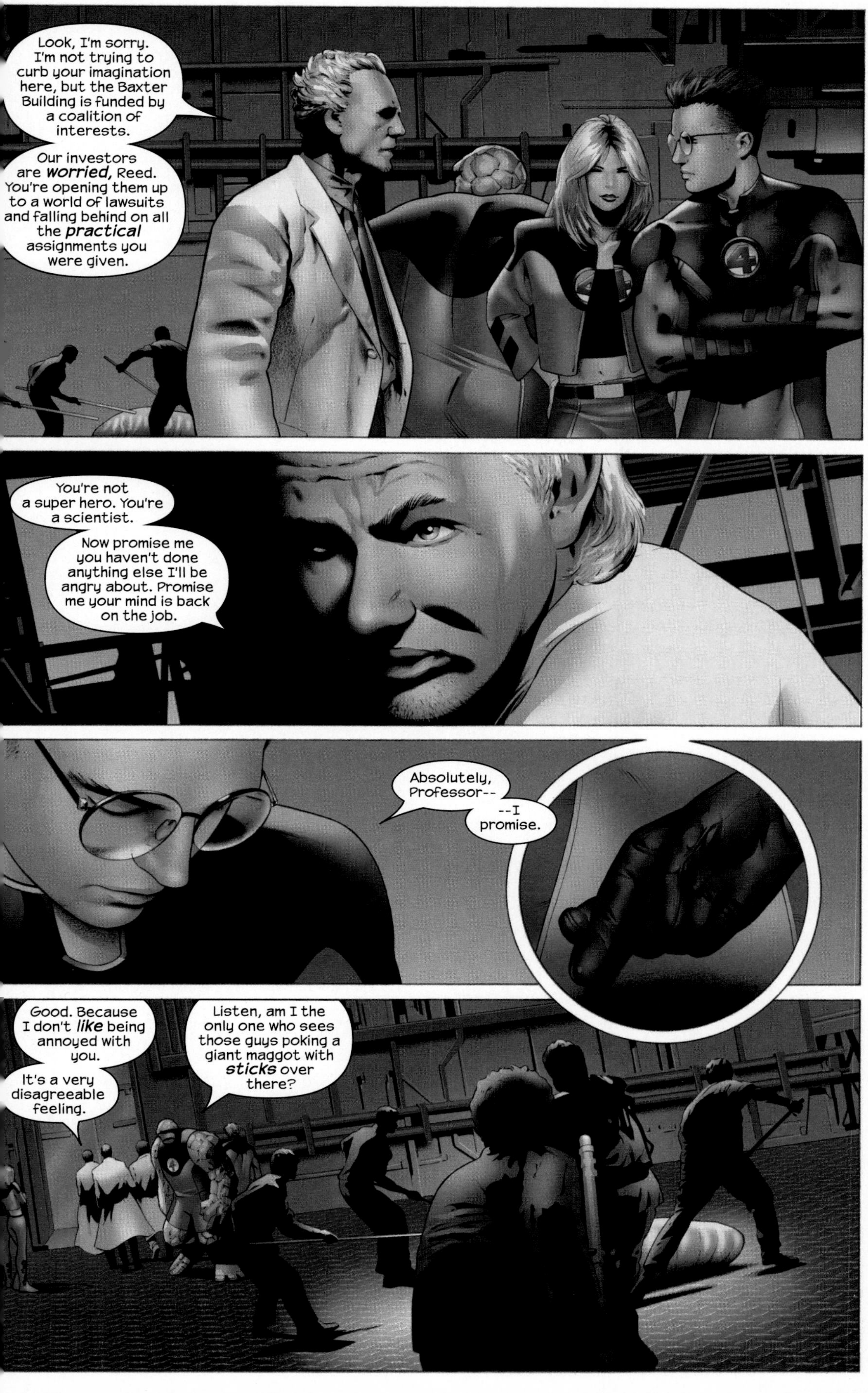
Look, I'm sorry. I'm not trying to curb your imagination here, but the Baxter Building is funded by a coalition of interests.
Our investors are *worried,* Reed. You're opening them up to a world of lawsuits and falling behind on all the *practical* assignments you were given.
You're not a super hero. You're a scientist.
Now promise me you haven't done anything else I'll be angry about. Promise me your mind is back on the job.
Absolutely, Professor--
--I promise.
Good. Because I don't *like* being annoyed with you.
It's a very disagreeable feeling.
Listen, am I the only one who sees those guys poking a giant maggot with *sticks* over there?

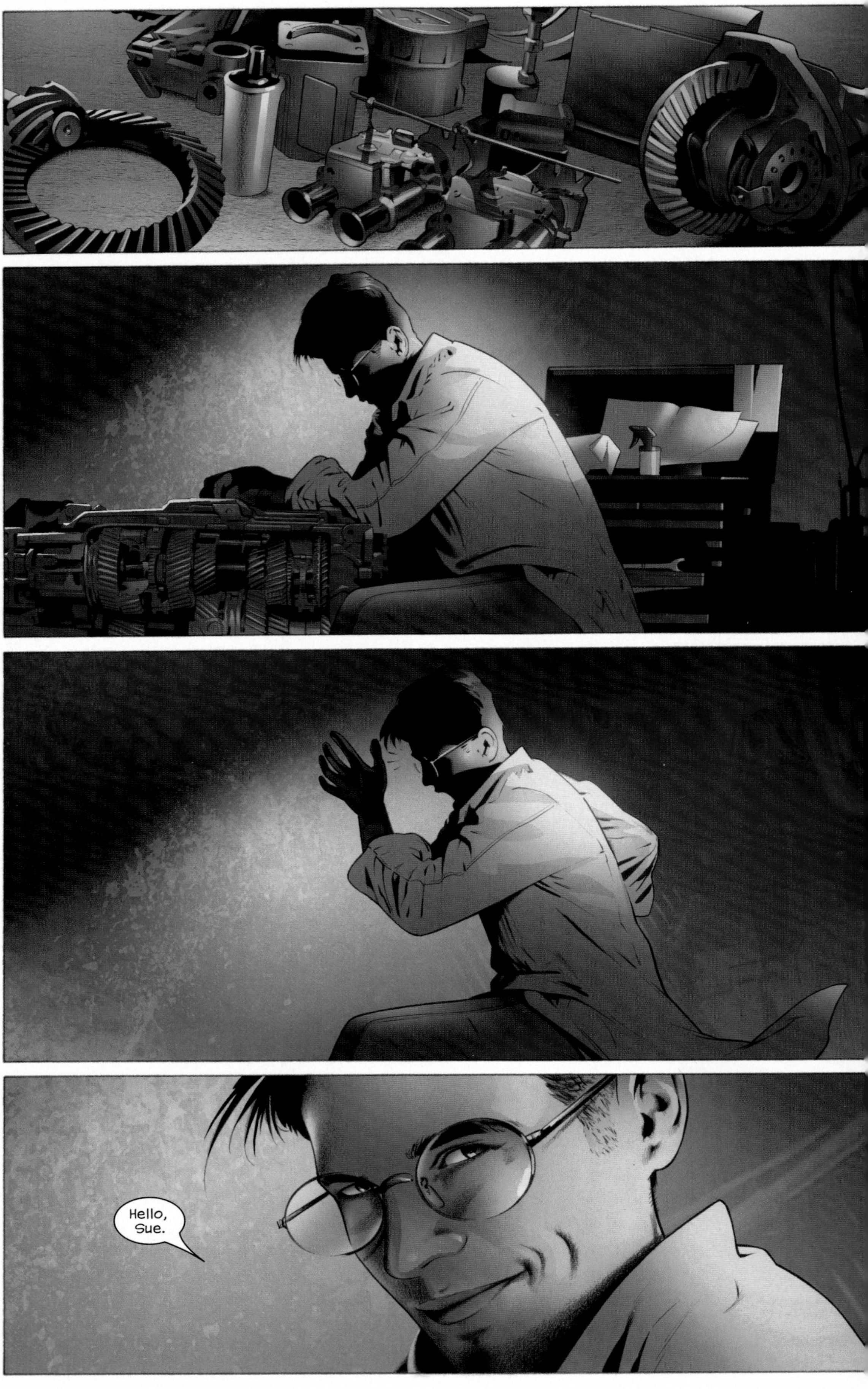
Hello, Sue.

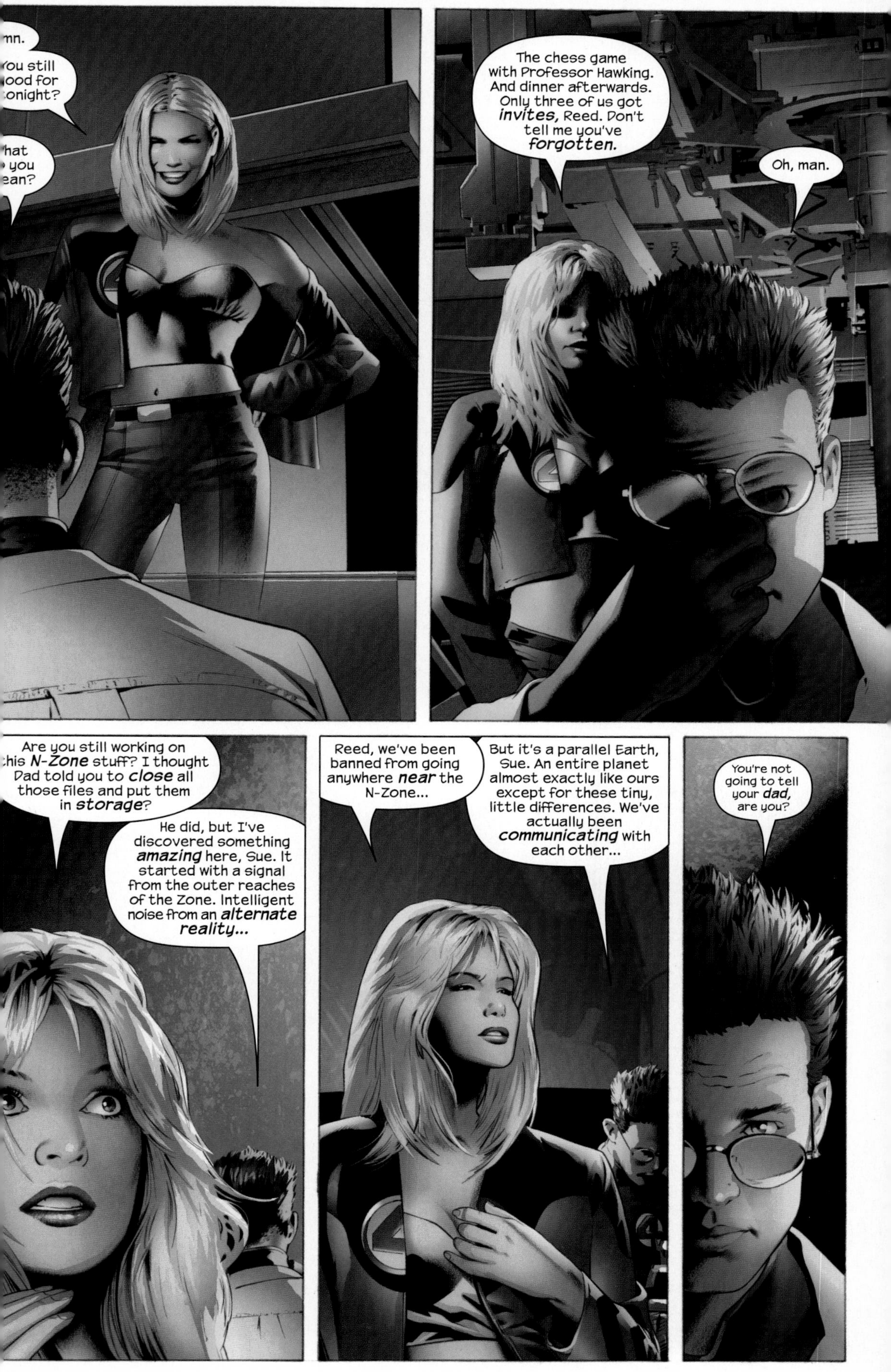
mn.
You still
good for
tonight?
hat
you
ean?
The chess game with Professor Hawking. And dinner afterwards. Only three of us got *invites*, Reed. Don't tell me you've *forgotten.*
Oh, man.
Are you still working on this *N-Zone* stuff? I thought Dad told you to *close* all those files and put them in *storage*?
He did, but I've discovered something *amazing* here, Sue. It started with a signal from the outer reaches of the Zone. Intelligent noise from an *alternate reality...*
Reed, we've been banned from going anywhere *near* the N-Zone...
But it's a parallel Earth, Sue. An entire planet almost exactly like ours except for these tiny, little differences. We've actually been *communicating* with each other...
You're not going to tell your *dad,* are you?

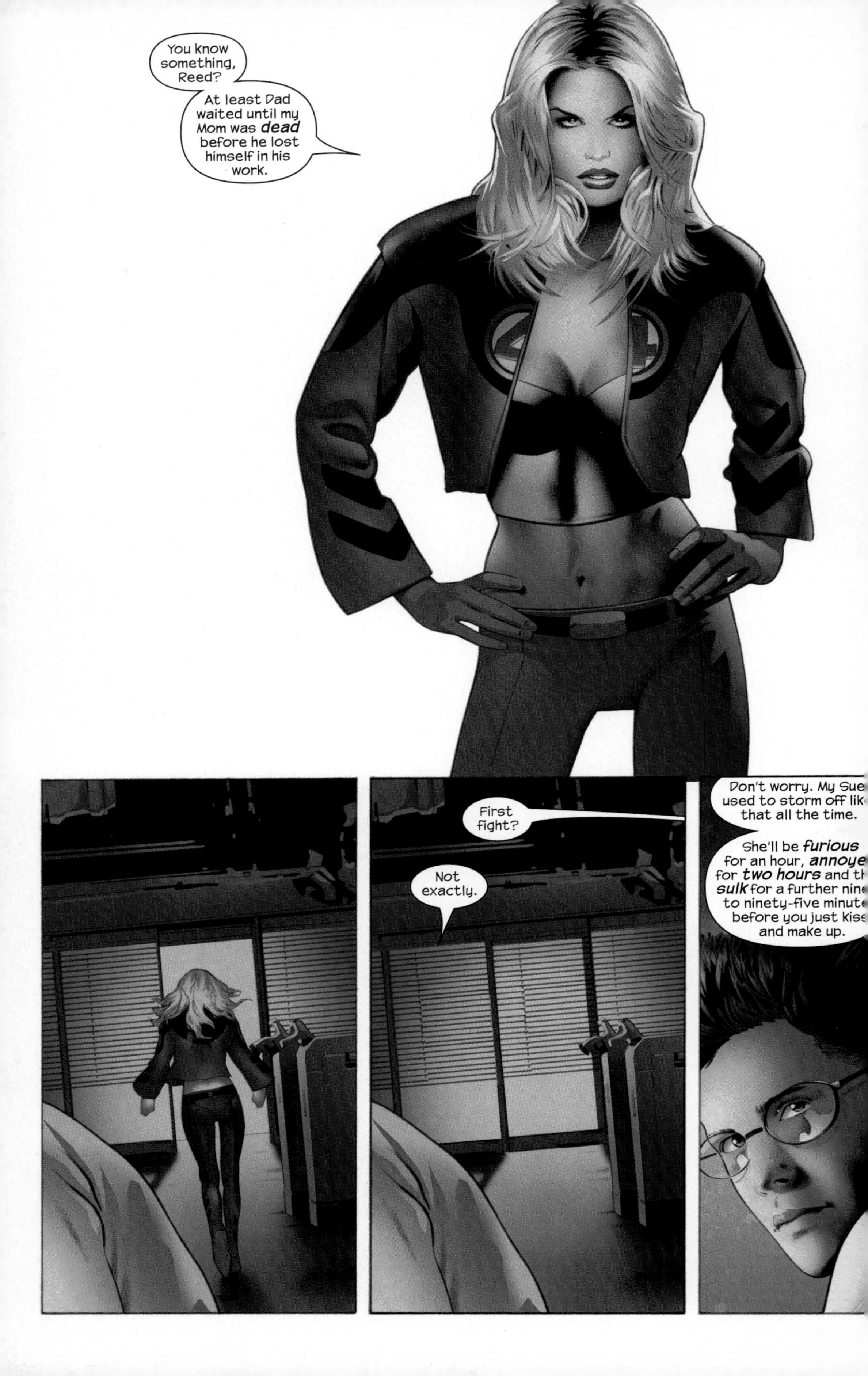

You know something, Reed?
At least Dad waited until my Mom was *dead* before he lost himself in his work.
First fight?
Not exactly.
Don't worry. My Sue used to storm off lik
that all the time.
She'll be *furious* for an hour, *annoye* for *two hours* and th *sulk* for a further nine to ninety-five minut before you just kiss and make up.

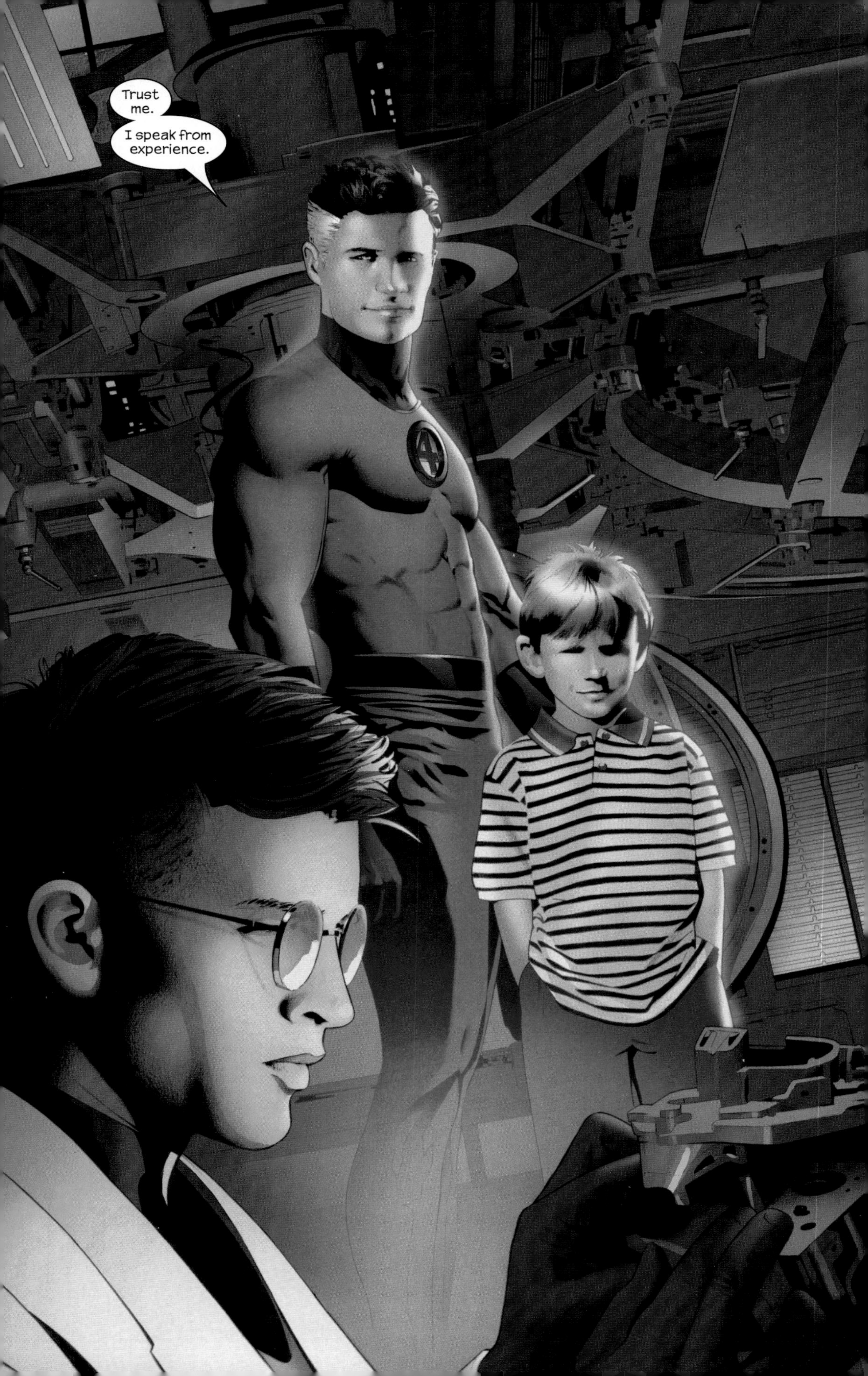
Trust me.
I speak from experience.

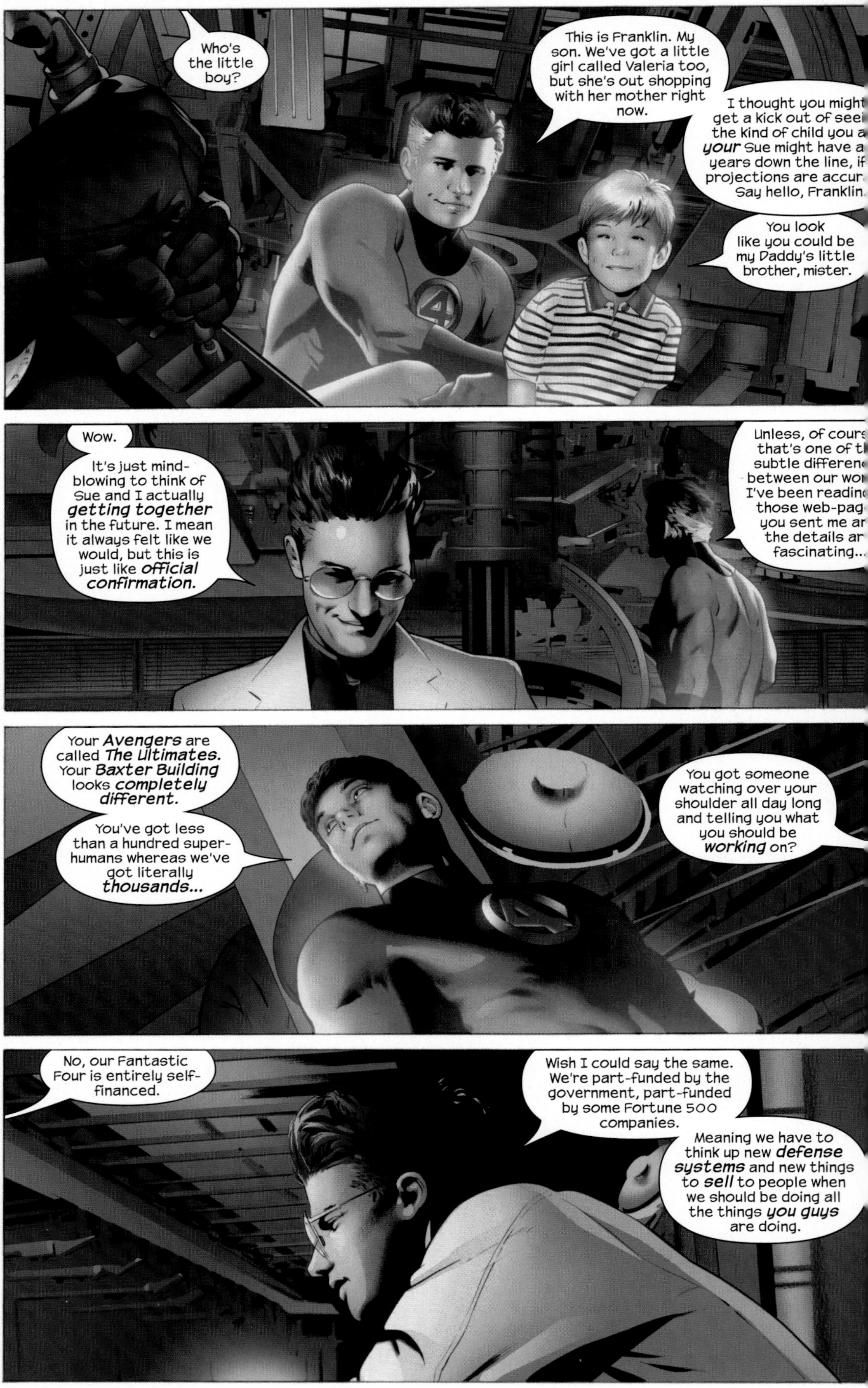

Who's the little boy?
This is Franklin. My son. We've got a little girl called Valeria too, but she's out shopping with her mother right now.
I thought you might get a kick out of seei the kind of child you a *your* Sue might have a years down the line, if projections are accur. Say hello, Franklin.
You look like you could be my Daddy's little brother, mister.
Wow.
It's just mind-blowing to think of Sue and I actually *getting together* in the future. I mean it always felt like we would, but this is just like *official confirmation.*
Unless, of cours that's one of t subtle differen between our wo I've been readin those web-pag you sent me a the details a fascinating...
Your *Avengers* are called *The Ultimates.* Your *Baxter Building* looks *completely different.*
You've got less than a hundred super-humans whereas we've got literally *thousands...*
You got someone watching over your shoulder all day long and telling you what you should be *working* on?
No, our Fantastic Four is entirely self-financed.
Wish I could say the same. We're part-funded by the government, part-funded by some Fortune 500 companies.
Meaning we have to think up new *defense systems* and new things to *sell* to people when we should be doing all the things *you guys* are doing.

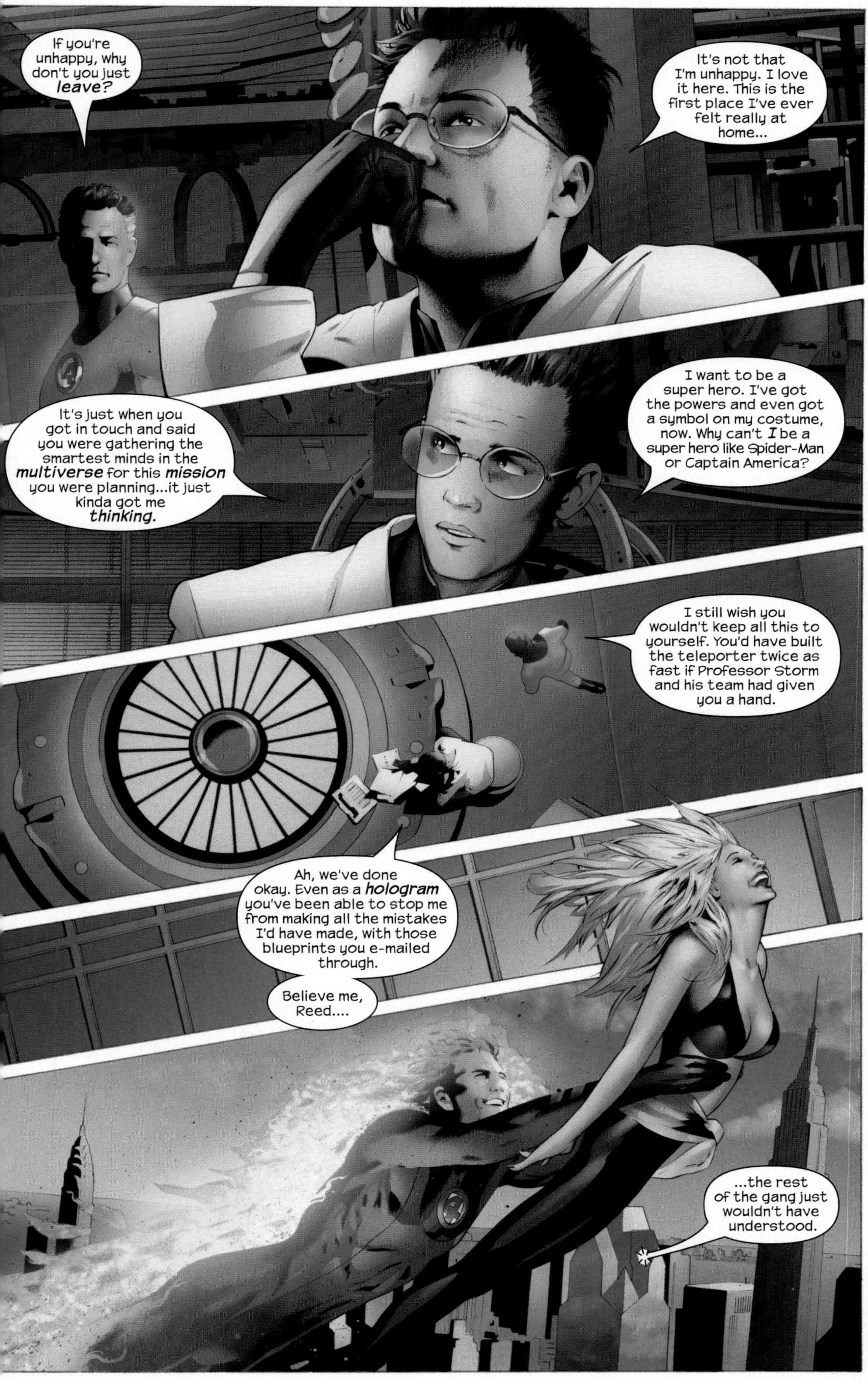
If you're unhappy, why don't you just leave?
It's not that I'm unhappy. I love it here. This is the first place I've ever felt really at home...
It's just when you got in touch and said you were gathering the smartest minds in the multiverse for this mission you were planning...it just kinda got me thinking.
I want to be a super hero. I've got the powers and even got a symbol on my costume, now. Why can't I be a super hero like Spider-Man or Captain America?
I still wish you wouldn't keep all this to yourself. You'd have built the teleporter twice as fast if Professor Storm and his team had given you a hand.
Ah, we've done okay. Even as a hologram you've been able to stop me from making all the mistakes I'd have made, with those blueprints you e-mailed through.
Believe me, Reed....
...the rest of the gang just wouldn't have understood.

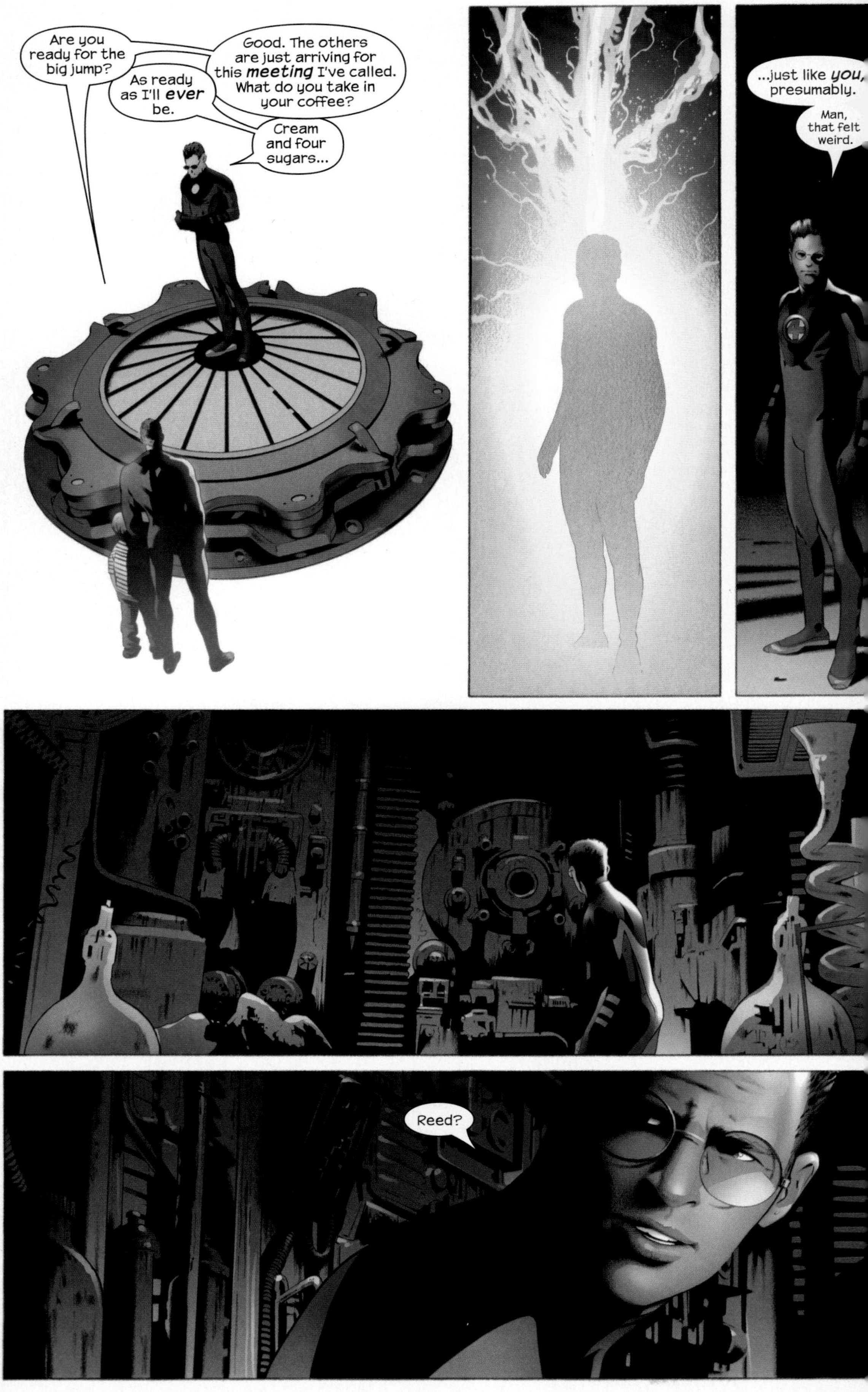

Are you ready for the big jump?
Good. The others are just arriving for this *meeting* I've called. What do you take in your coffee?
As ready as I'll *ever* be.
Cream and four sugars...
...just like *you*, presumably.
Man, that felt weird.
Reed?

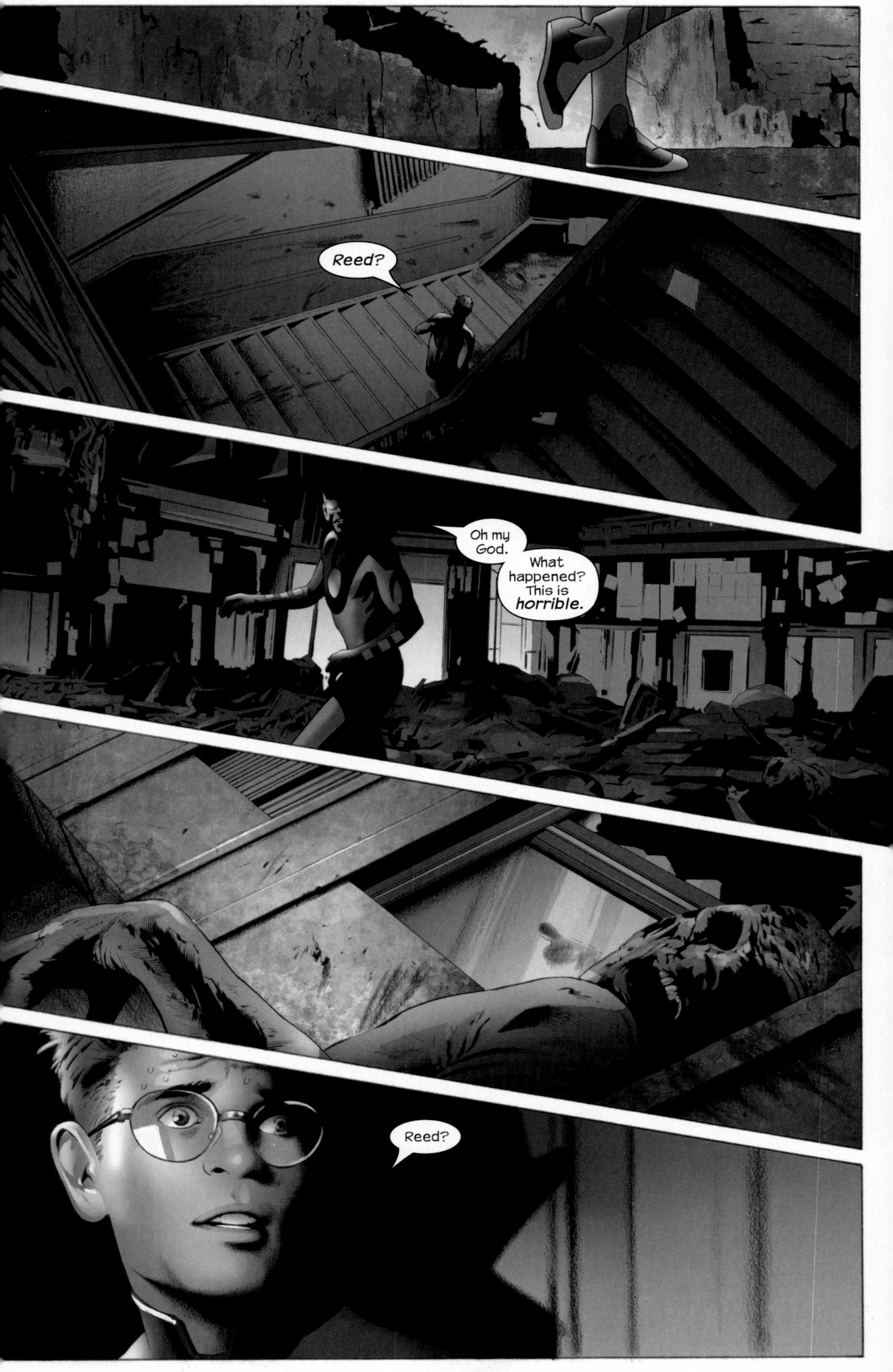
Reed?
Oh my God.
What happened? This is *horrible.*
Reed?

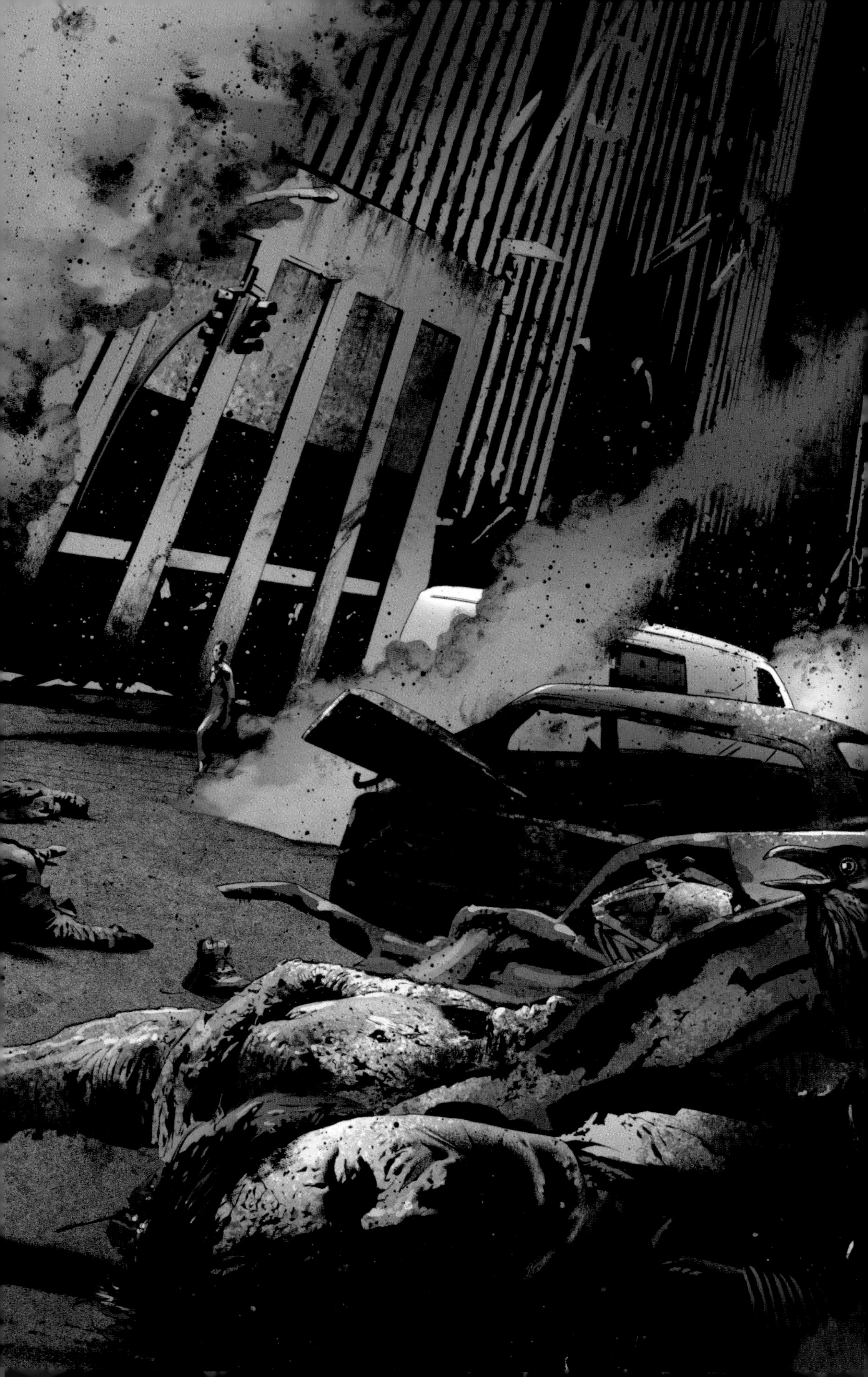

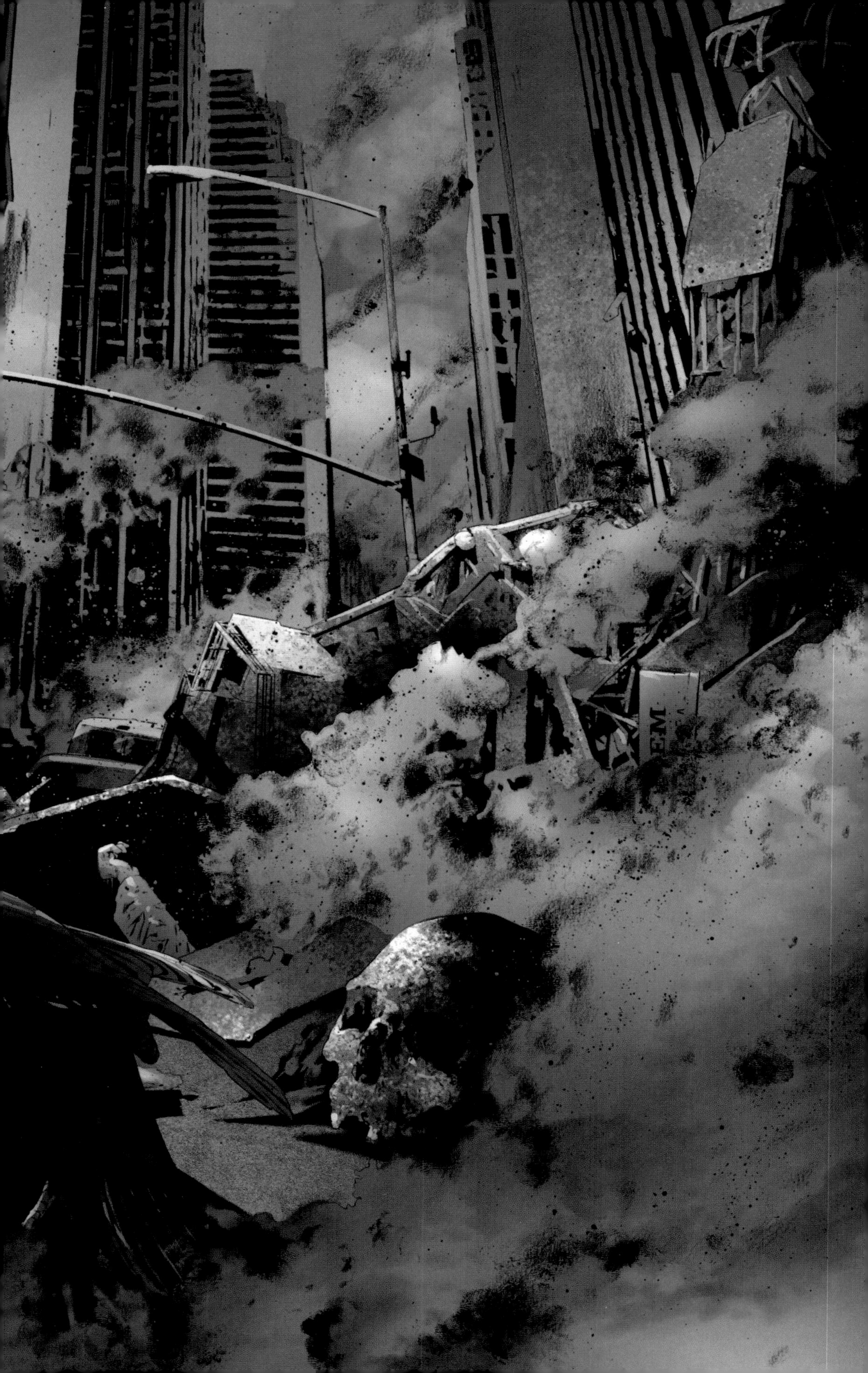

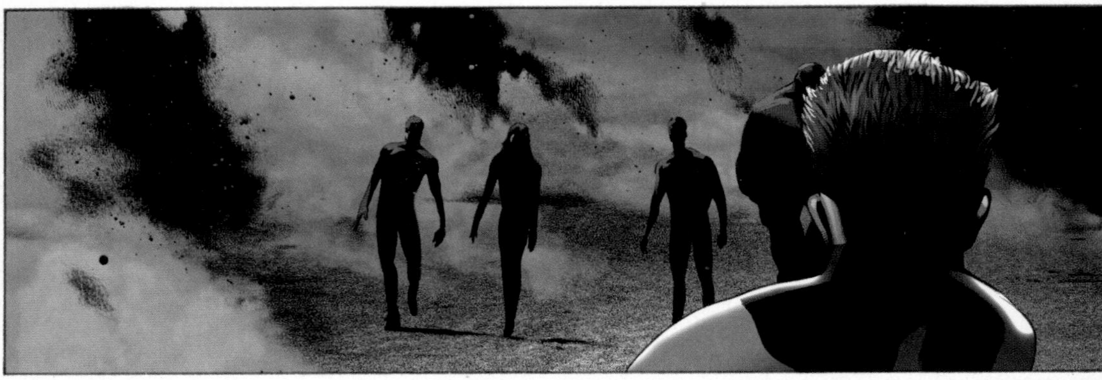

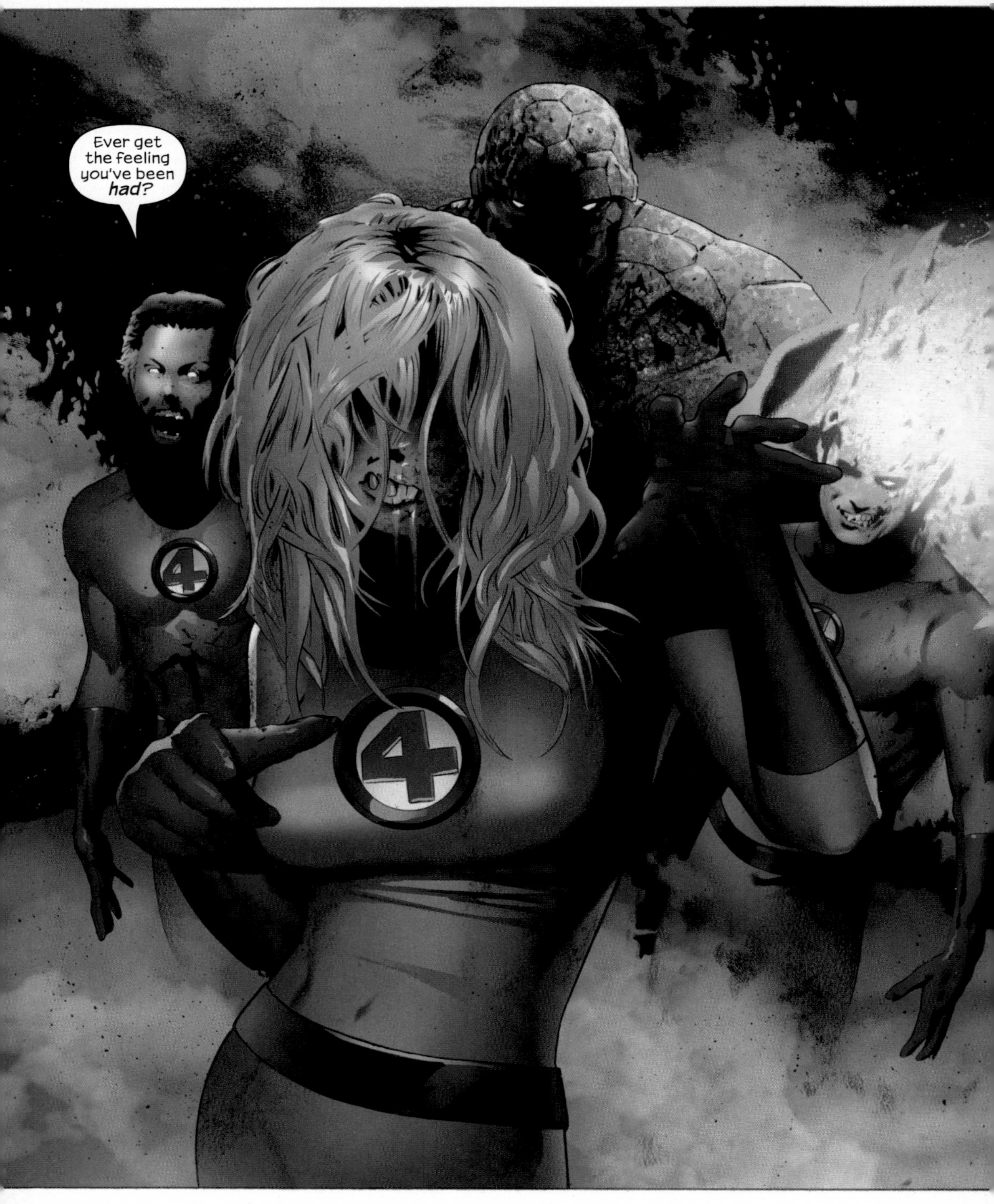
Ever get the feeling you've been *had*?

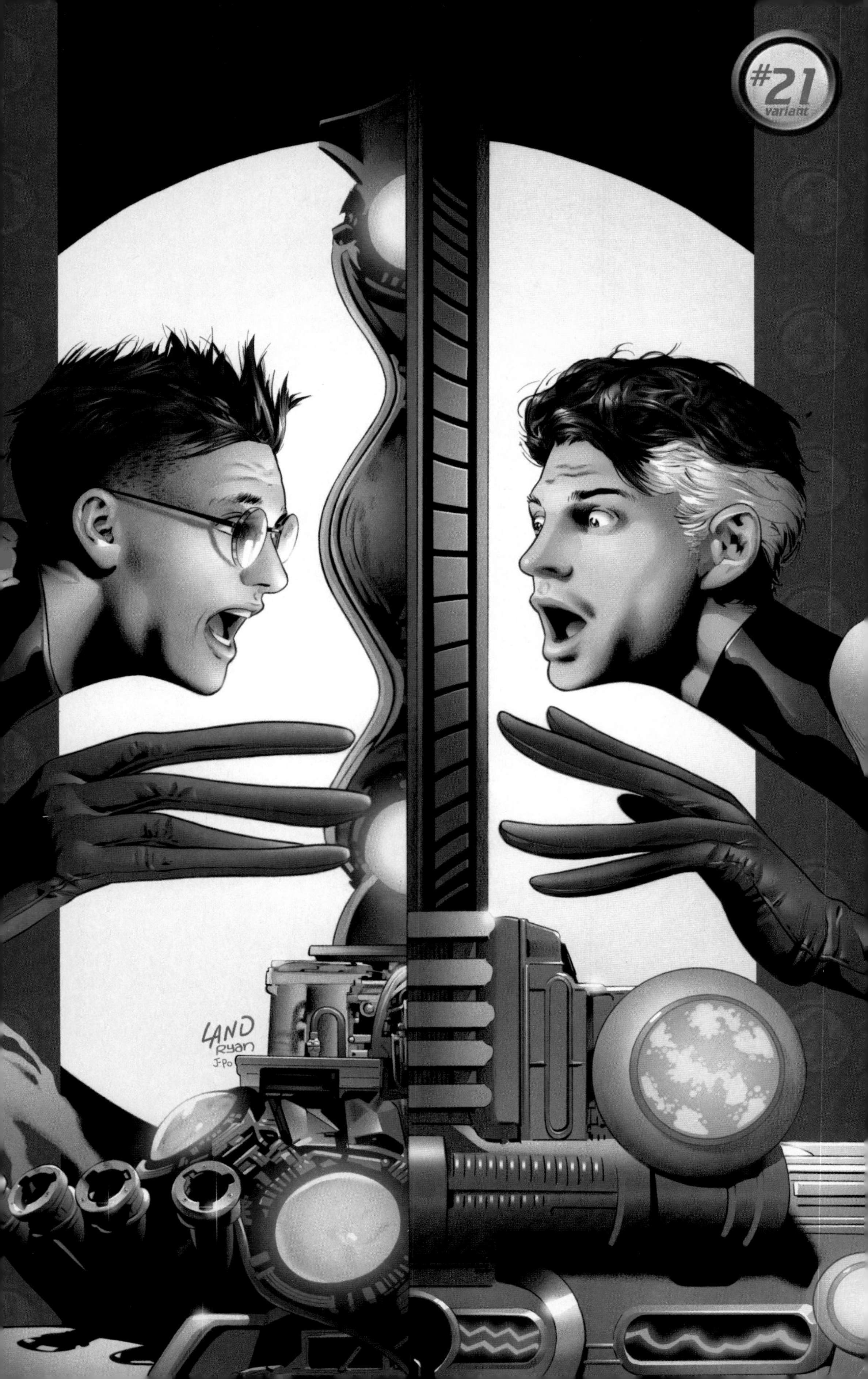
#21
variant
LAND
Ryan
J-Po

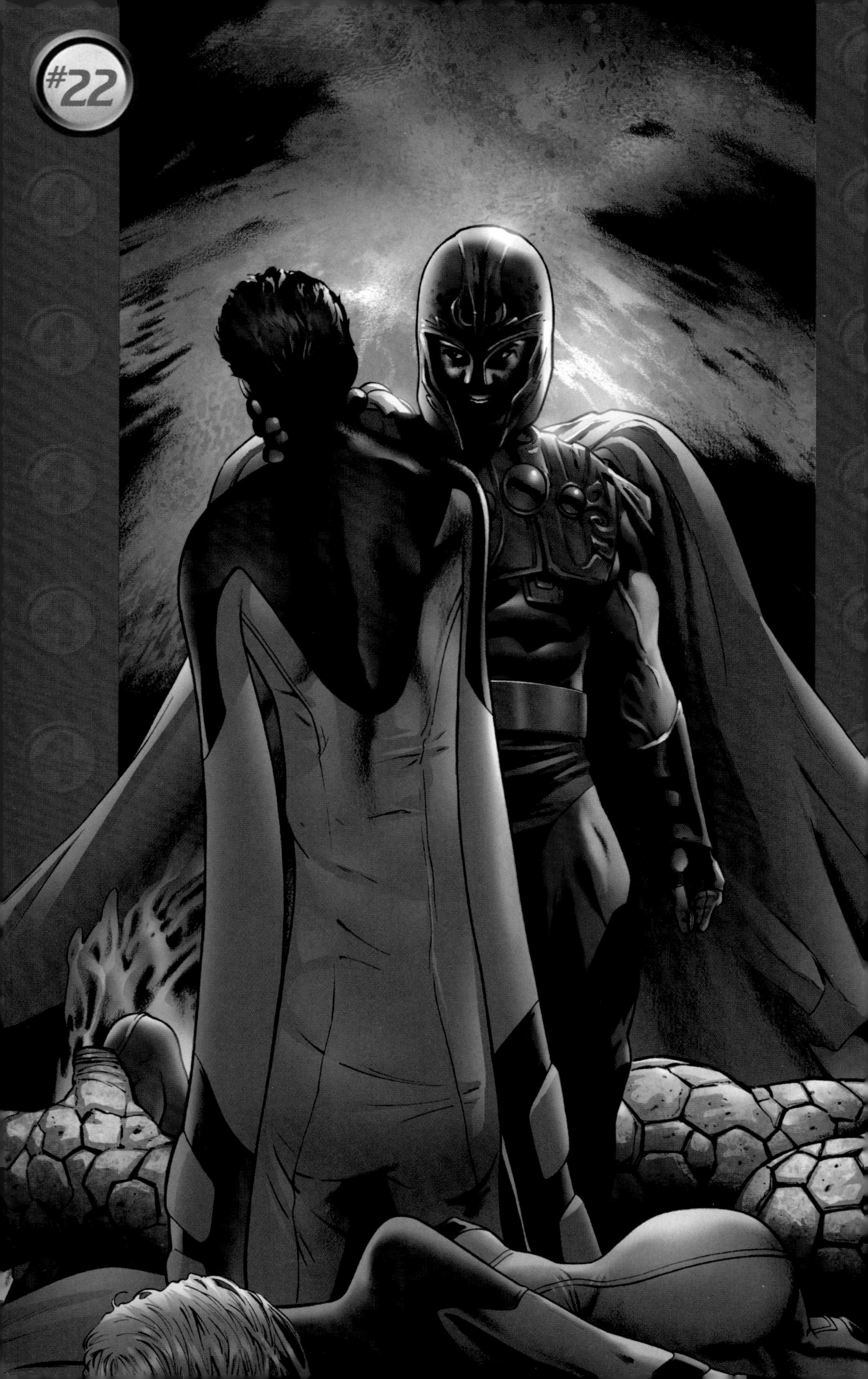
#22

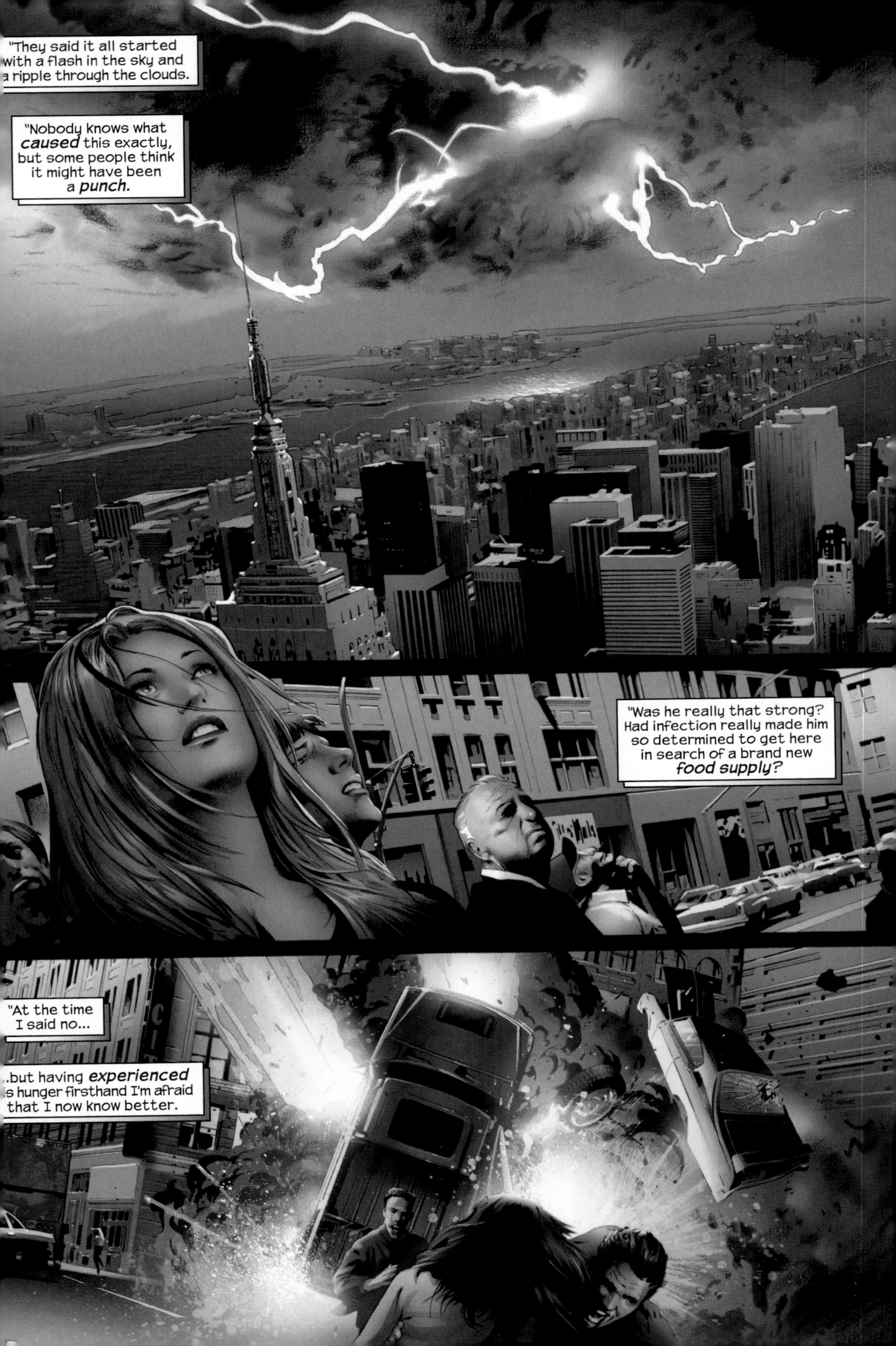
"They said it all started with a flash in the sky and a ripple through the clouds.
"Nobody knows what *caused* this exactly, but some people think it might have been a *punch.*
"Was he really that strong? Had infection really made him so determined to get here in search of a brand new *food supply?*
"At the time I said no...
..but having *experienced* s hunger firsthand I'm afraid that I now know better.

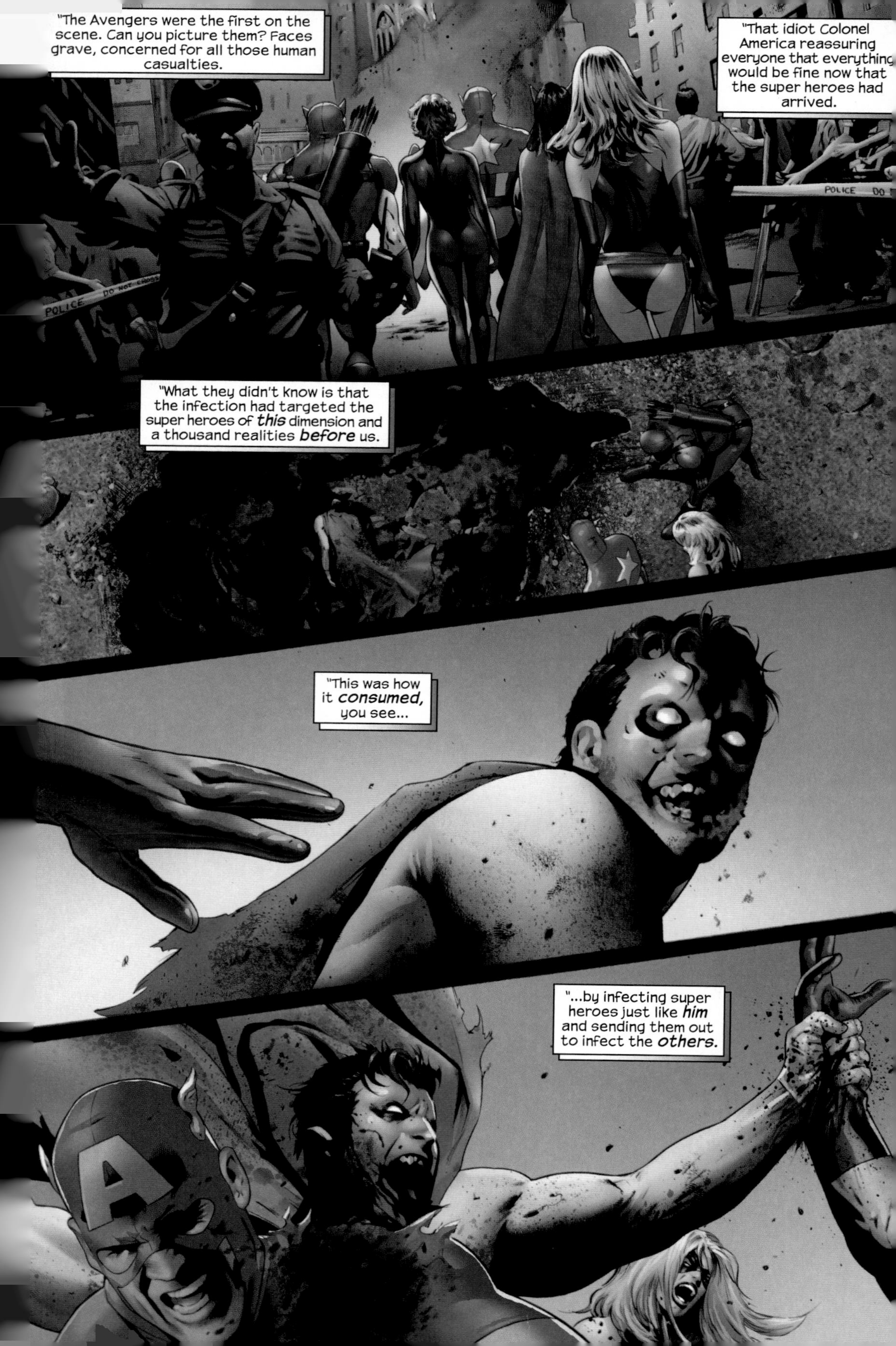
"The Avengers were the first on the scene. Can you picture them? Faces grave, concerned for all those human casualties.
"That idiot Colonel America reassuring everyone that everything would be fine now that the super heroes had arrived.
POLICE DO NOT CROSS
POLICE DO
"What they didn't know is that the infection had targeted the super heroes of *this* dimension and a thousand realities *before* us.
"This was how it *consumed,* you see...
"...by infecting super heroes just like *him* and sending them out to infect the *others.*

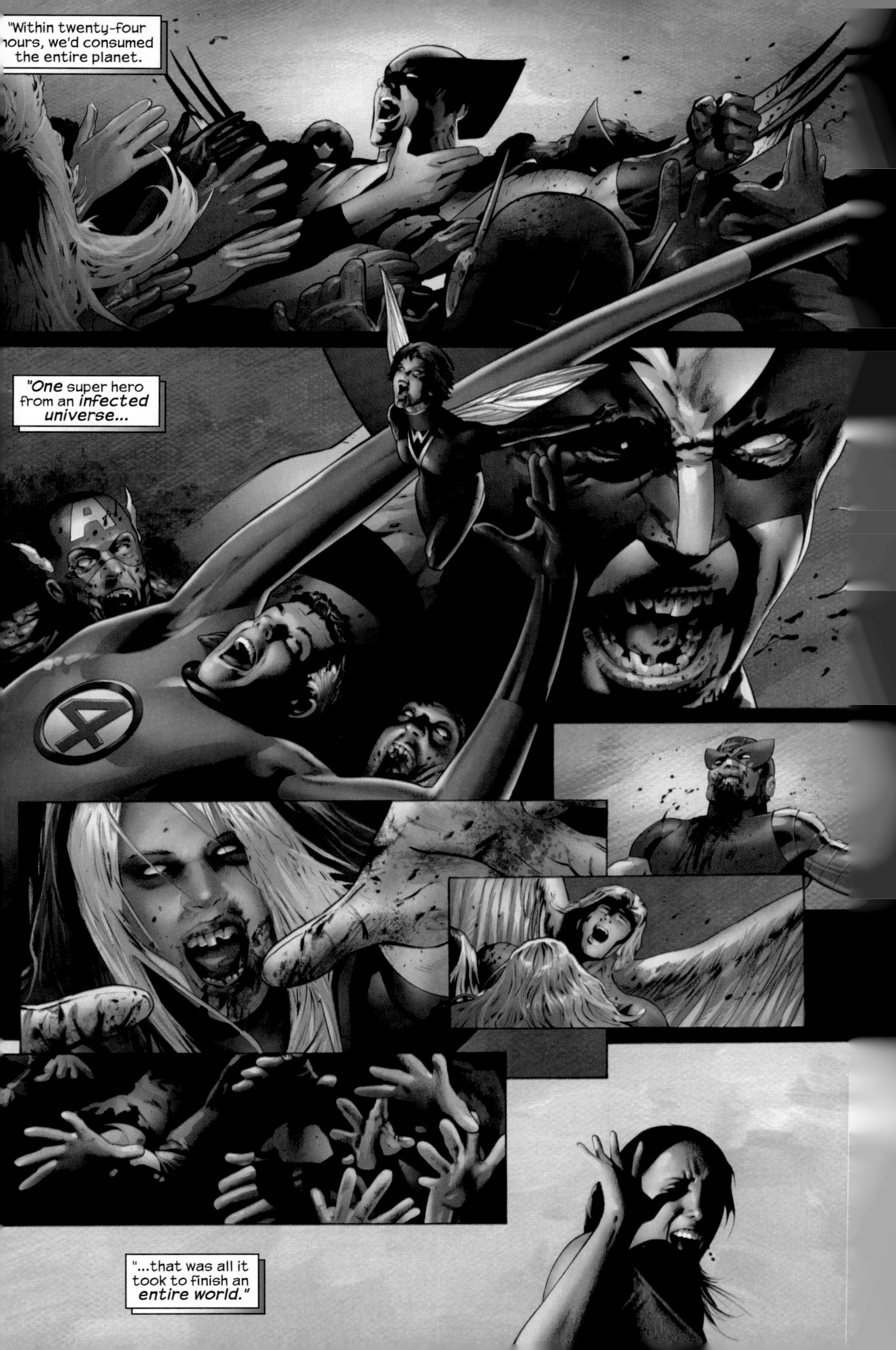
"Within twenty-four hours, we'd consumed the entire planet.
"One super hero from an infected universe...
"...that was all it took to finish an entire world."

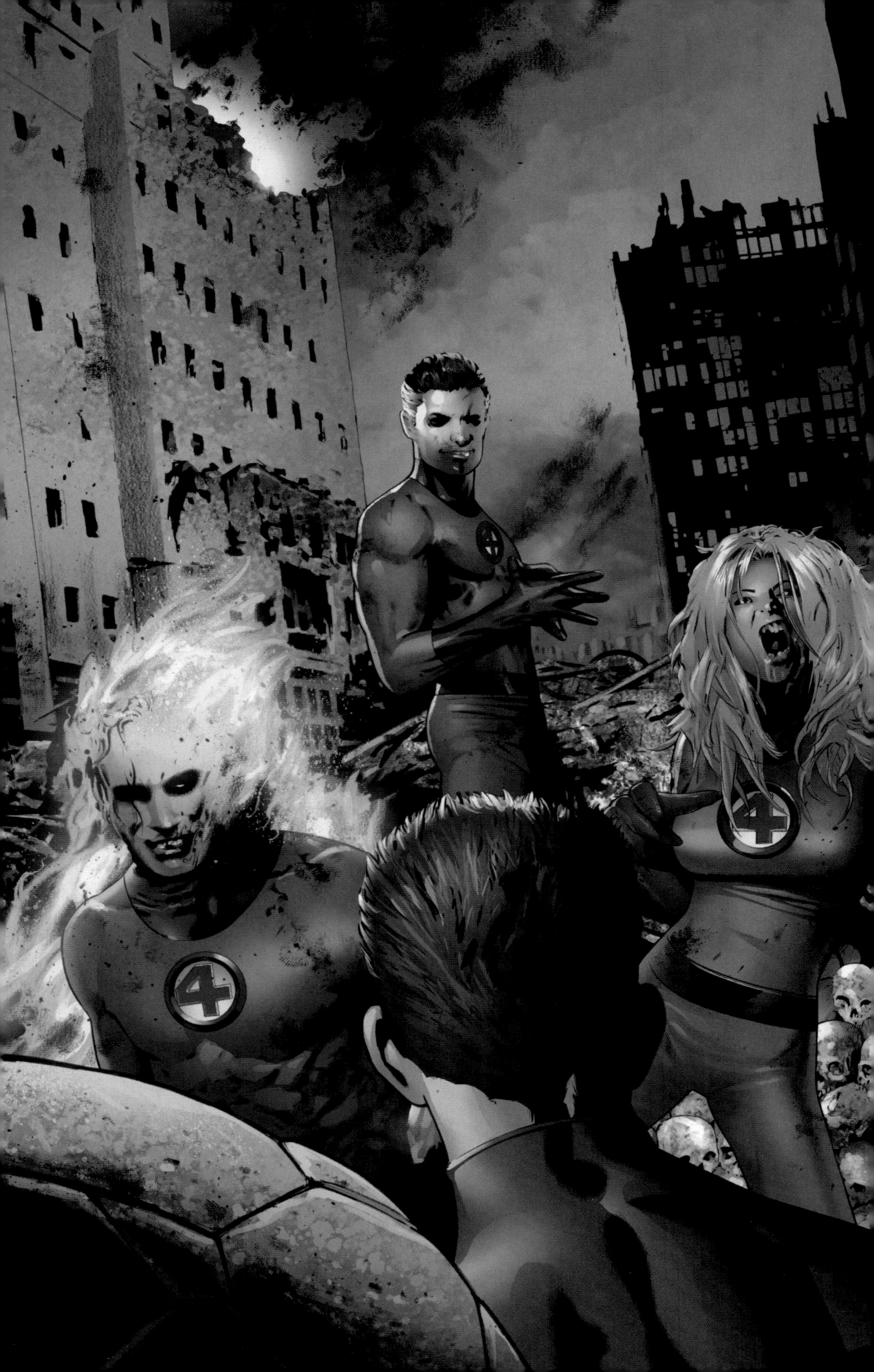

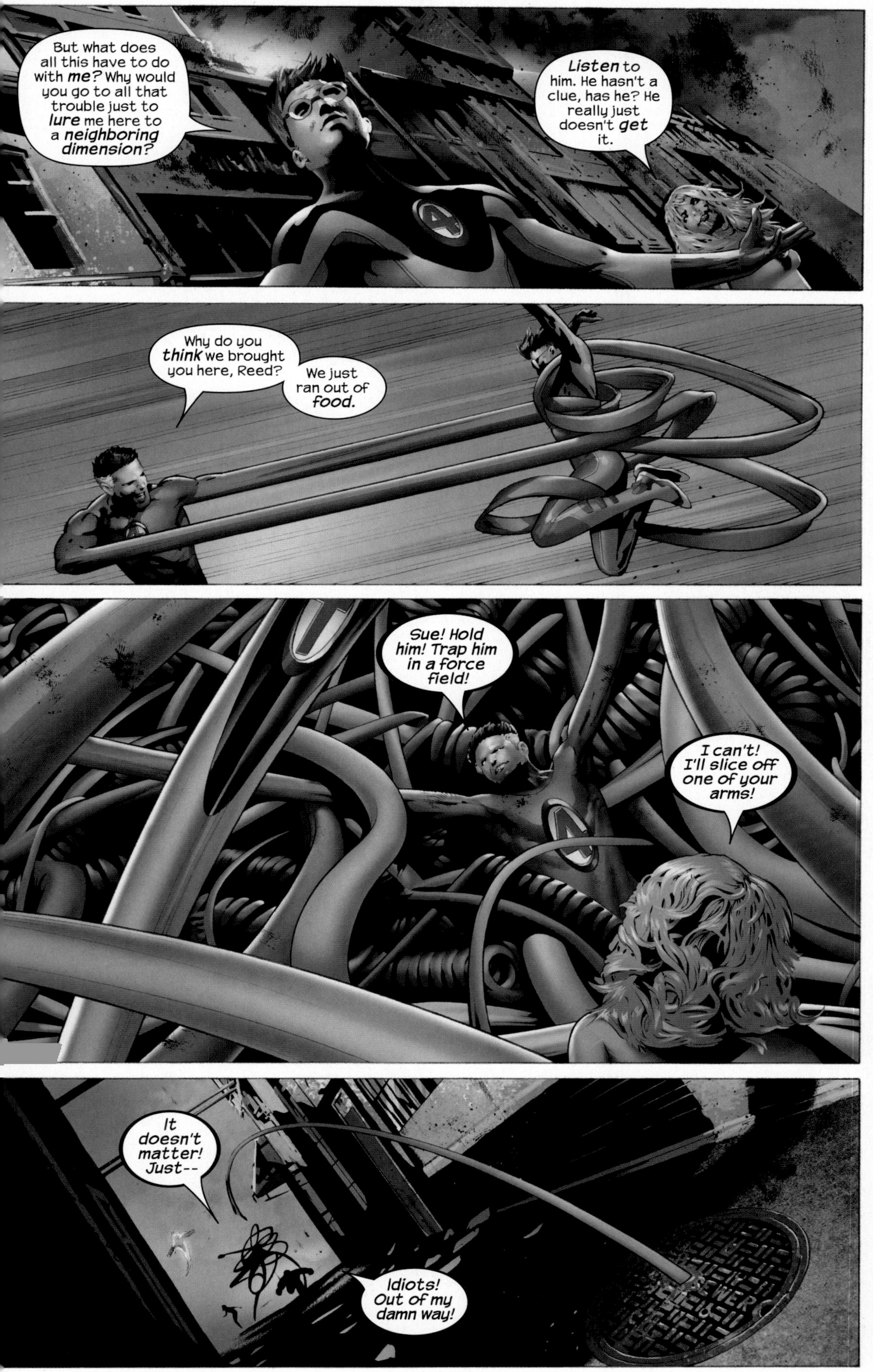

But what does all this have to do with *me*? Why would you go to all that trouble just to *lure* me here to a *neighboring dimension*?
Listen to him. He hasn't a clue, has he? He really just doesn't *get* it.
Why do you *think* we brought you here, Reed?
We just ran out of *food.*
Sue! Hold him! Trap him in a force field!
I can't! I'll slice off one of your arms!
It doesn't matter! Just--
Idiots! Out of my damn way!
SEWER

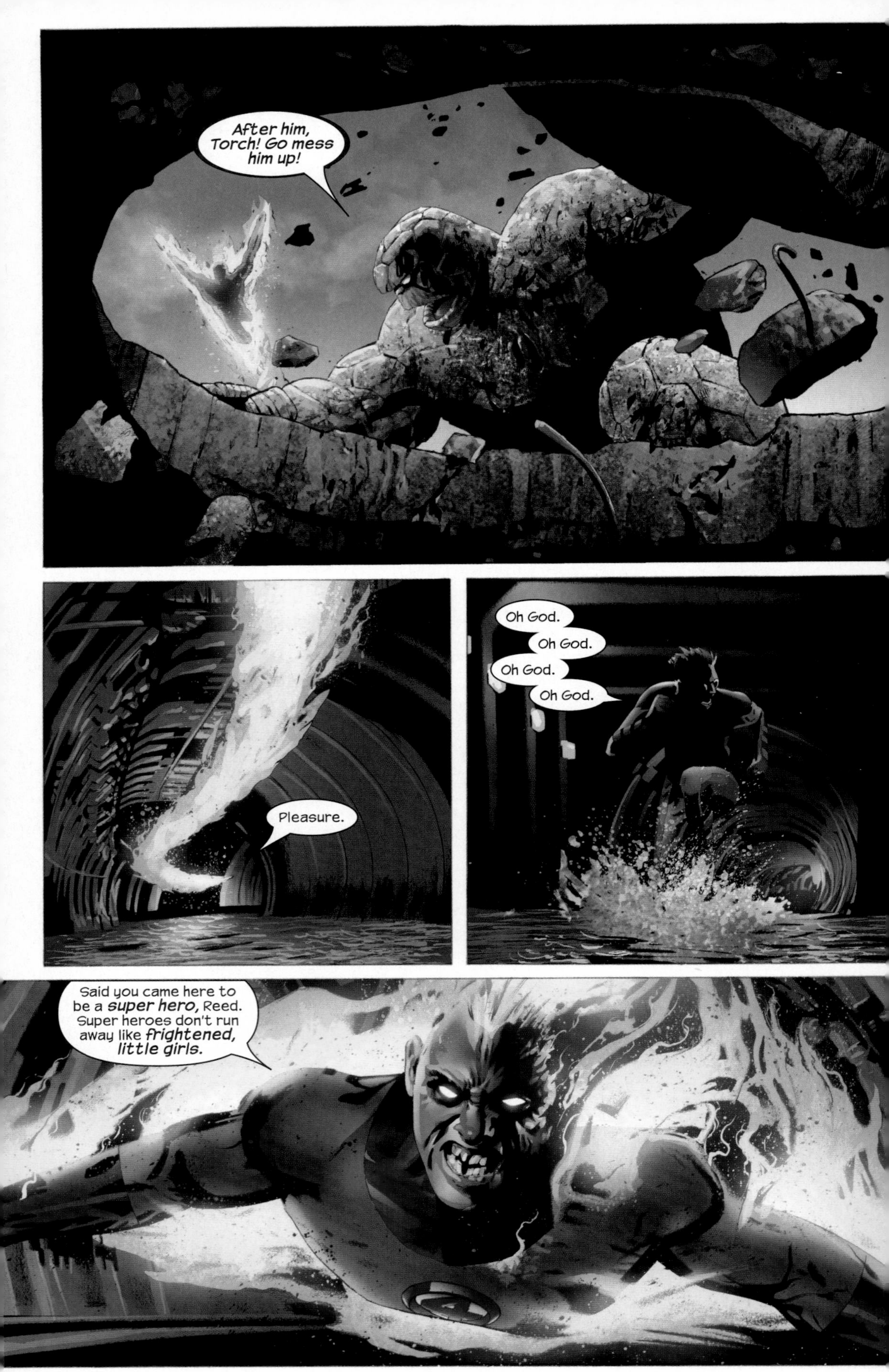
After him, Torch! Go mess him up!
Pleasure.
Oh God.
Oh God.
Oh God.
Oh God.
Said you came here to be a *super hero,* Reed. Super heroes don't run away like *frightened, little girls.*

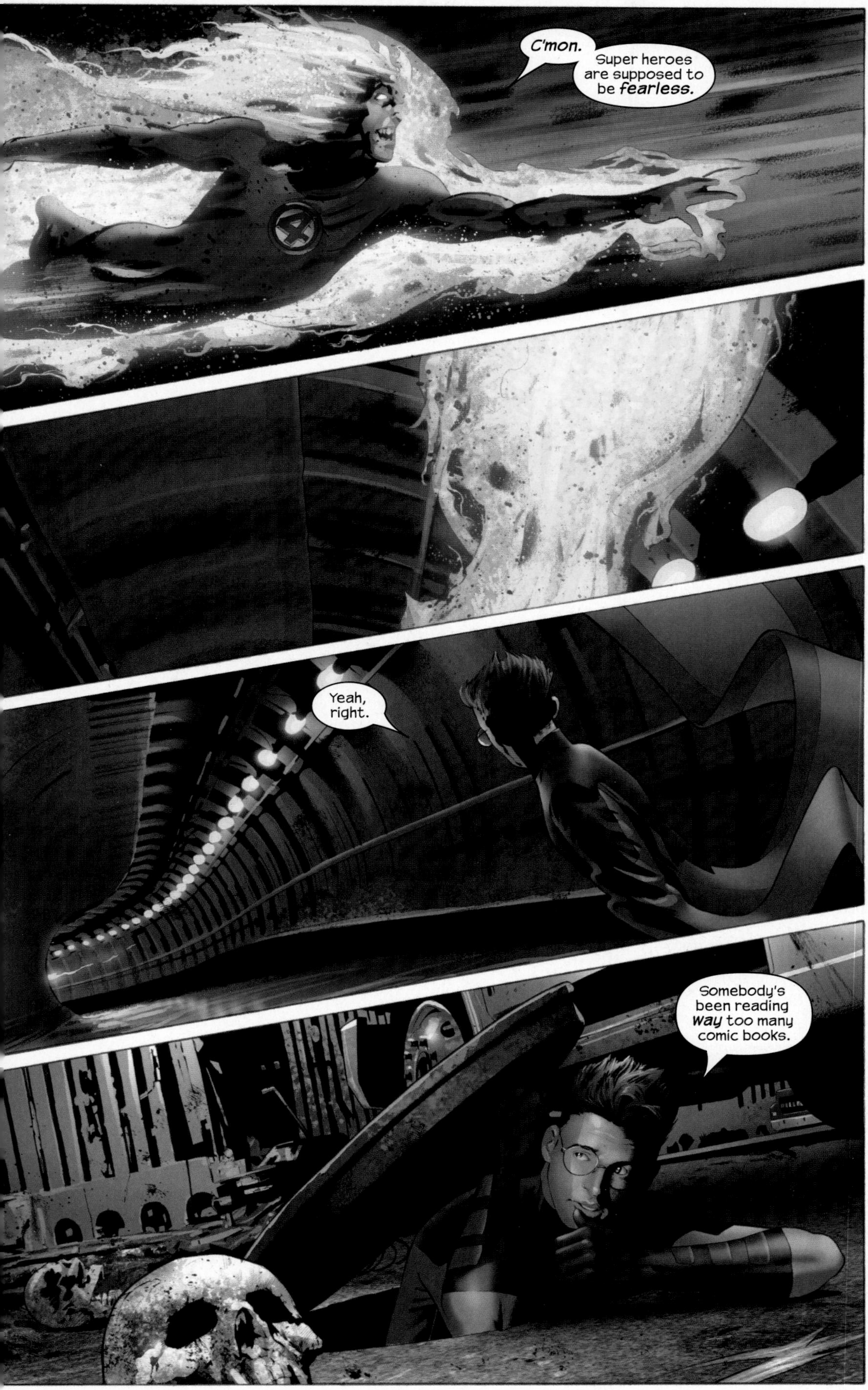
C'mon.
Super heroes are supposed to be fearless.
Yeah, right.
Somebody's been reading way too many comic books.

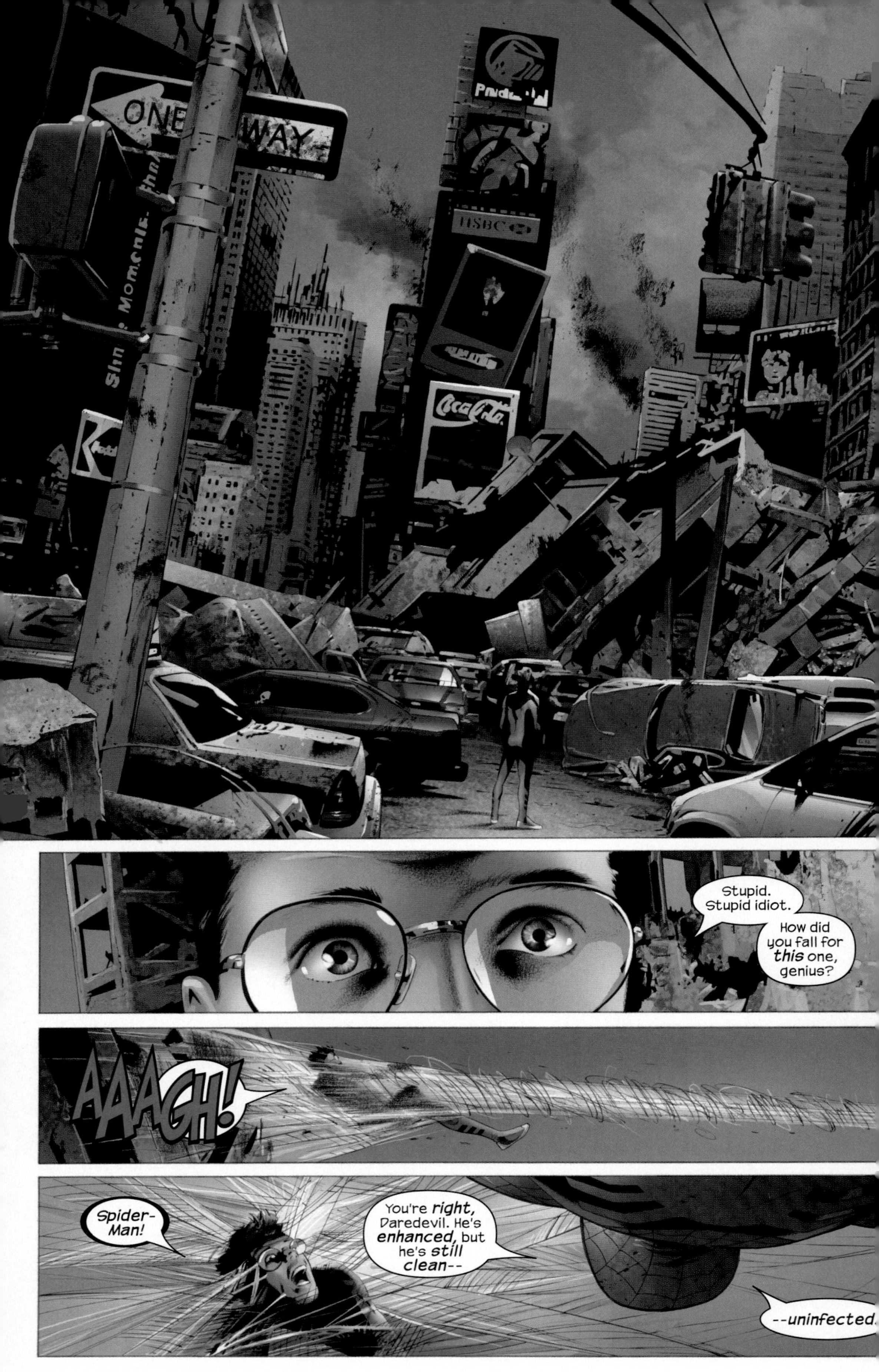
ONE WAY
HSBC
Coca-Cola
Stupid. Stupid idiot.
How did you fall for *this* one, genius?
AAAGH!
Spider-Man!
You're *right*, Daredevil. He's *enhanced*, but he's *still clean*--
--*uninfected*.

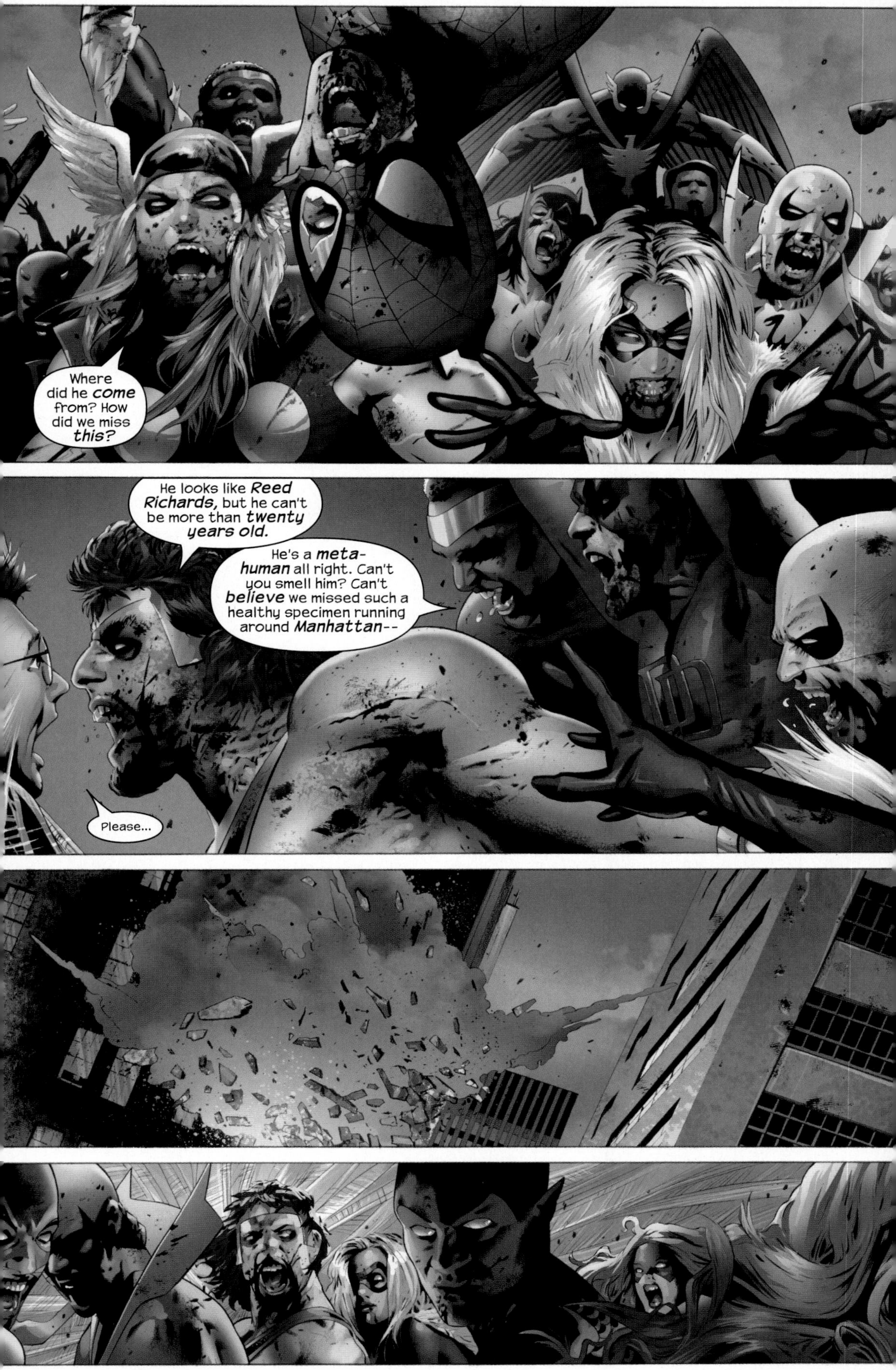
Where did he come from? How did we miss this?
He looks like Reed Richards, but he can't be more than twenty years old.
He's a meta-human all right. Can't you smell him? Can't believe we missed such a healthy specimen running around Manhattan--
Please...

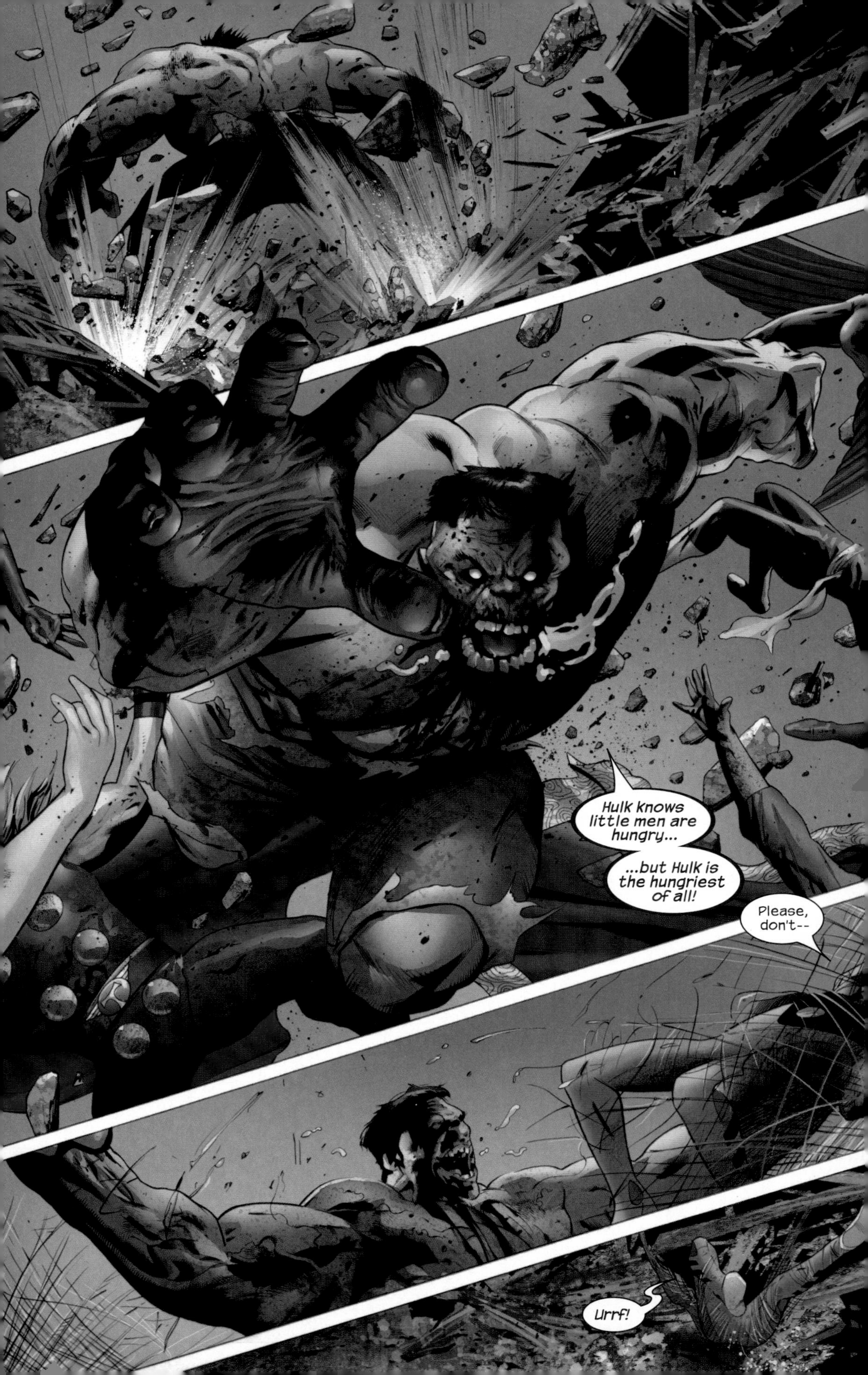
Hulk knows little men are hungry...
...but Hulk is the hungriest of all!
Please, don't--
Urrf!

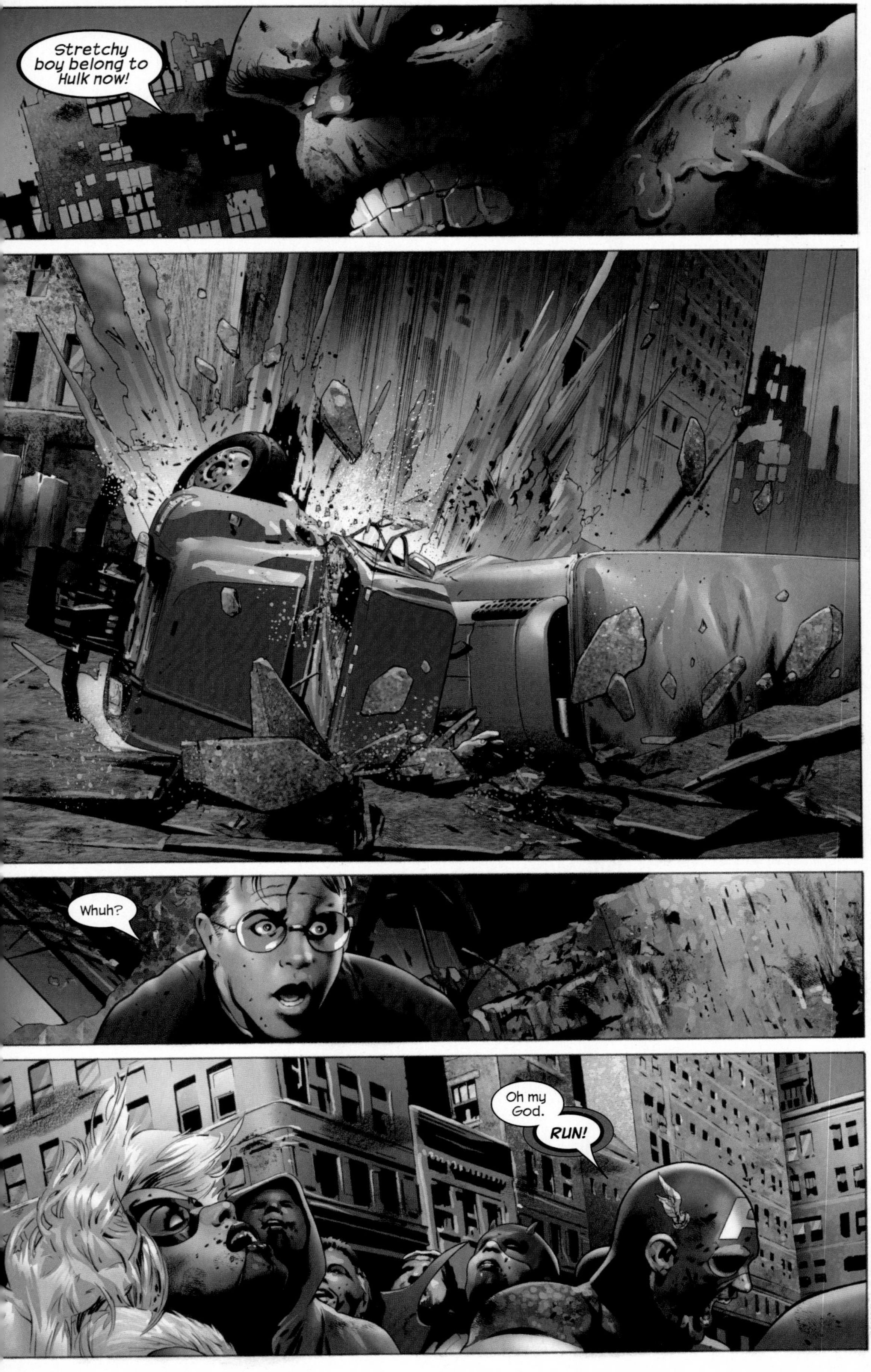
Stretchy boy belong to Hulk now!
Whuh?
Oh my God.
RUN!

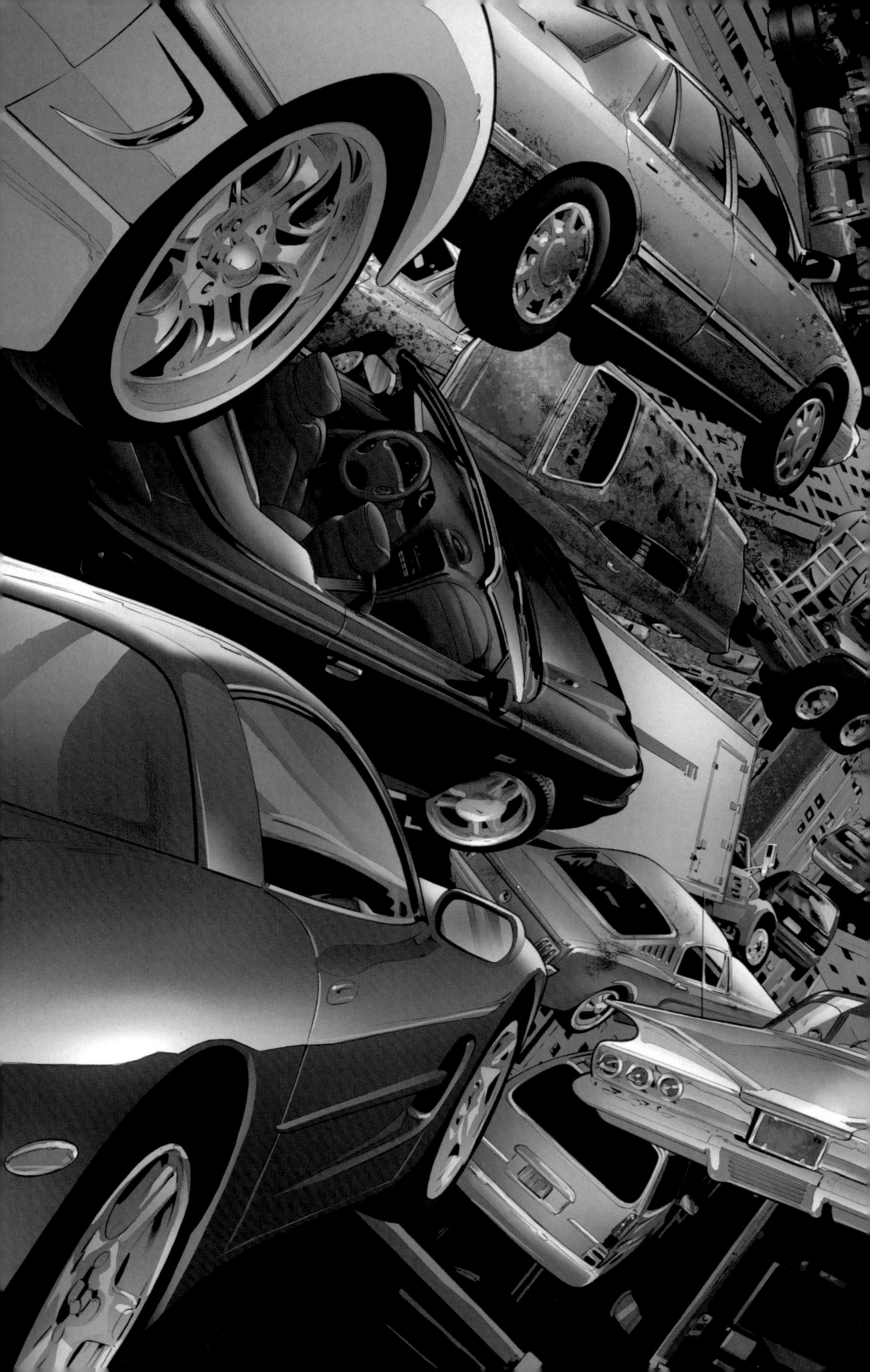

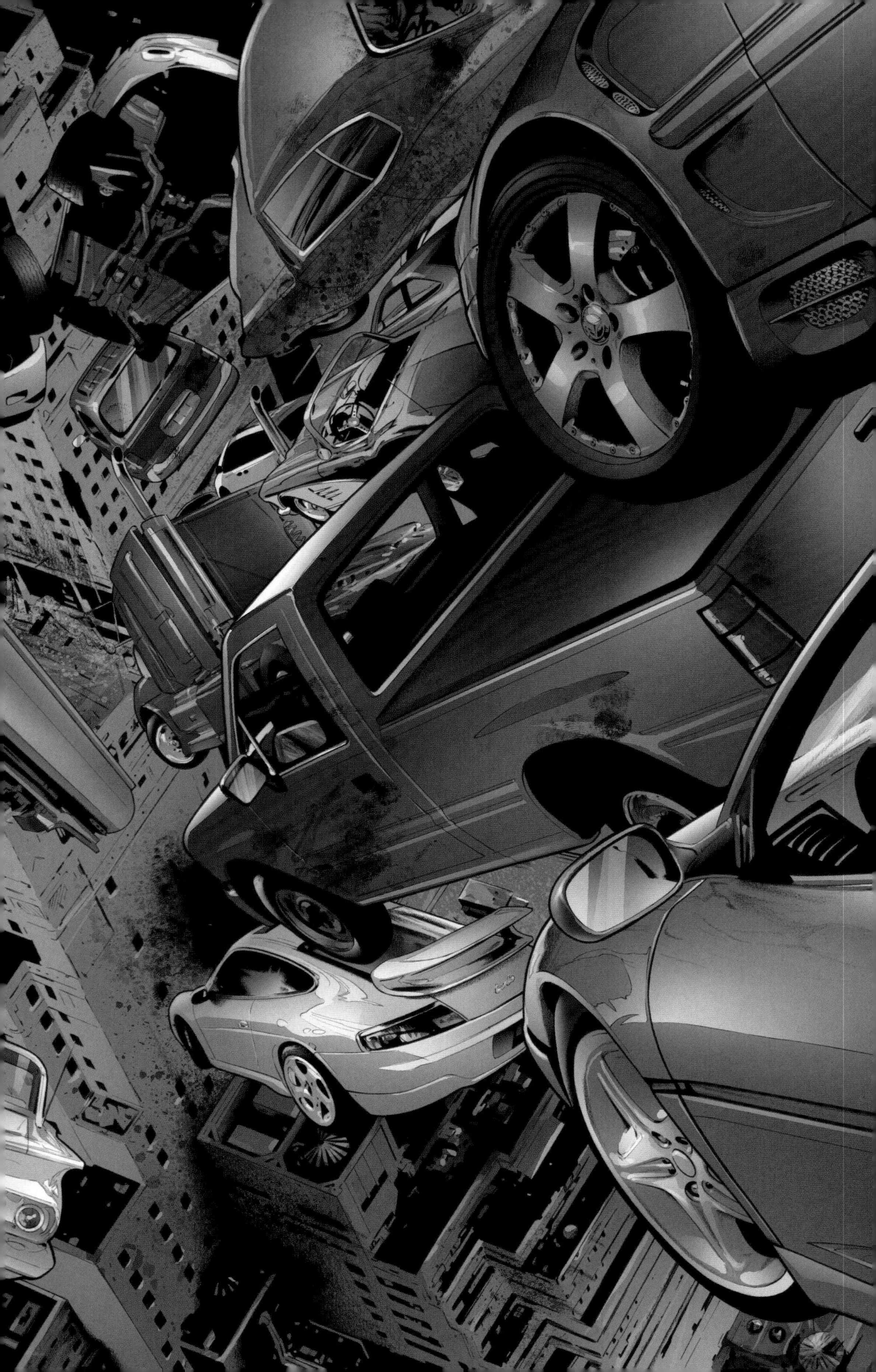

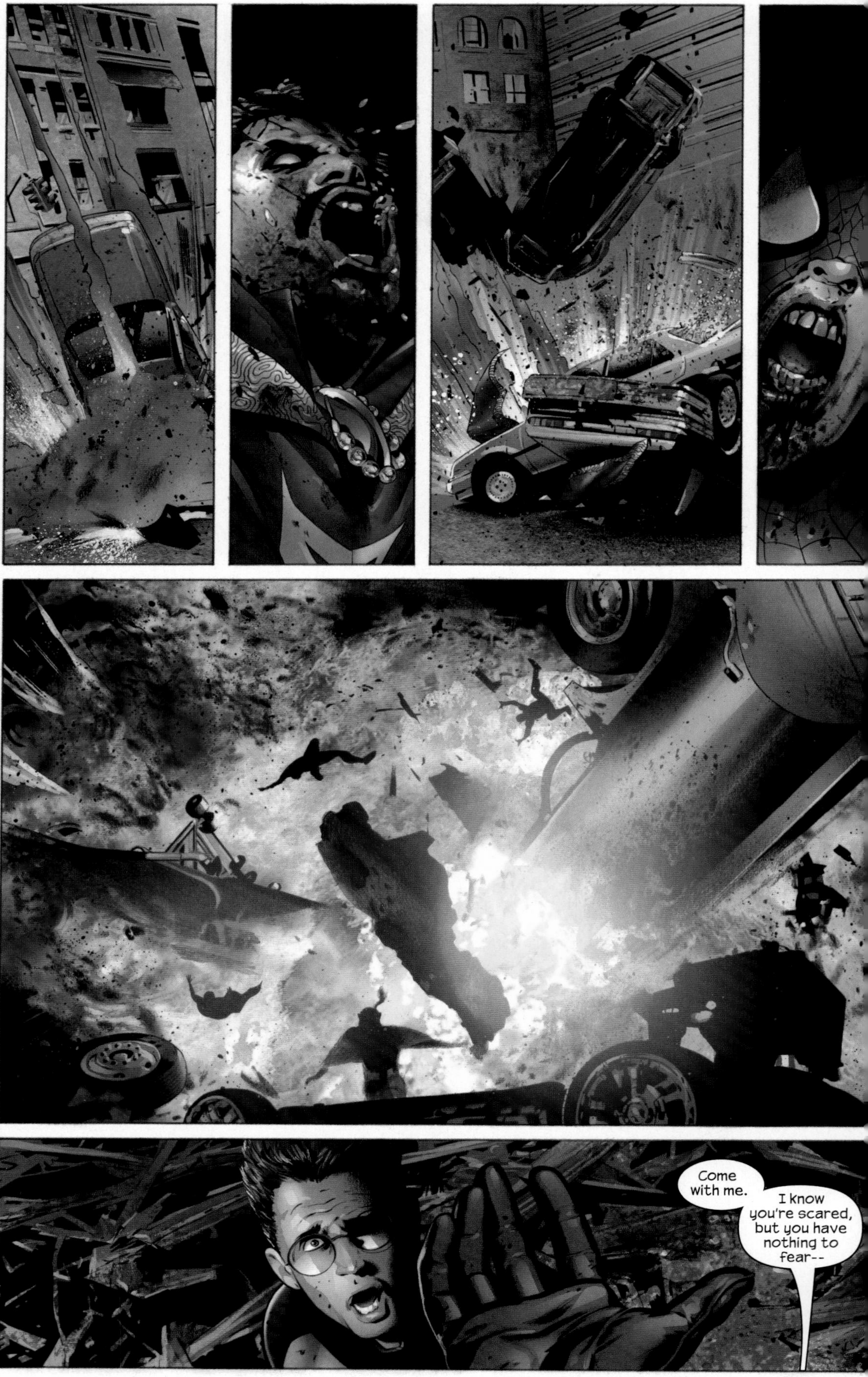
Come with me.
I know you're scared, but you have nothing to fear--

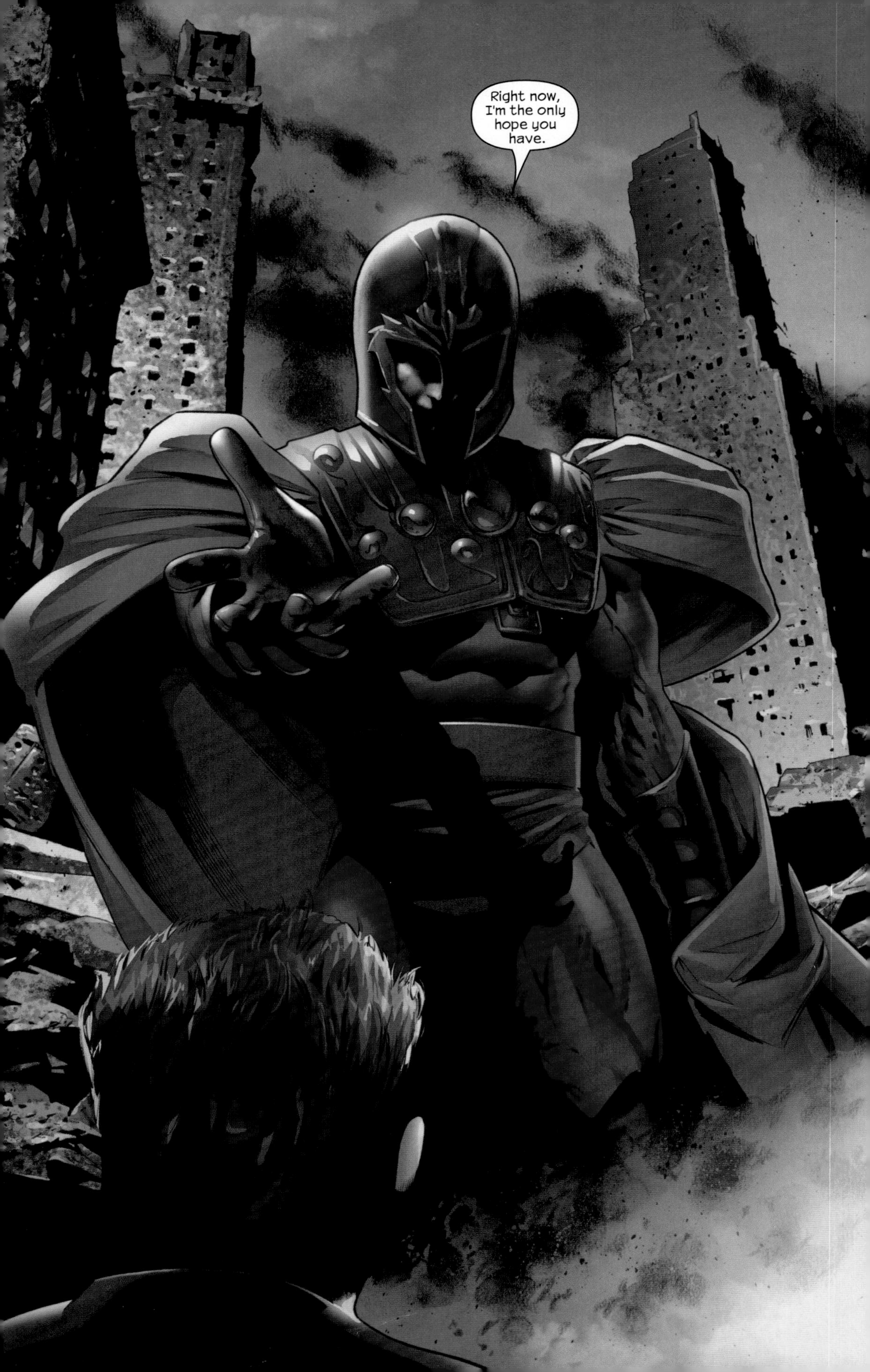
Right now, I'm the only hope you have.

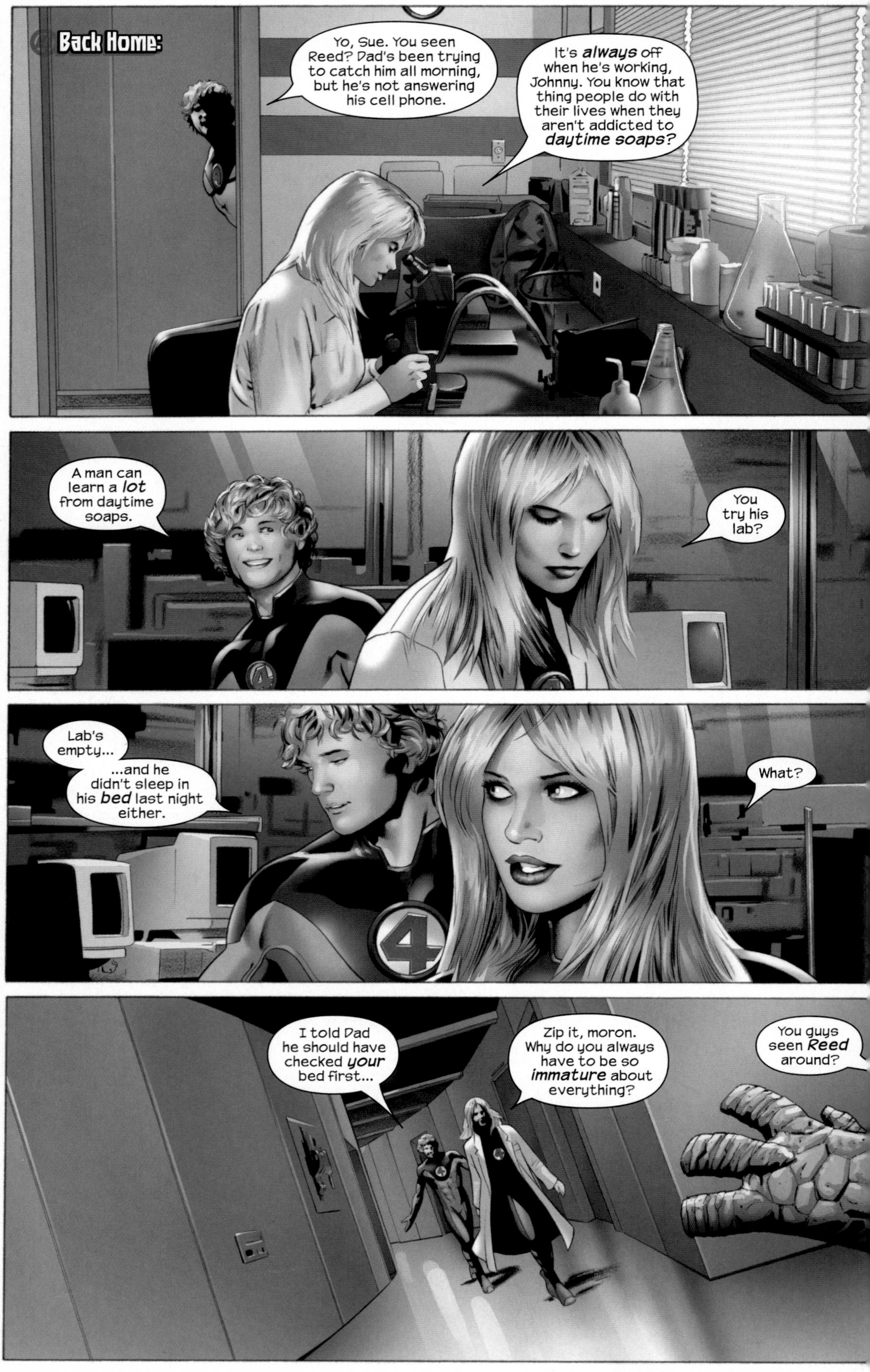
Back Home:
Yo, Sue. You seen Reed? Dad's been trying to catch him all morning, but he's not answering his cell phone.
It's *always* off when he's working, Johnny. You know that thing people do with their lives when they aren't addicted to *daytime soaps?*
A man can learn a *lot* from daytime soaps.
You try his lab?
Lab's empty...
...and he didn't sleep in his *bed* last night either.
What?
I told Dad he should have checked *your* bed first...
Zip it, moron. Why do you always have to be so *immature* about everything?
You guys seen *Reed* around?

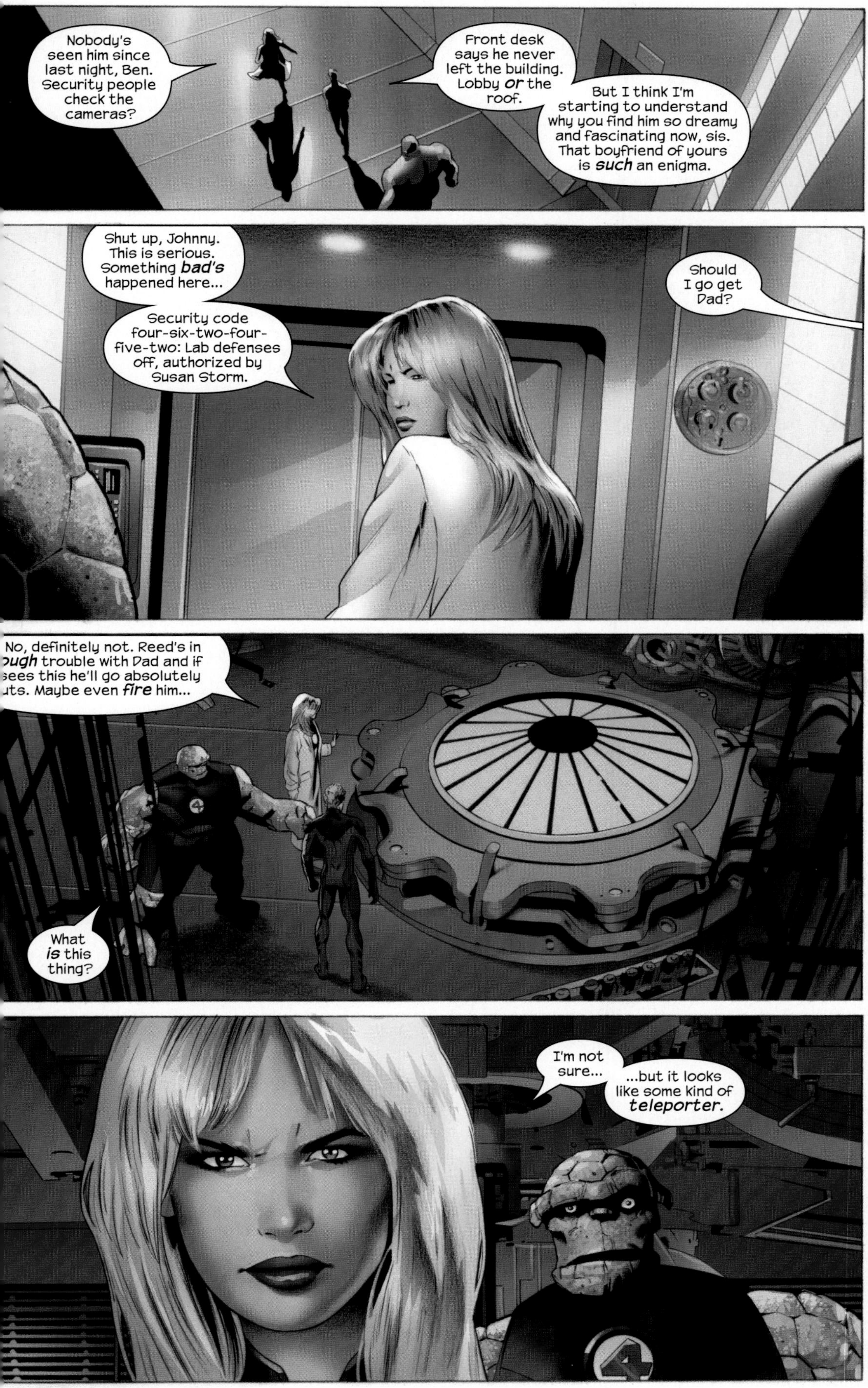
Nobody's seen him since last night, Ben. Security people check the cameras?
Front desk says he never left the building. Lobby *or* the roof.
But I think I'm starting to understand why you find him so dreamy and fascinating now, sis. That boyfriend of yours is *such* an enigma.
Shut up, Johnny. This is serious. Something *bad's* happened here...
Security code four-six-two-four-five-two: Lab defenses off, authorized by Susan Storm.
Should I go get Dad?
No, definitely not. Reed's in ough trouble with Dad and if sees this he'll go absolutely uts. Maybe even *fire* him...
What *is* this thing?
I'm not sure...
...but it looks like some kind of *teleporter*.

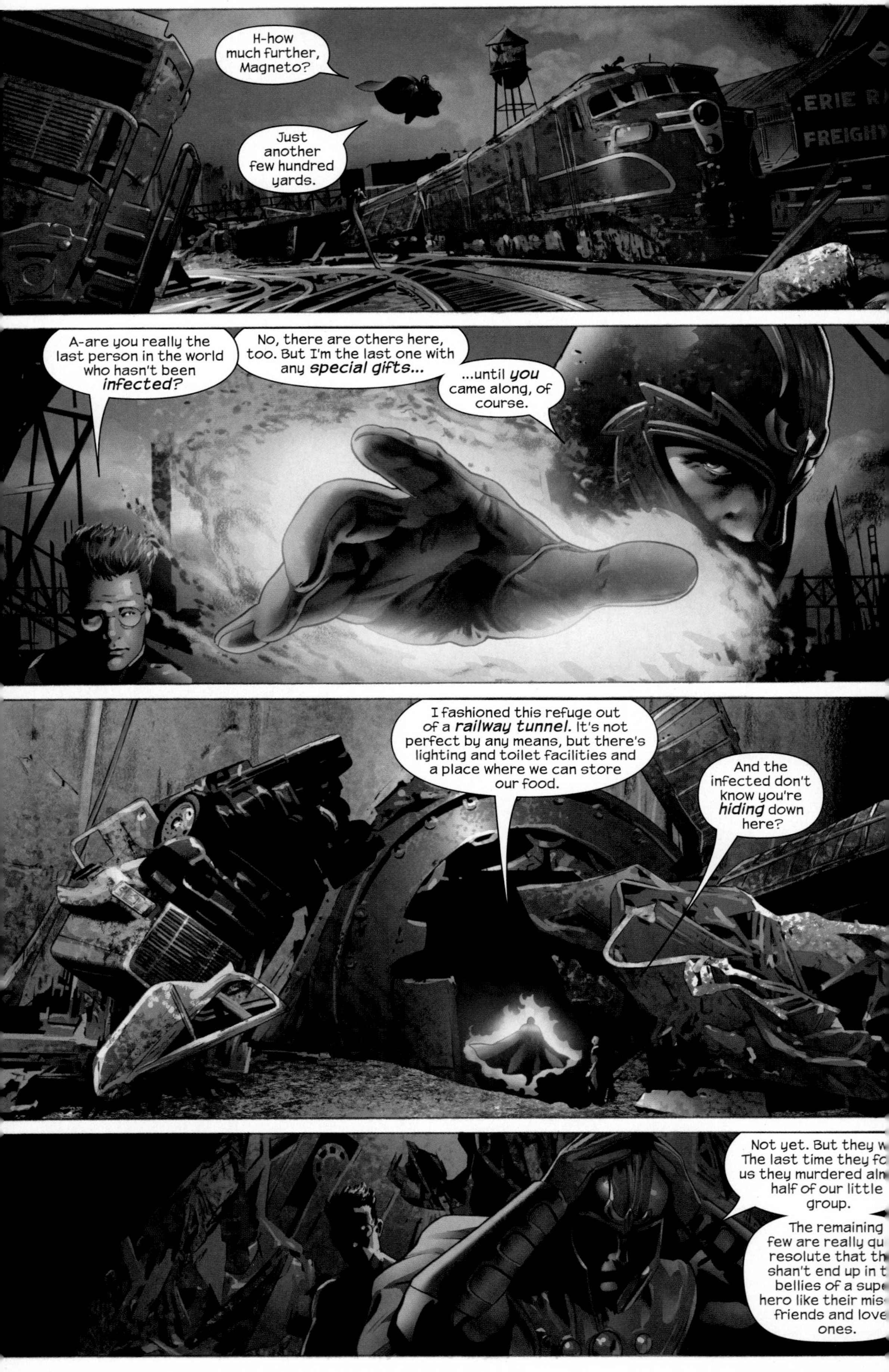

H-how much further, Magneto?
Just another few hundred yards.
ERIE
FREIGH
A-are you really the last person in the world who hasn't been *infected*?
No, there are others here, too. But I'm the last one with any *special gifts...*
...until *you* came along, of course.
I fashioned this refuge out of a *railway tunnel.* It's not perfect by any means, but there's lighting and toilet facilities and a place where we can store our food.
And the infected don't know you're *hiding* down here?
Not yet. But they
The last time they
us they murdered al
half of our little
group.
The remaining
few are really
resolute that
shan't end up in
bellies of a sup
hero like their mi
friends and love
ones.

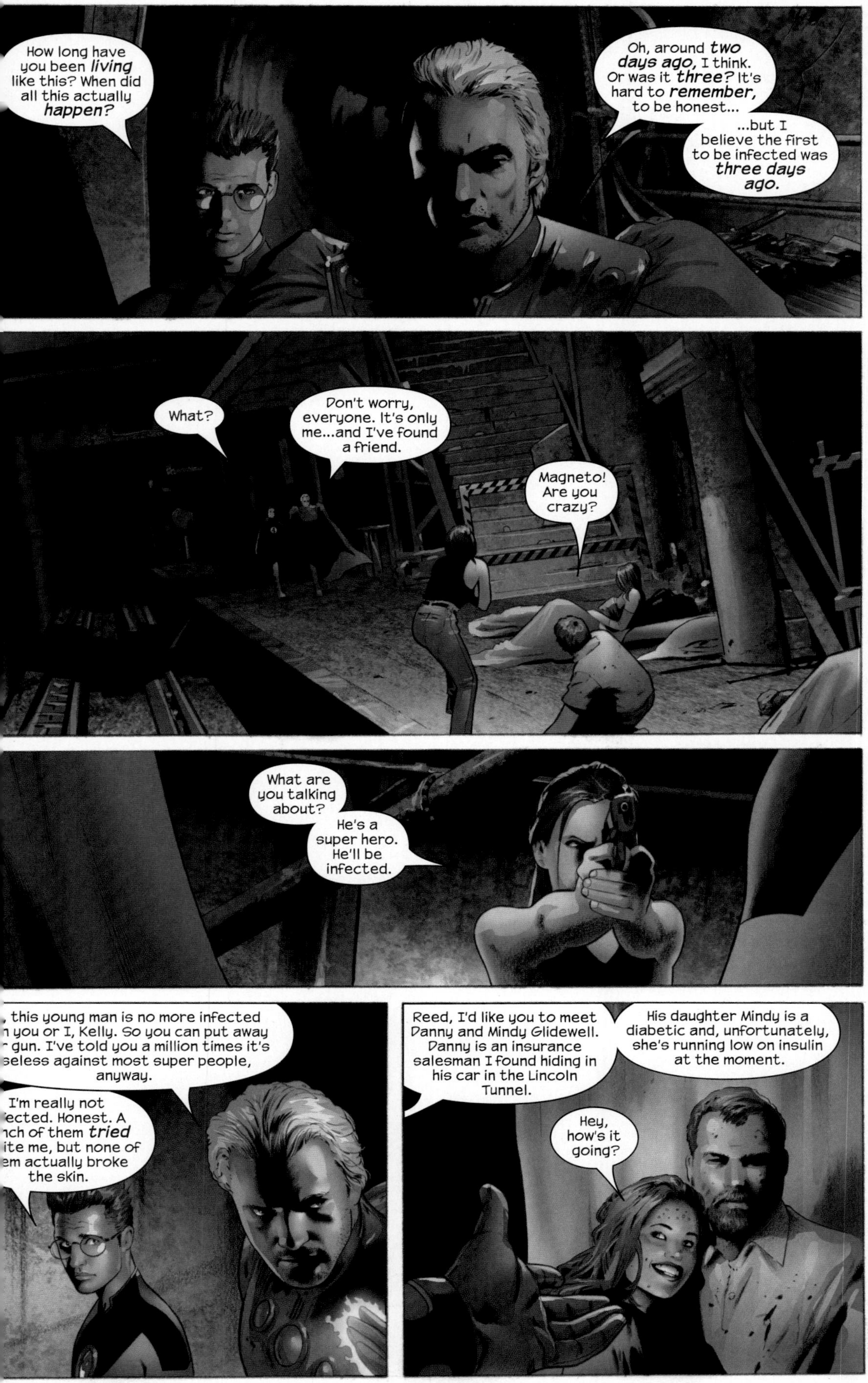
How long have you been living like this? When did all this actually happen?
Oh, around two days ago, I think. Or was it three? It's hard to remember, to be honest...
...but I believe the first to be infected was three days ago.
What?
Don't worry, everyone. It's only me...and I've found a friend.
Magneto! Are you crazy?
What are you talking about?
He's a super hero. He'll be infected.
this young man is no more infected n you or I, Kelly. So you can put away gun. I've told you a million times it's seless against most super people, anyway.
I'm really not fected. Honest. A nch of them tried ite me, but none of em actually broke the skin.
Reed, I'd like you to meet Danny and Mindy Glidewell. Danny is an insurance salesman I found hiding in his car in the Lincoln Tunnel.
His daughter Mindy is a diabetic and, unfortunately, she's running low on insulin at the moment.
Hey, how's it going?

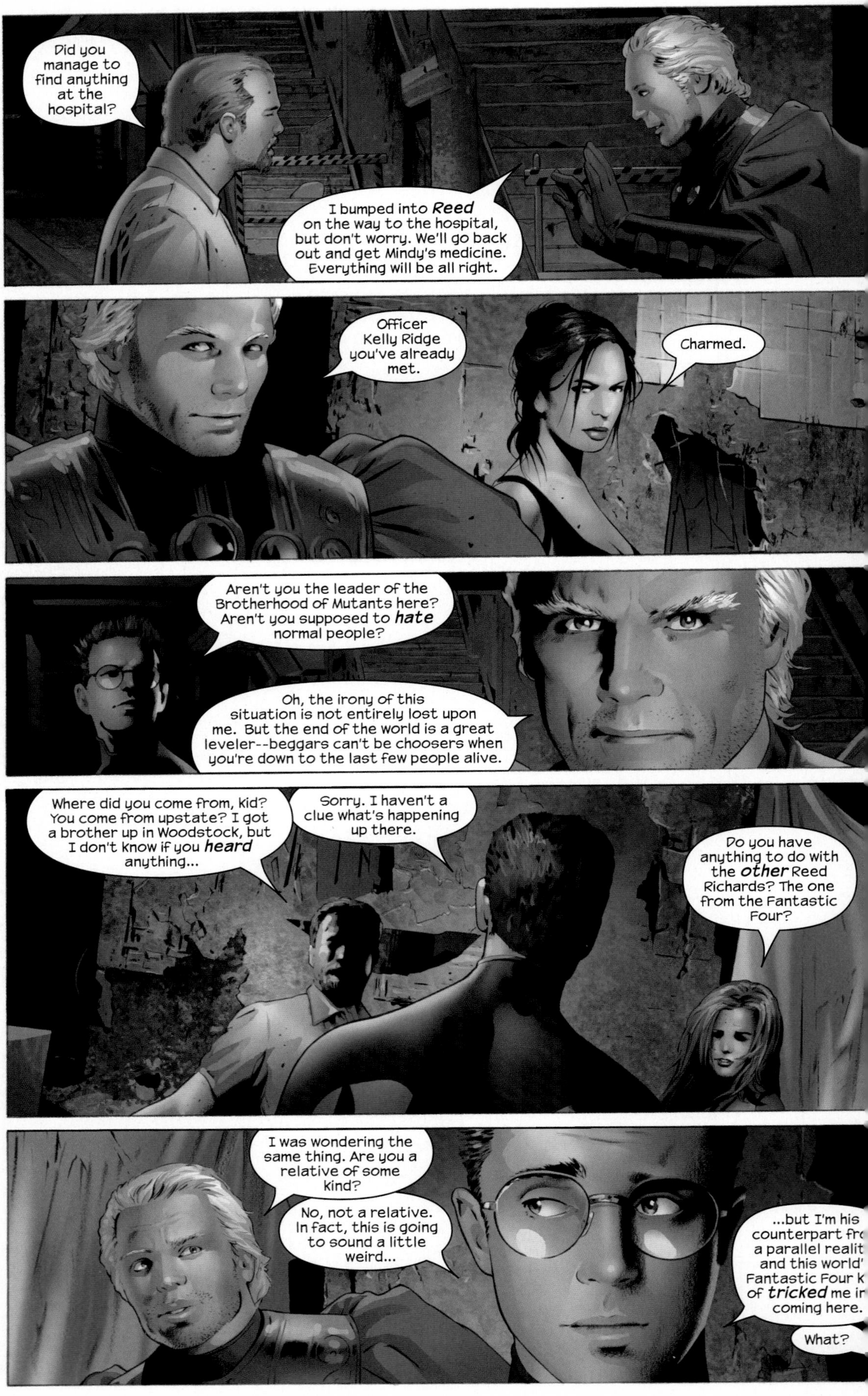

Did you manage to find anything at the hospital?
I bumped into *Reed* on the way to the hospital, but don't worry. We'll go back out and get Mindy's medicine. Everything will be all right.
Officer Kelly Ridge you've already met.
Charmed.
Aren't you the leader of the Brotherhood of Mutants here? Aren't you supposed to *hate* normal people?
Oh, the irony of this situation is not entirely lost upon me. But the end of the world is a great leveler--beggars can't be choosers when you're down to the last few people alive.
Where did you come from, kid? You come from upstate? I got a brother up in Woodstock, but I don't know if you *heard* anything...
Sorry. I haven't a clue what's happening up there.
Do you have anything to do with the *other* Reed Richards? The one from the Fantastic Four?
I was wondering the same thing. Are you a relative of some kind?
No, not a relative. In fact, this is going to sound a little weird...
...but I'm his counterpart fr a parallel realit and this world' Fantastic Four k of *tricked* me i coming here.
What?

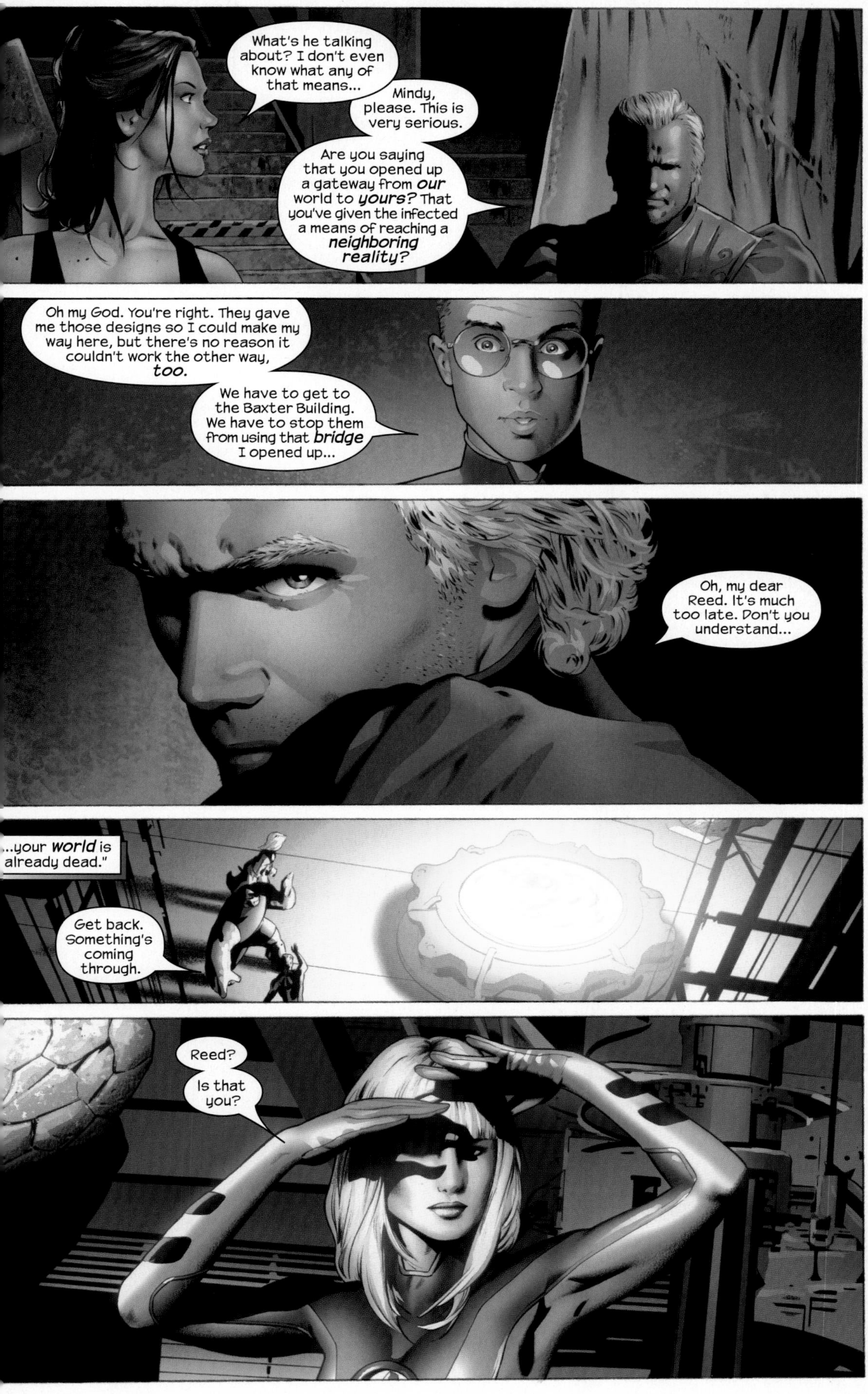
What's he talking about? I don't even know what any of that means...
Mindy, please. This is very serious.
Are you saying that you opened up a gateway from *our* world to *yours?* That you've given the infected a means of reaching a *neighboring reality?*
Oh my God. You're right. They gave me those designs so I could make my way here, but there's no reason it couldn't work the other way, *too.*
We have to get to the Baxter Building. We have to stop them from using that *bridge* I opened up...
Oh, my dear Reed. It's much too late. Don't you understand...
...your *world* is already dead."
Get back. Something's coming through.
Reed?
Is that you?

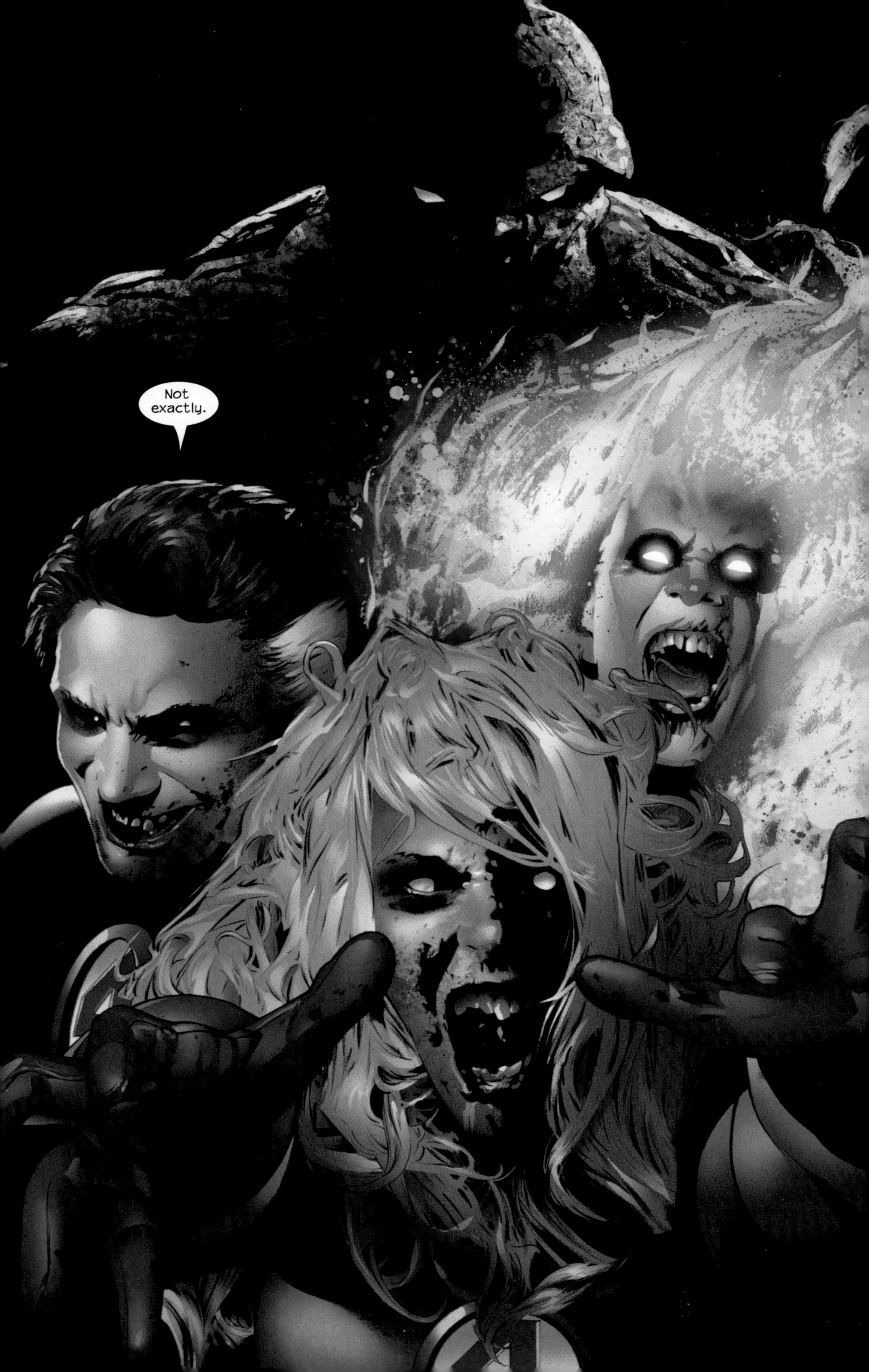
Not exactly.

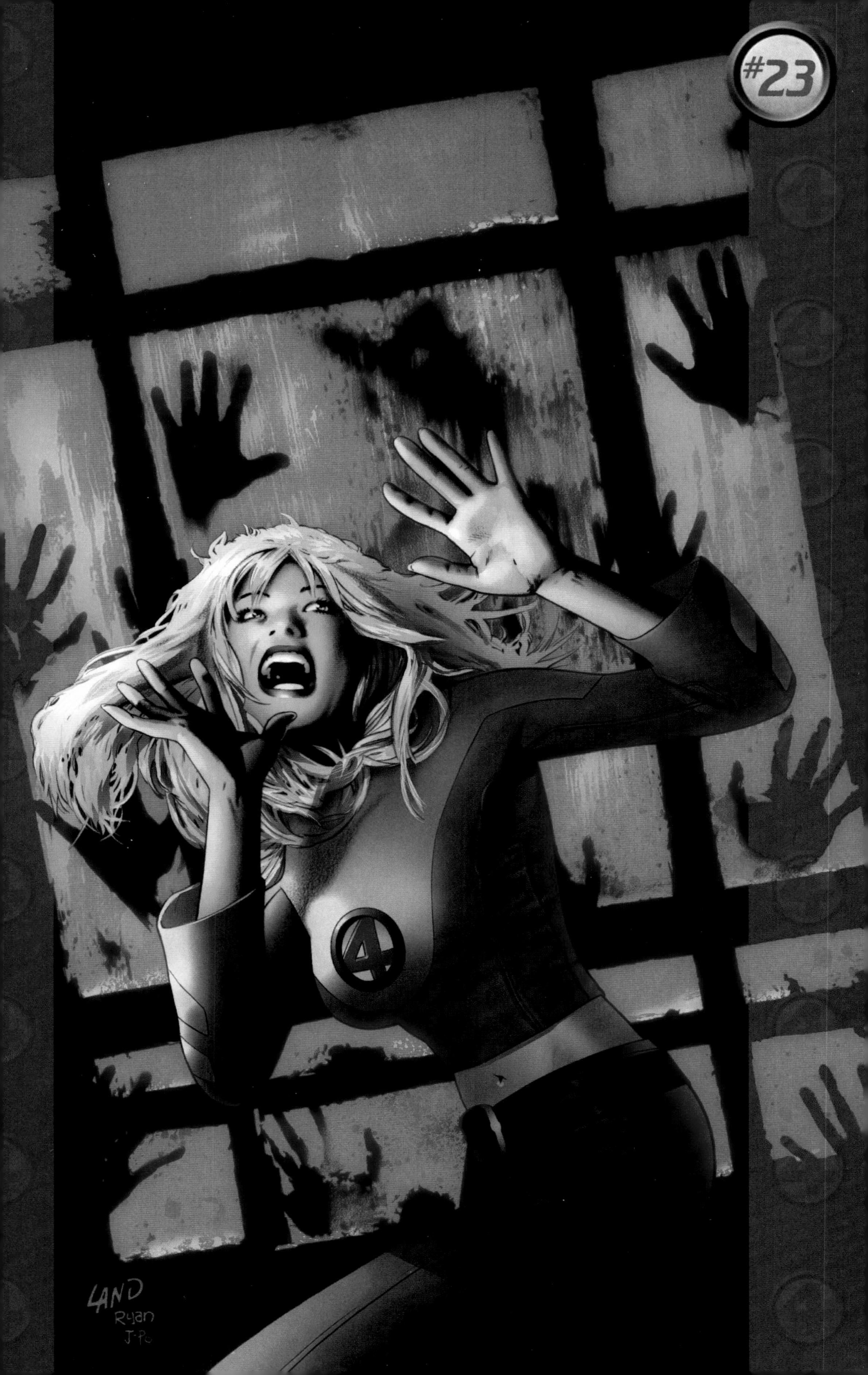
#23
LAND
Ryan
J-Po

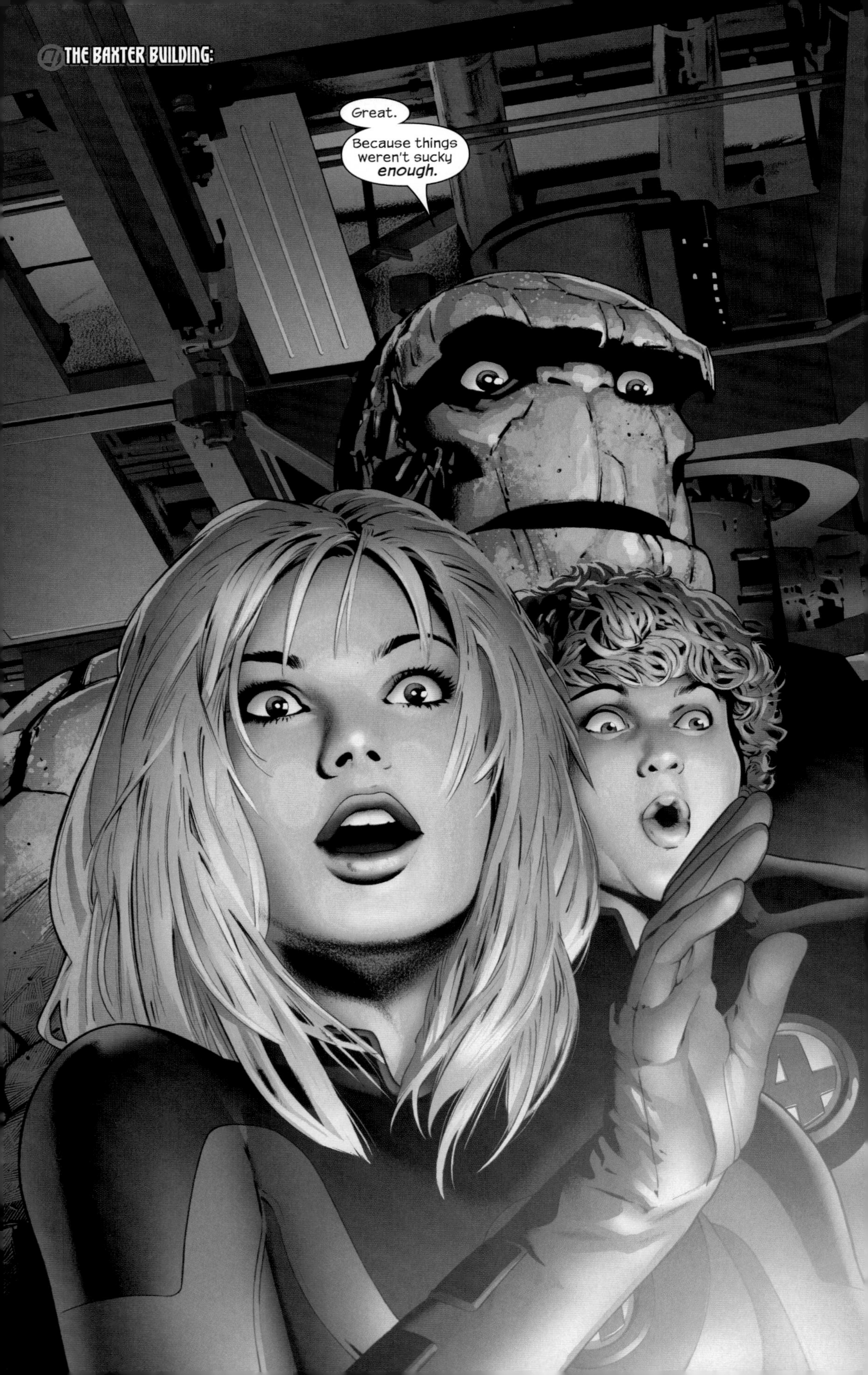
THE BAXTER BUILDING:
Great.
Because things weren't sucky *enough*.

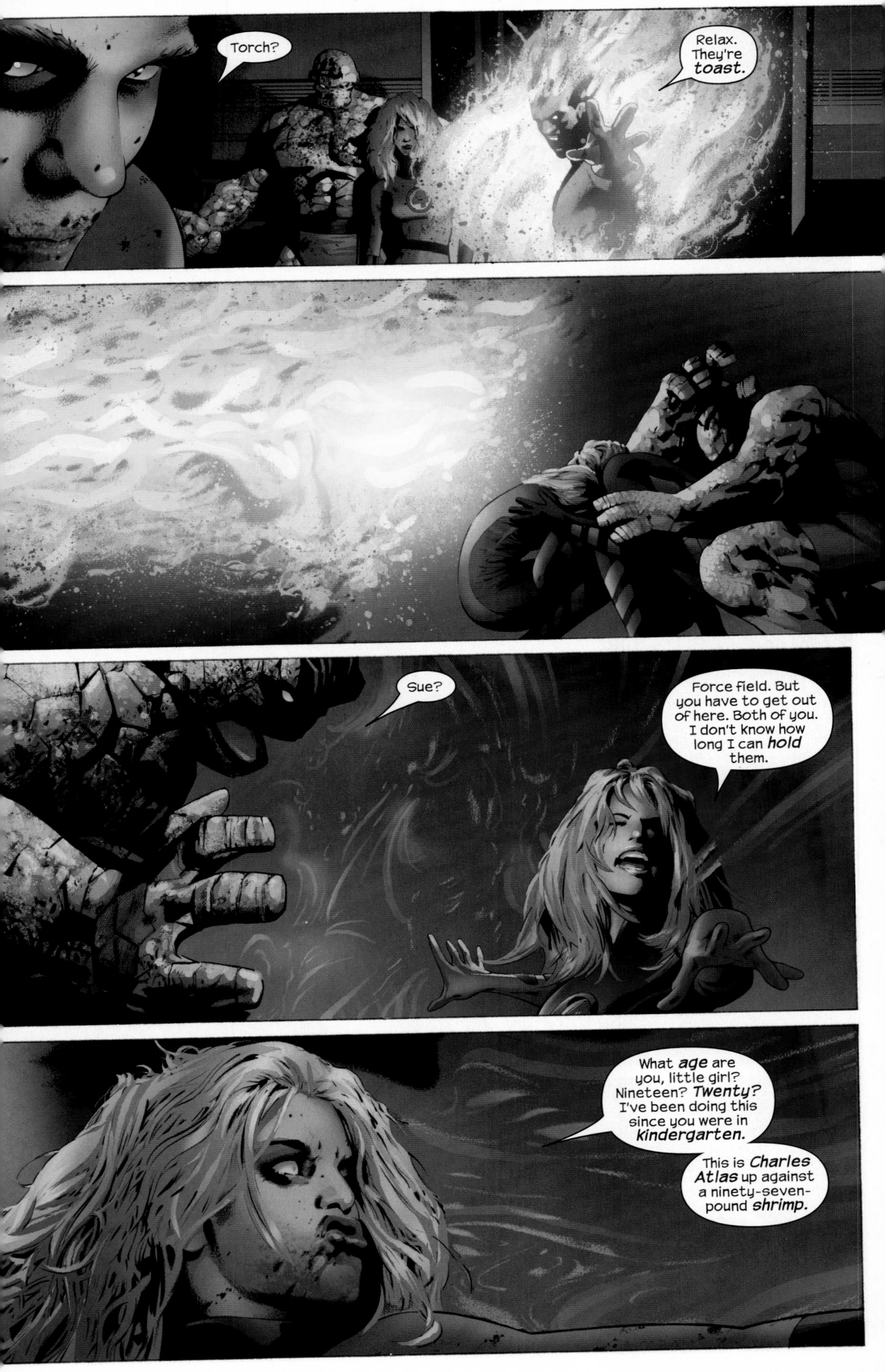
Torch?
Relax. They're toast.
Sue?
Force field. But you have to get out of here. Both of you. I don't know how long I can hold them.
What age are you, little girl? Nineteen? Twenty? I've been doing this since you were in kindergarten.
This is Charles Atlas up against a ninety-seven-pound shrimp.

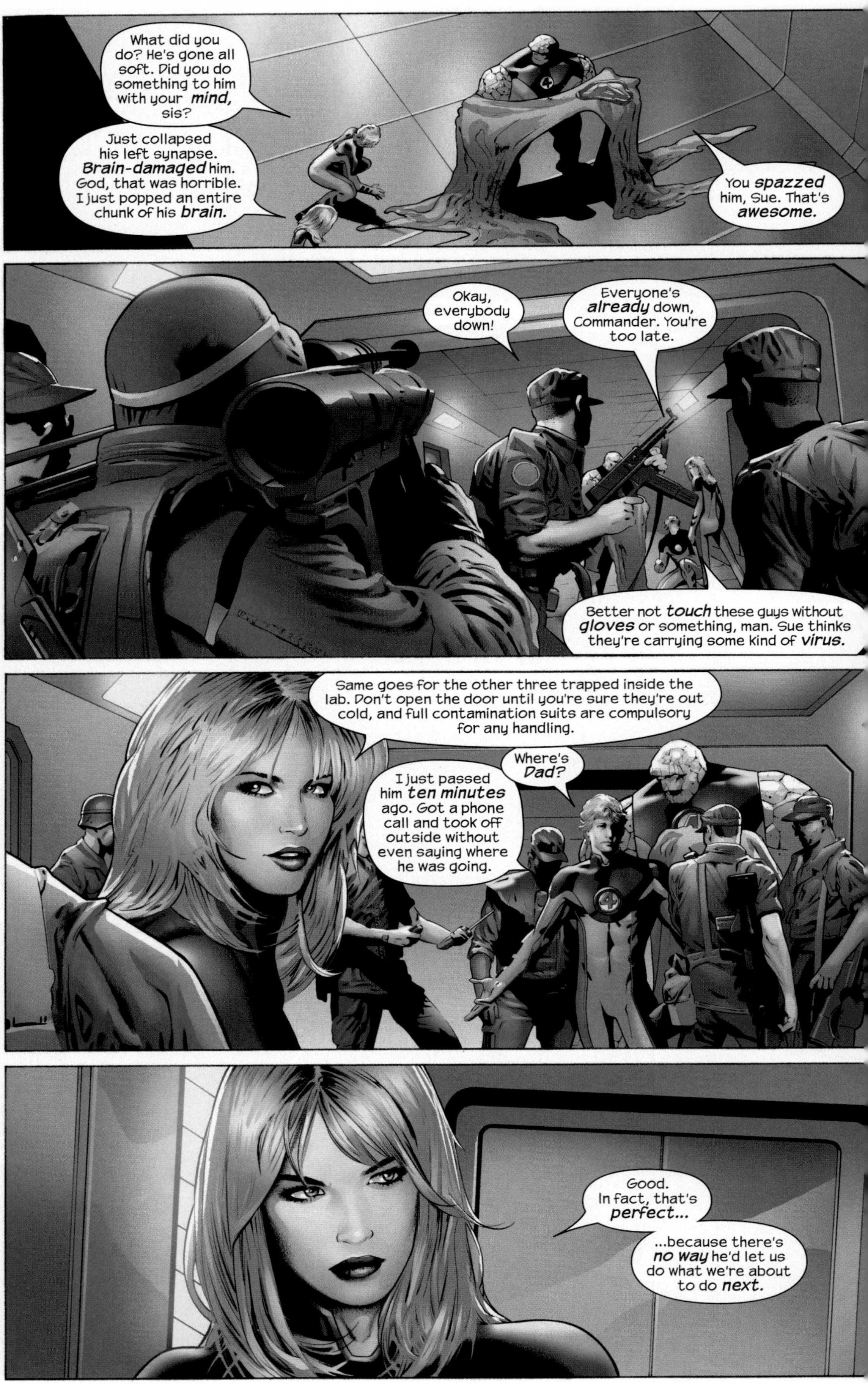
What did you do? He's gone all soft. Did you do something to him with your mind, sis?
Just collapsed his left synapse. Brain-damaged him. God, that was horrible. I just popped an entire chunk of his brain.
You spazzed him, Sue. That's awesome.
Okay, everybody down!
Everyone's already down, Commander. You're too late.
Better not touch these guys without gloves or something, man. Sue thinks they're carrying some kind of virus.
Same goes for the other three trapped inside the lab. Don't open the door until you're sure they're out cold, and full contamination suits are compulsory for any handling.
Where's Dad?
I just passed him ten minutes ago. Got a phone call and took off outside without even saying where he was going.
Good. In fact, that's perfect...
...because there's no way he'd let us do what we're about to do next.

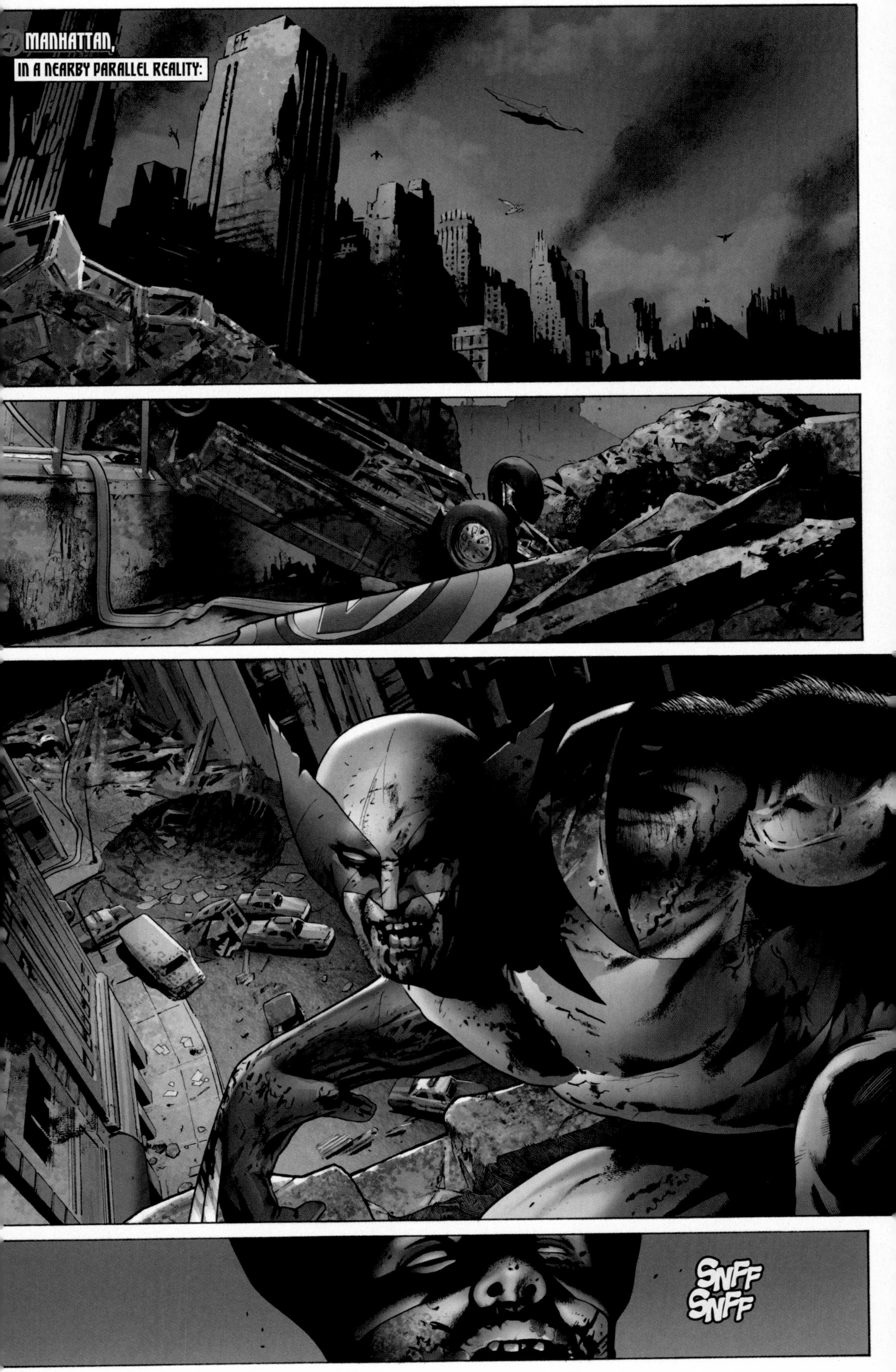
MANHATTAN,
IN A NEARBY PARALLEL REALITY:
SNFF SNFF

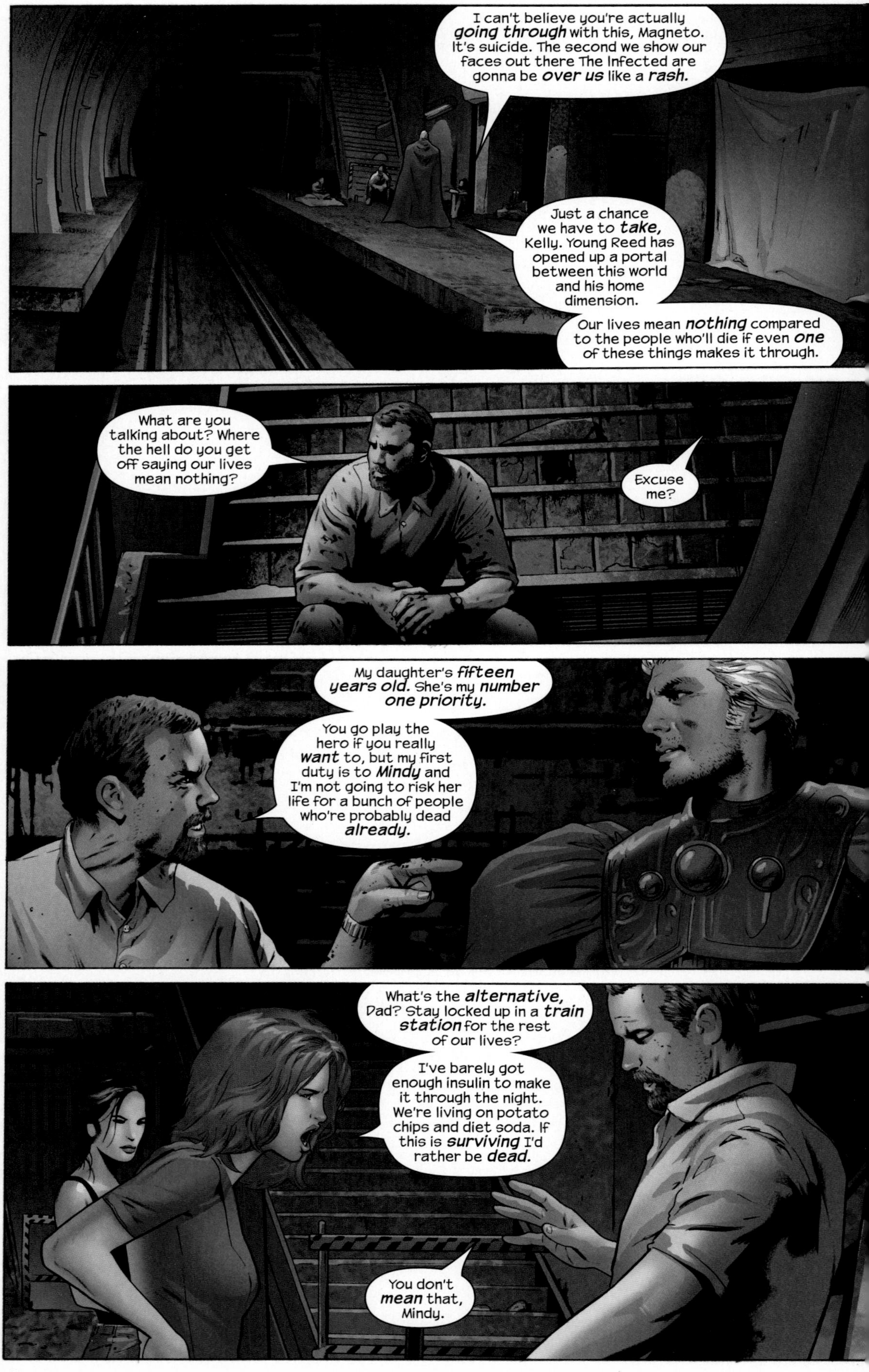
I can't believe you're actually going through with this, Magneto. It's suicide. The second we show our faces out there The Infected are gonna be over us like a rash.
Just a chance we have to take, Kelly. Young Reed has opened up a portal between this world and his home dimension.
Our lives mean nothing compared to the people who'll die if even one of these things makes it through.
What are you talking about? Where the hell do you get off saying our lives mean nothing?
Excuse me?
My daughter's fifteen years old. She's my number one priority.
You go play the hero if you really want to, but my first duty is to Mindy and I'm not going to risk her life for a bunch of people who're probably dead already.
What's the alternative, Dad? Stay locked up in a train station for the rest of our lives?
I've barely got enough insulin to make it through the night. We're living on potato chips and diet soda. If this is surviving I'd rather be dead.
You don't mean that, Mindy.

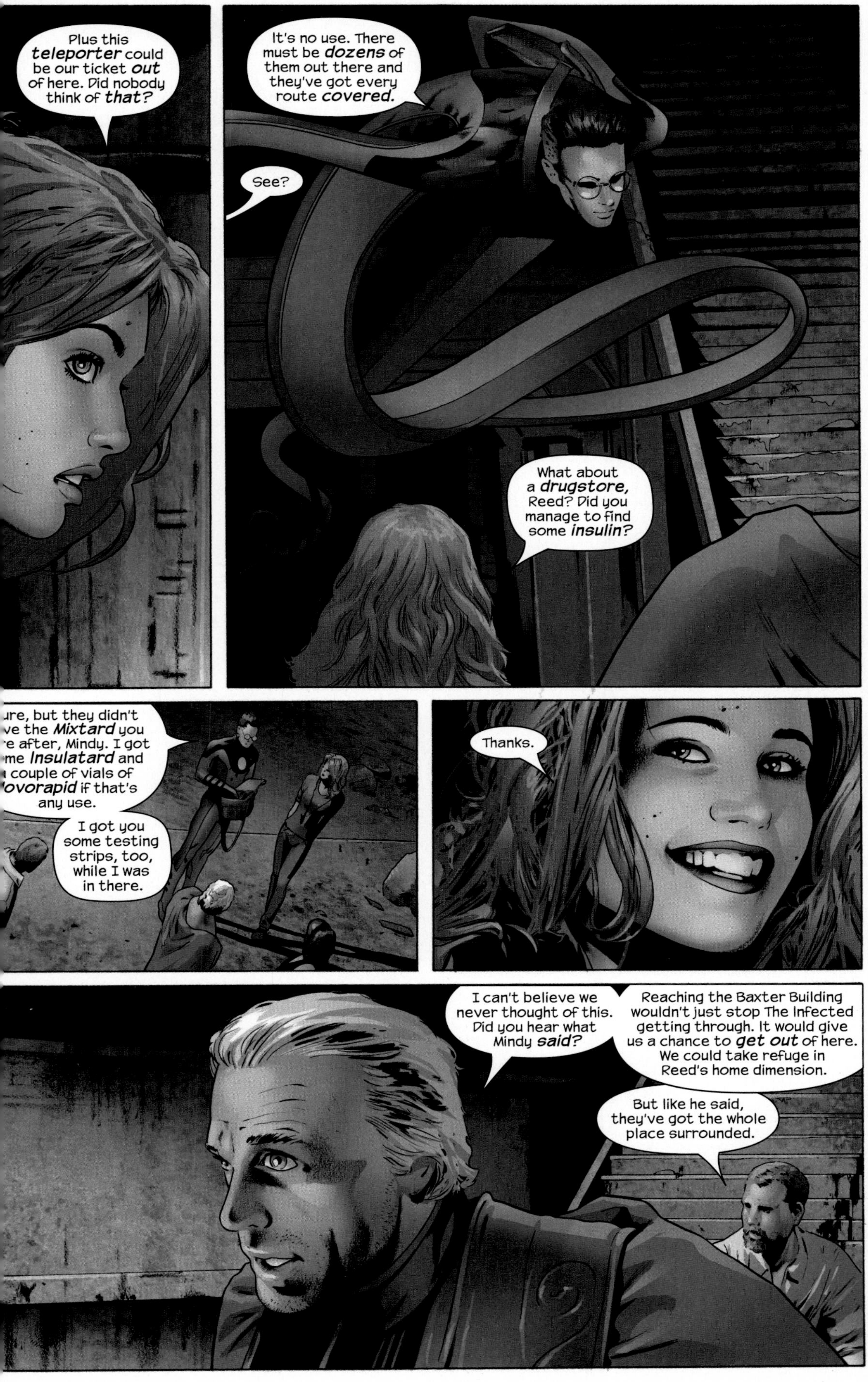
Plus this teleporter could be our ticket out of here. Did nobody think of that?
It's no use. There must be dozens of them out there and they've got every route covered.
See?
What about a drugstore, Reed? Did you manage to find some insulin?
ure, but they didn't ve the Mixtard you e after, Mindy. I got me Insulatard and couple of vials of ovorapid if that's any use.
I got you some testing strips, too, while I was in there.
Thanks.
I can't believe we never thought of this. Did you hear what Mindy said?
Reaching the Baxter Building wouldn't just stop The Infected getting through. It would give us a chance to get out of here. We could take refuge in Reed's home dimension.
But like he said, they've got the whole place surrounded.

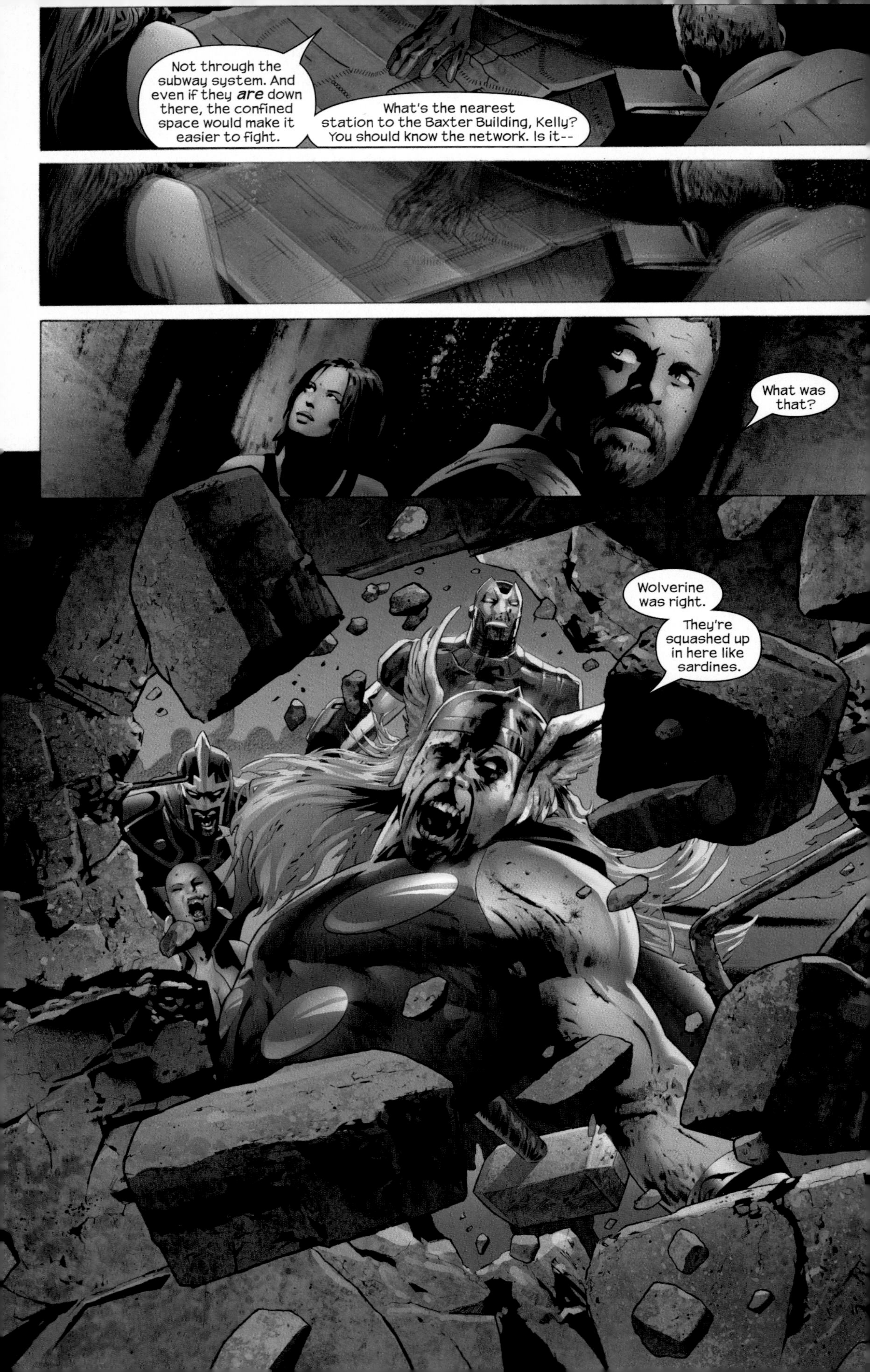
Not through the subway system. And even if they *are* down there, the confined space would make it easier to fight.
What's the nearest station to the Baxter Building, Kelly? You should know the network. Is it--
What was that?
Wolverine was right.
They're squashed up in here like sardines.

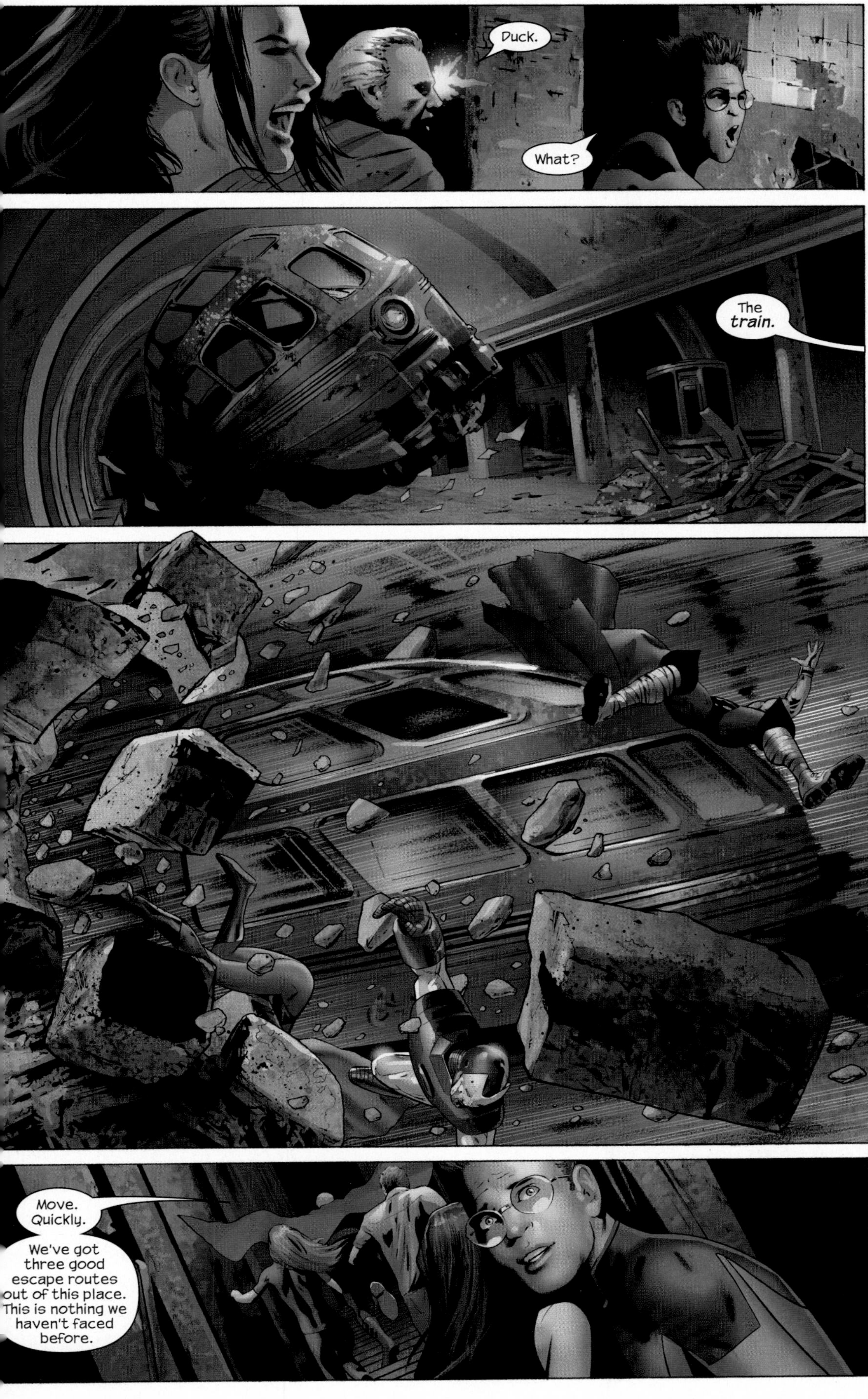
Duck.
What?
The *train.*
Move. Quickly.
We've got three good escape routes out of this place. This is nothing we haven't faced before.

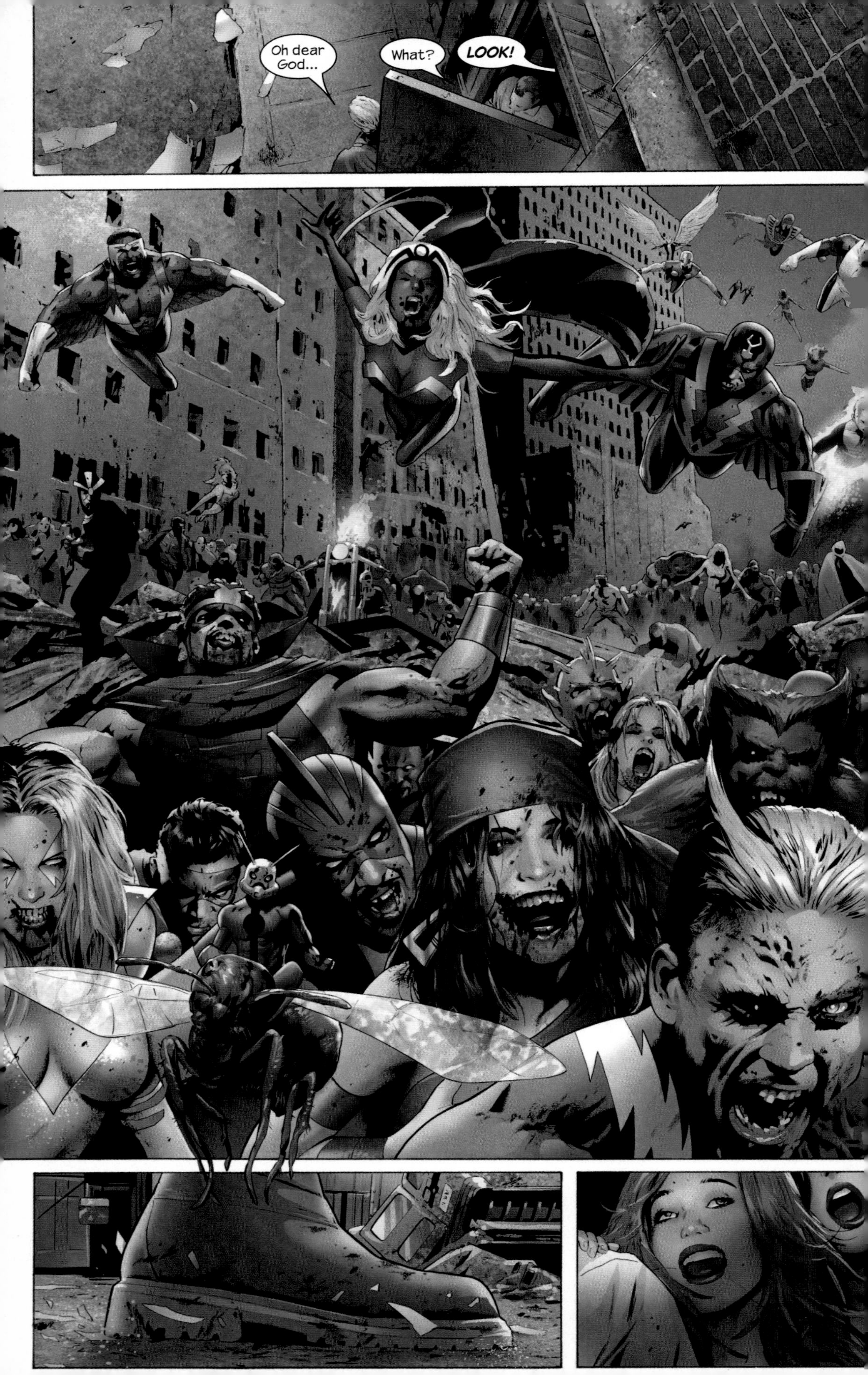
Oh dear God...
What?
LOOK!

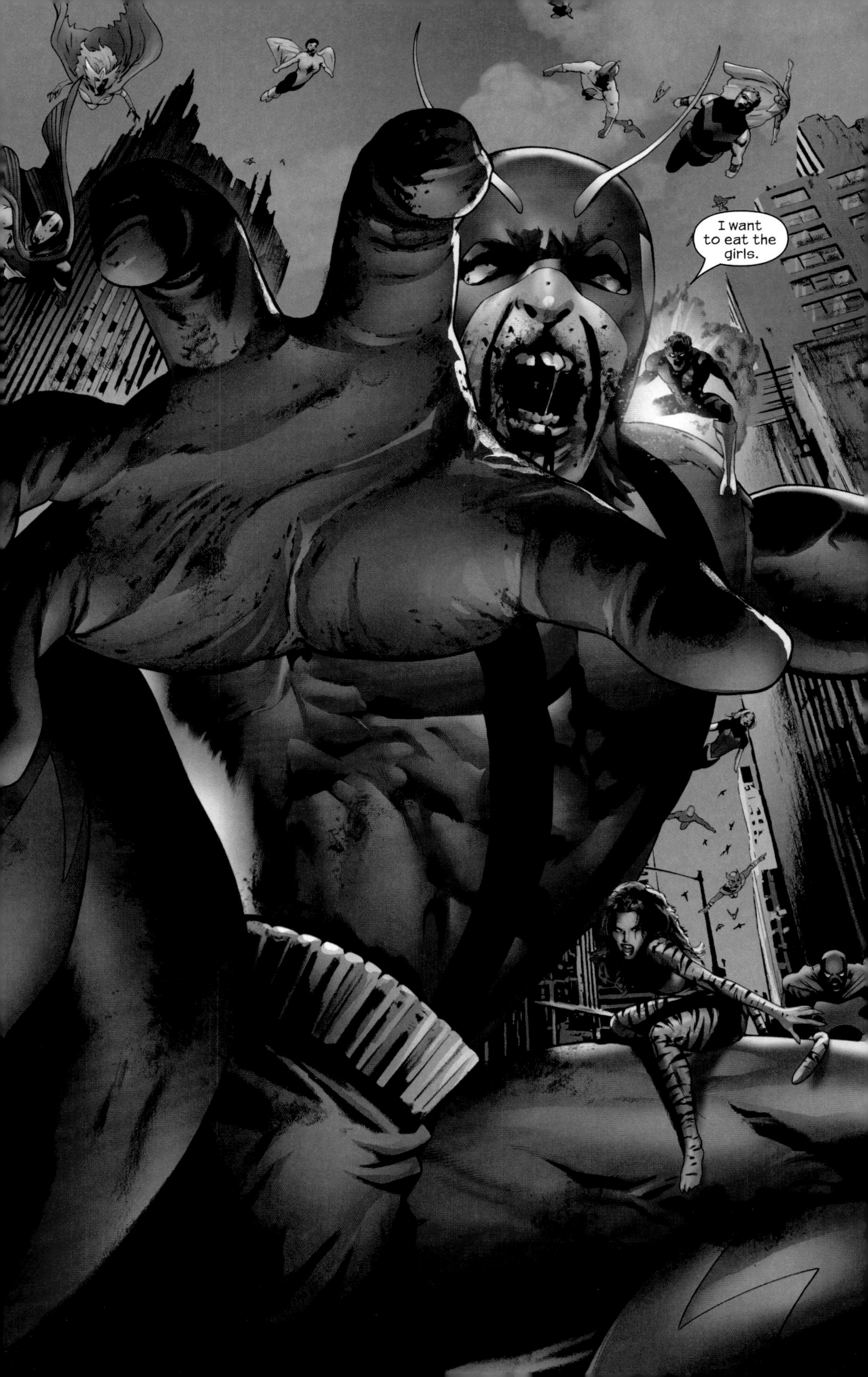
I want to eat the girls.

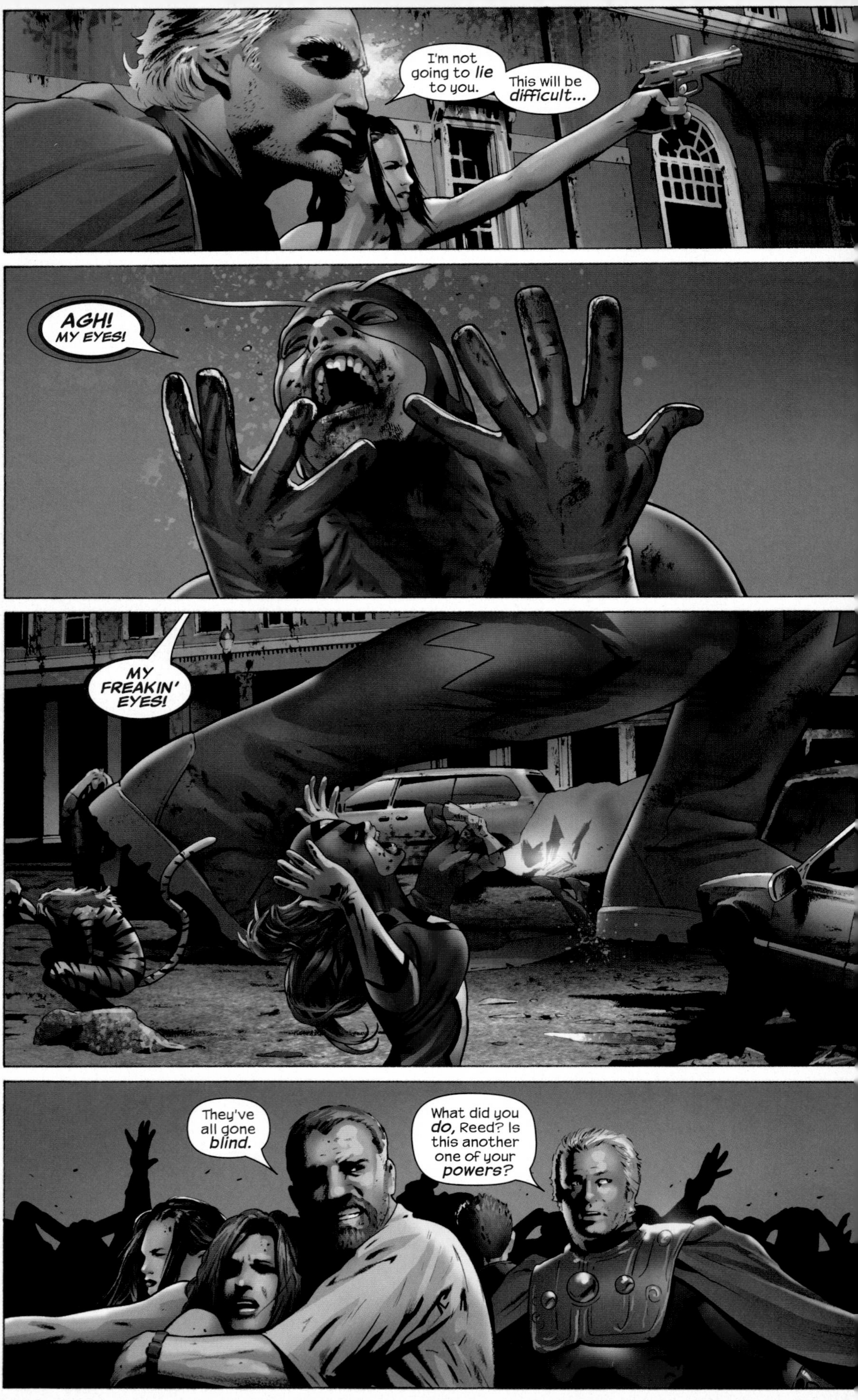
I'm not going to *lie* to you.
This will be *difficult...*
AGH! MY EYES!
MY FREAKIN' EYES!
They've all gone *blind.*
What did you *do,* Reed? Is this another one of your *powers?*

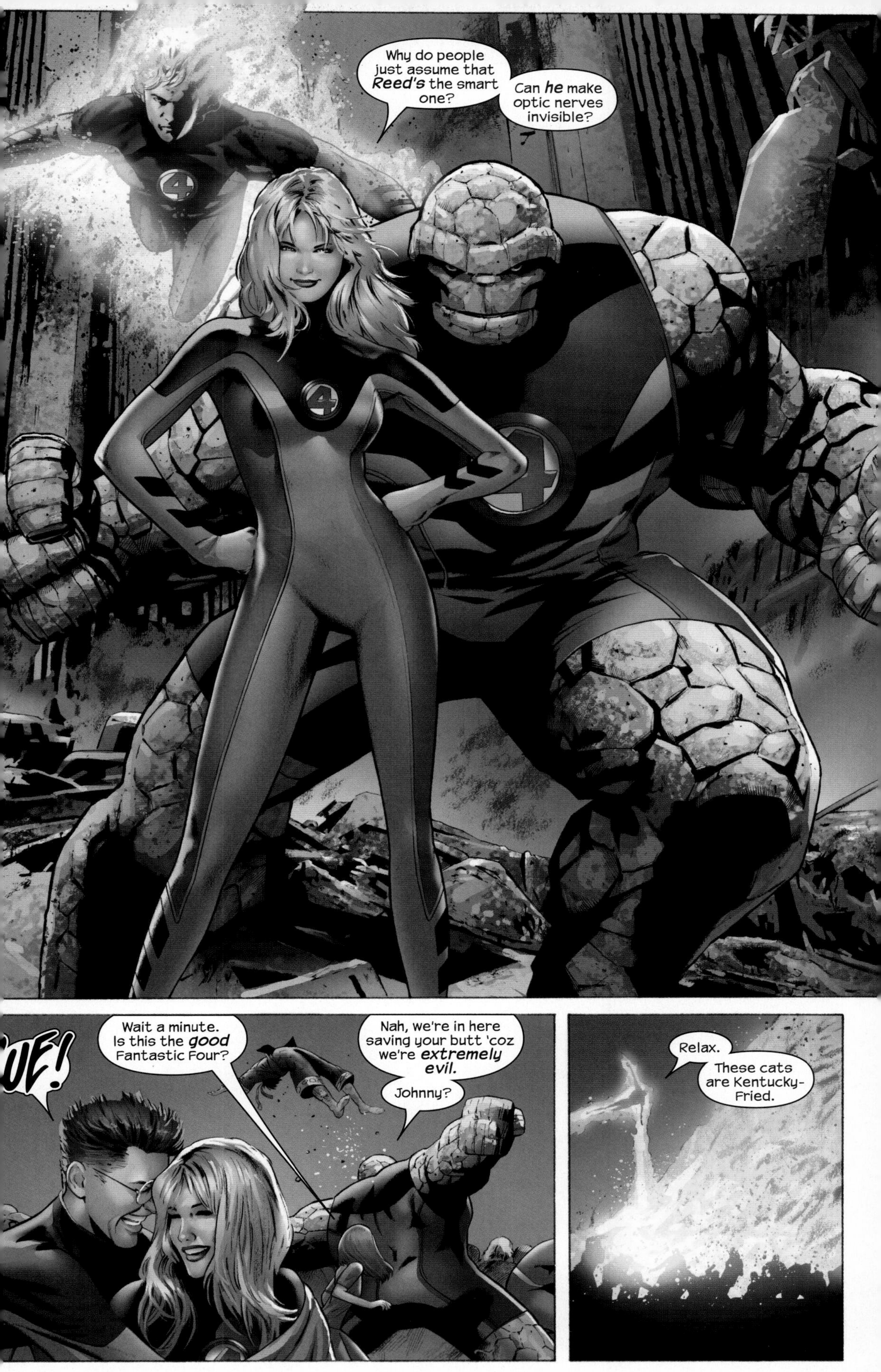
Why do people just assume that *Reed's* the smart one?
Can *he* make optic nerves invisible?
Wait a minute. Is this the *good* Fantastic Four?
Nah, we're in here saving your butt 'coz we're *extremely evil.*
Johnny?
Relax.
These cats are Kentucky-Fried.

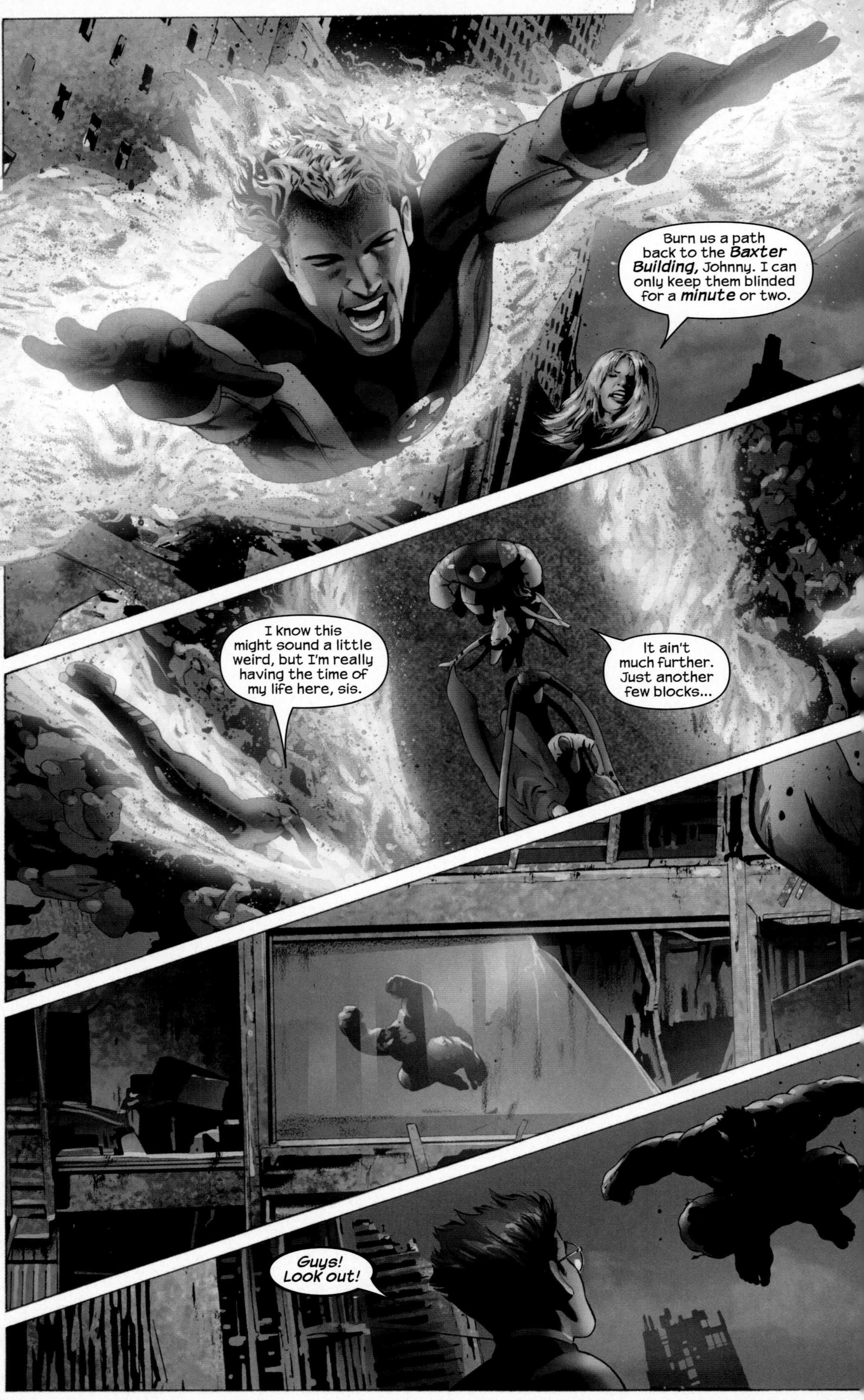
Burn us a path back to the Baxter Building, Johnny. I can only keep them blinded for a minute or two.
I know this might sound a little weird, but I'm really having the time of my life here, sis.
It ain't much further. Just another few blocks...
Guys! Look out!

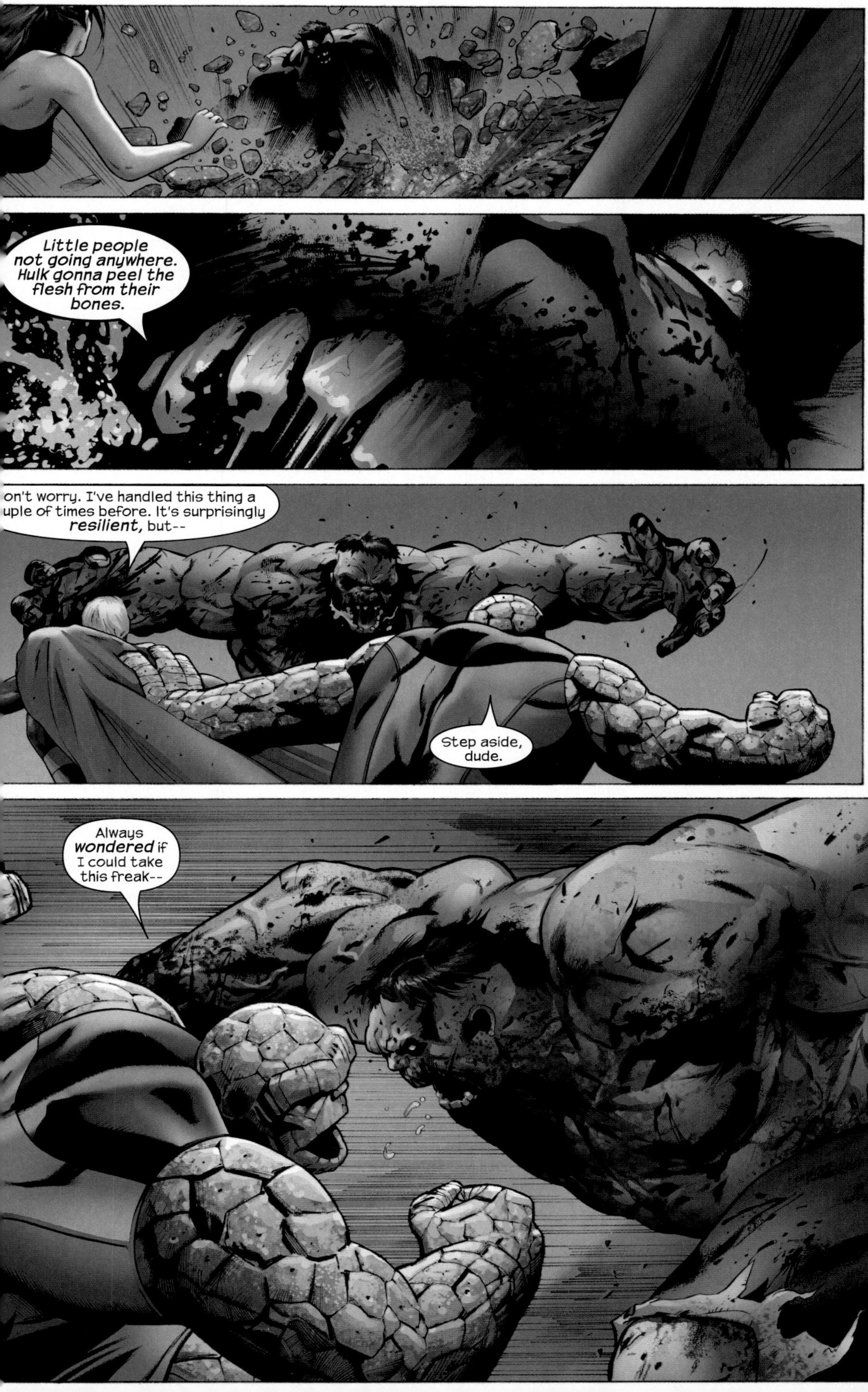
Little people not going anywhere. Hulk gonna peel the flesh from their bones.
on't worry. I've handled this thing a uple of times before. It's surprisingly resilient, but--
Step aside, dude.
Always wondered if I could take this freak--

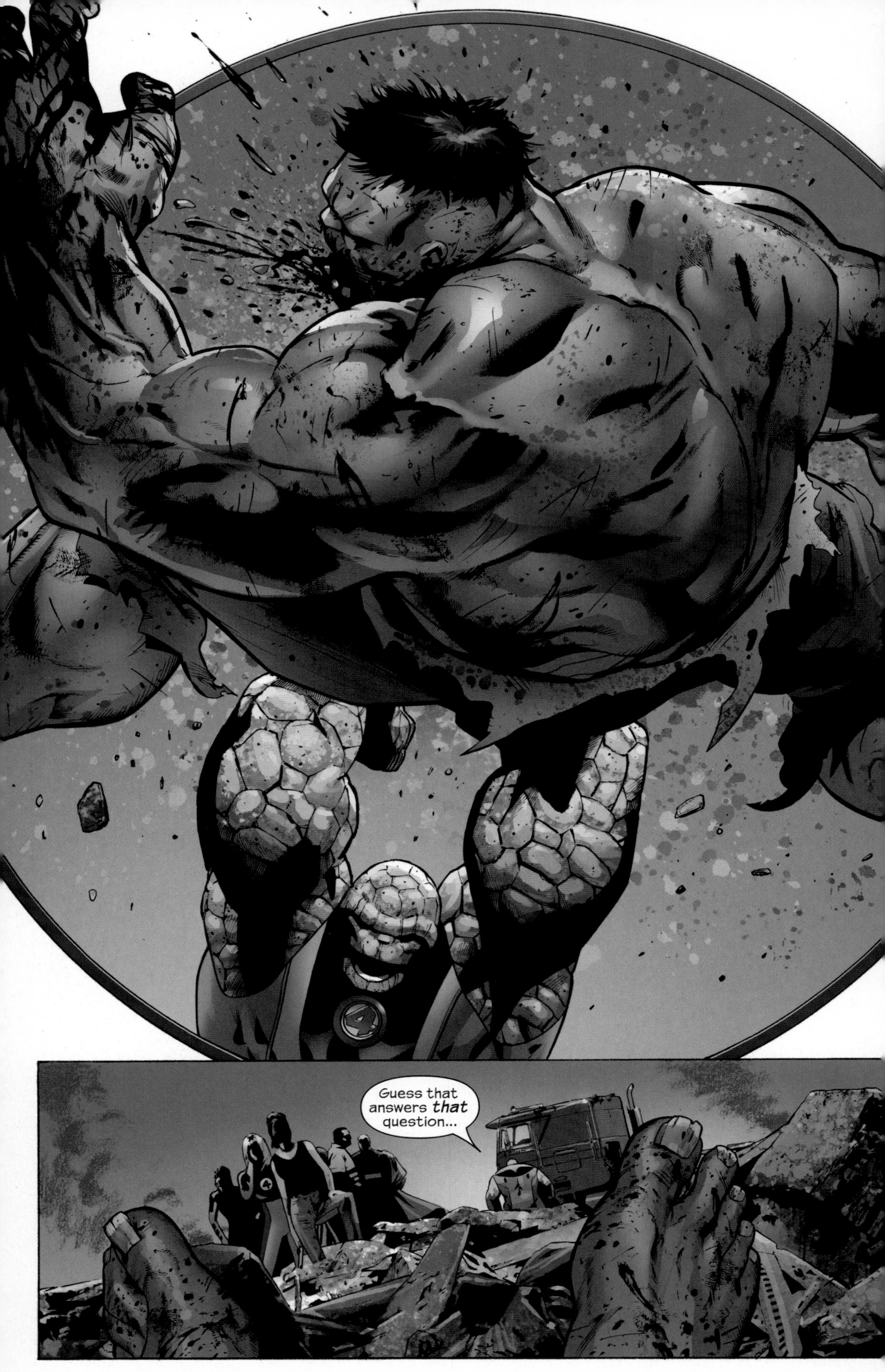
Guess that answers *that* question...

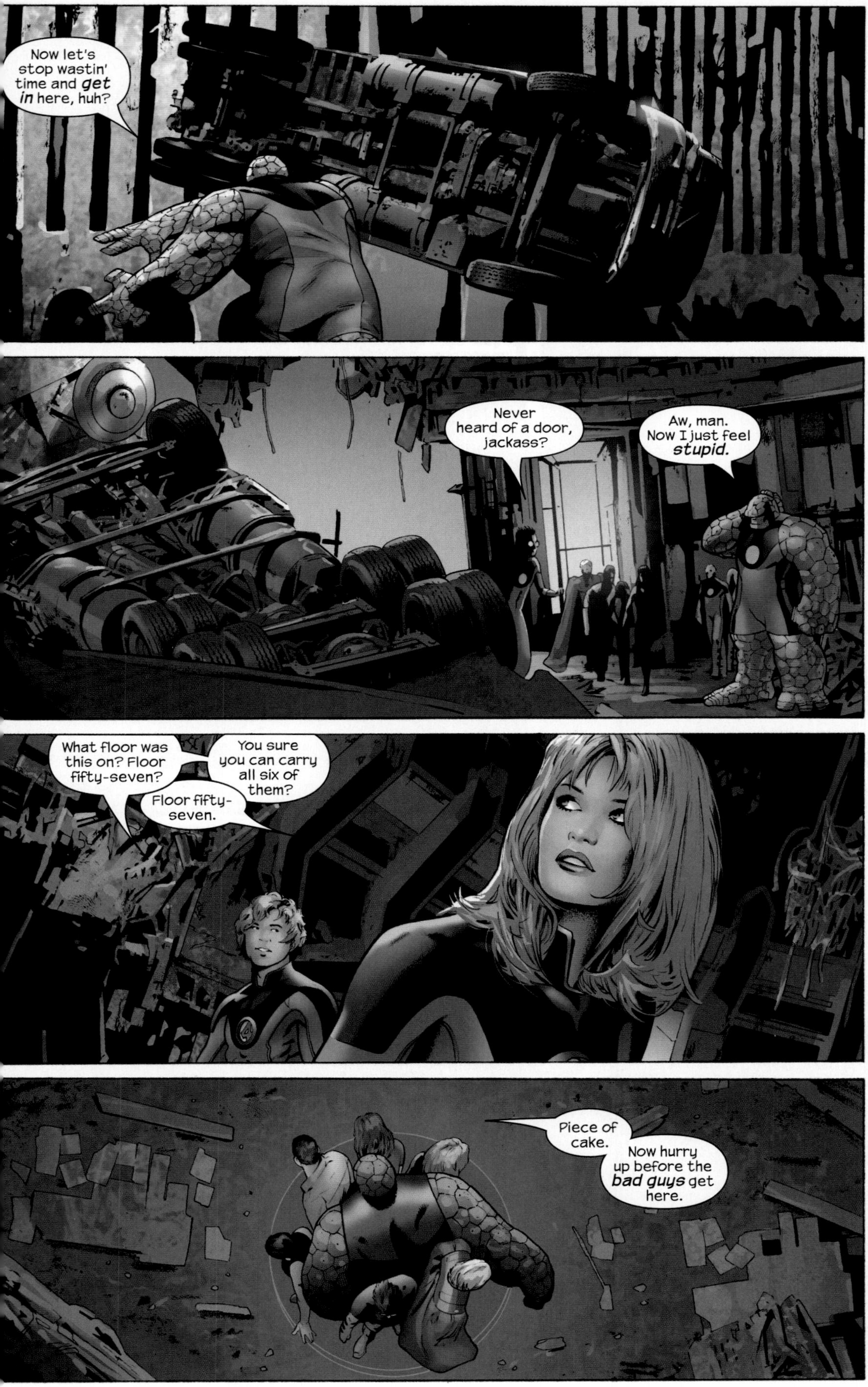
Now let's stop wastin' time and get in here, huh?
Never heard of a door, jackass?
Aw, man. Now I just feel stupid.
What floor was this on? Floor fifty-seven?
Floor fifty-seven.
You sure you can carry all six of them?
Piece of cake.
Now hurry up before the bad guys get here.

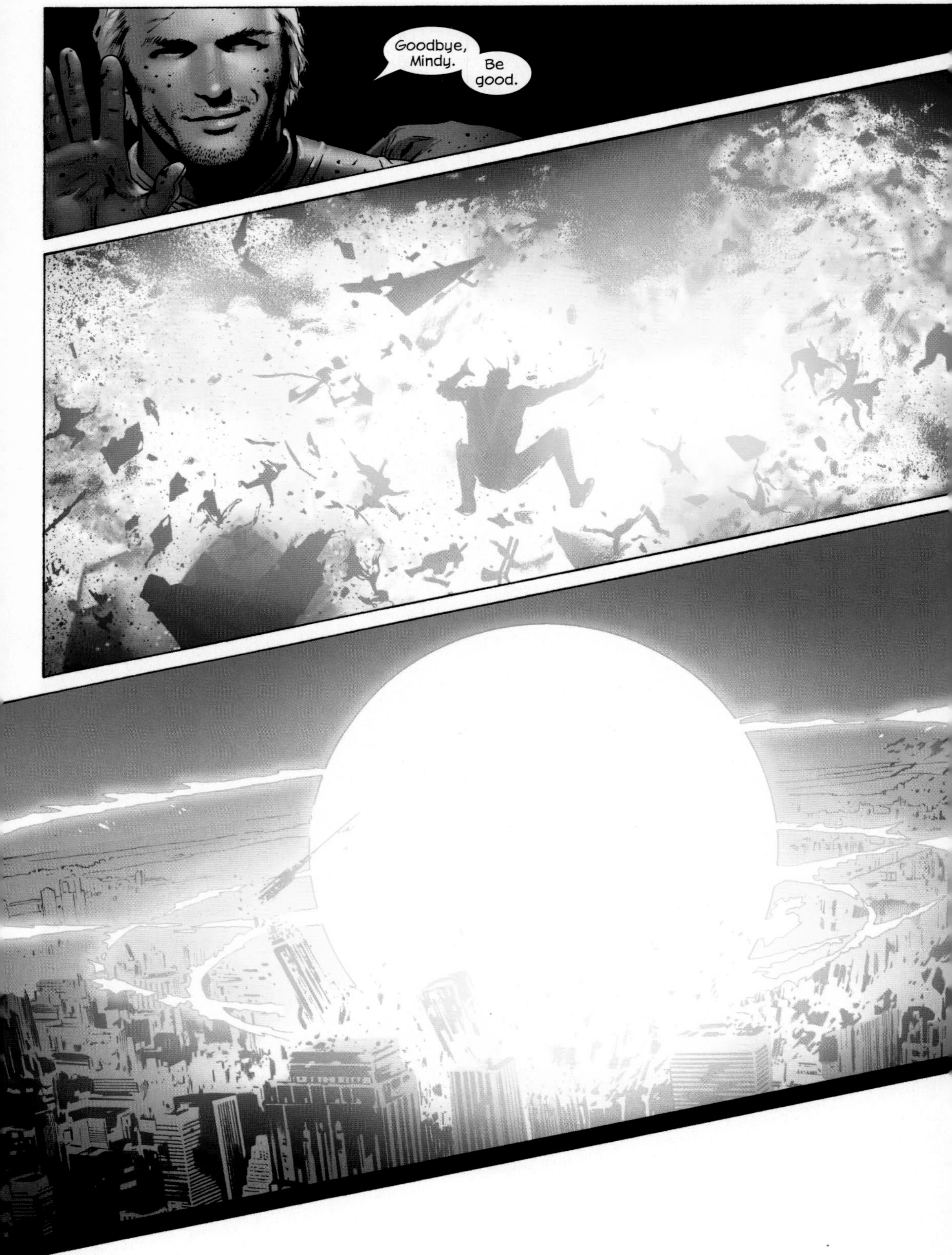
Goodbye, Mindy.
Be good.

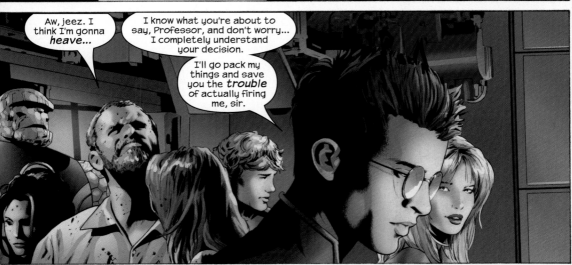

Aw, jeez. I think I'm gonna *heave...*

I know what you're about to say, Professor, and don't worry... I completely understand your decision.

I'll go pack my things and save you the *trouble* of actually firing me, sir.

I didn't *come* here to fire you, Reed. Obviously, I'm not happy about what you've done here, but I know about the creatures and we've contained them downstairs.

We can talk about your future *later.* I came here to talk to *Johnny and Sue.*

It's about--

Hello, my little darlings.

How's life been *treating* you the past fifteen years?

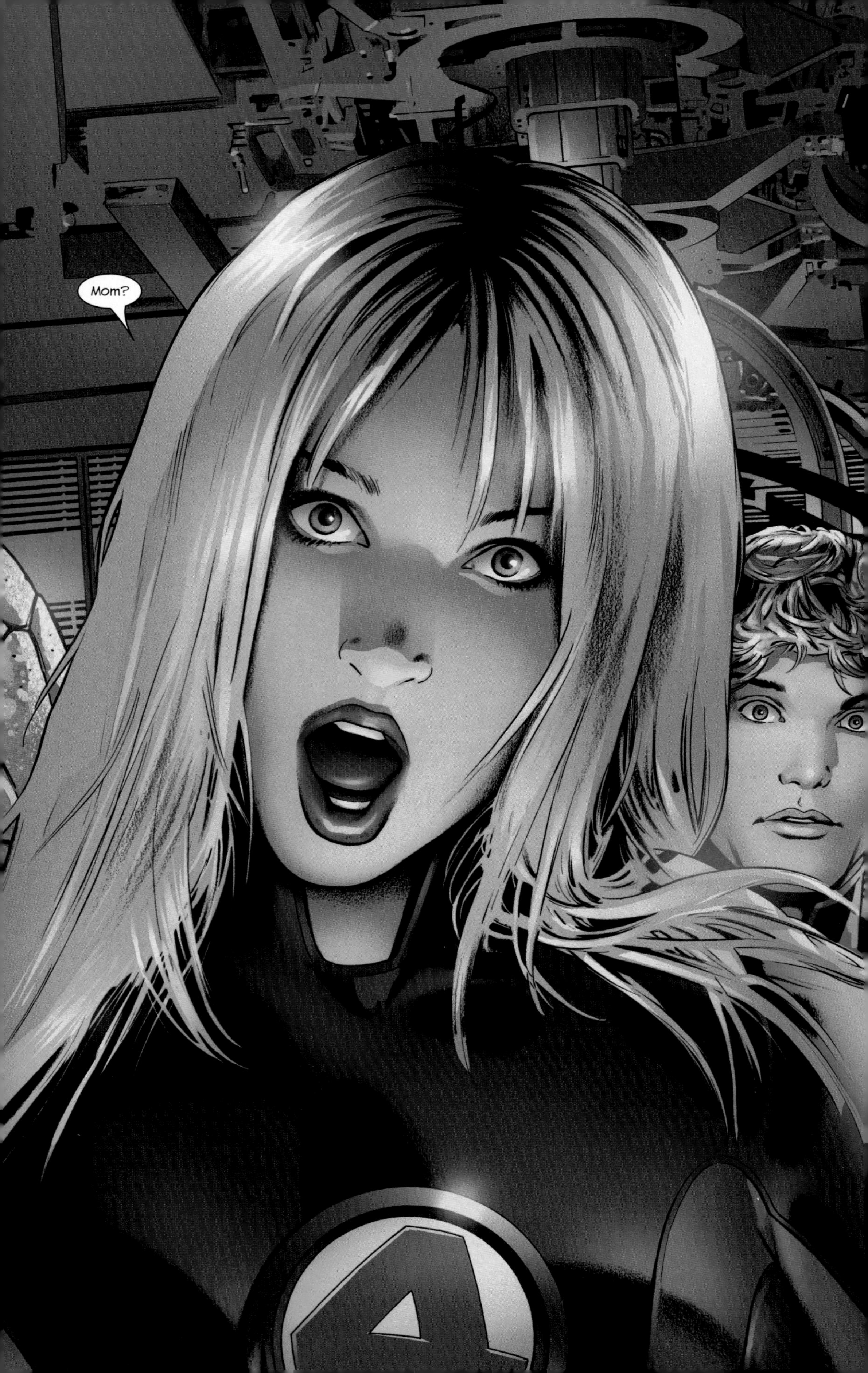
Mom?

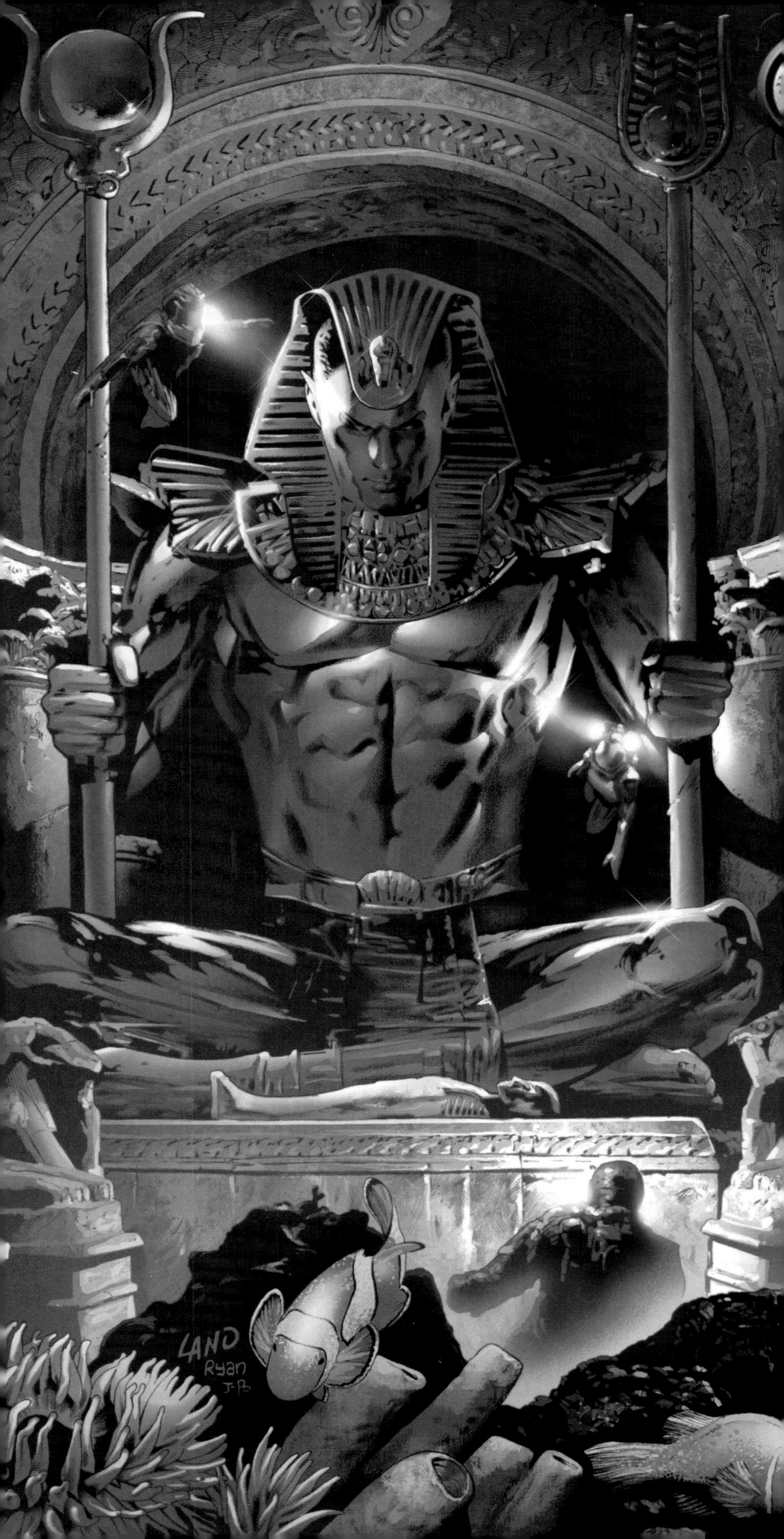

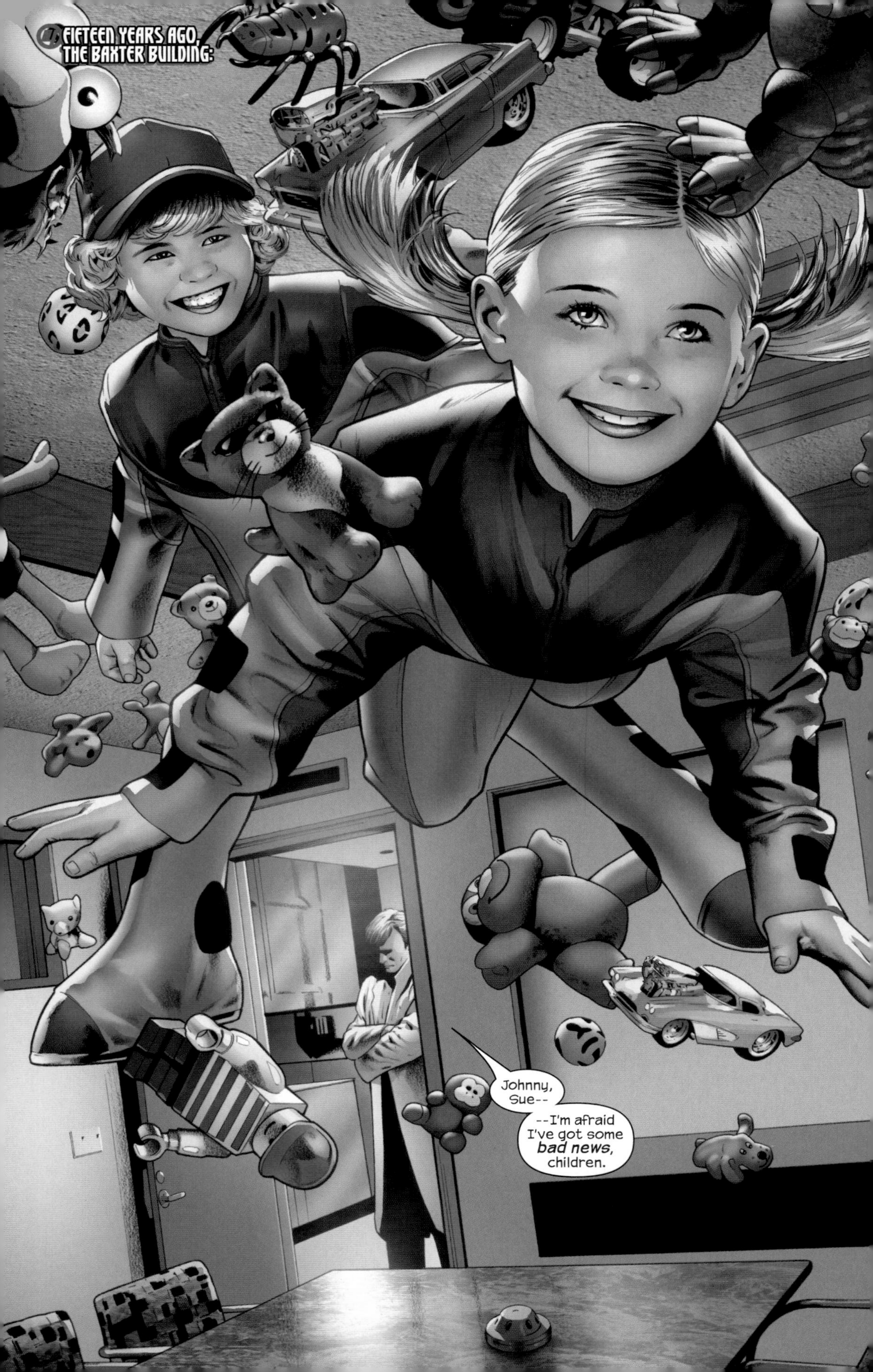
FIFTEEN YEARS AGO, THE BAXTER BUILDING:
Johnny, Sue--
--I'm afraid I've got some bad news, children.

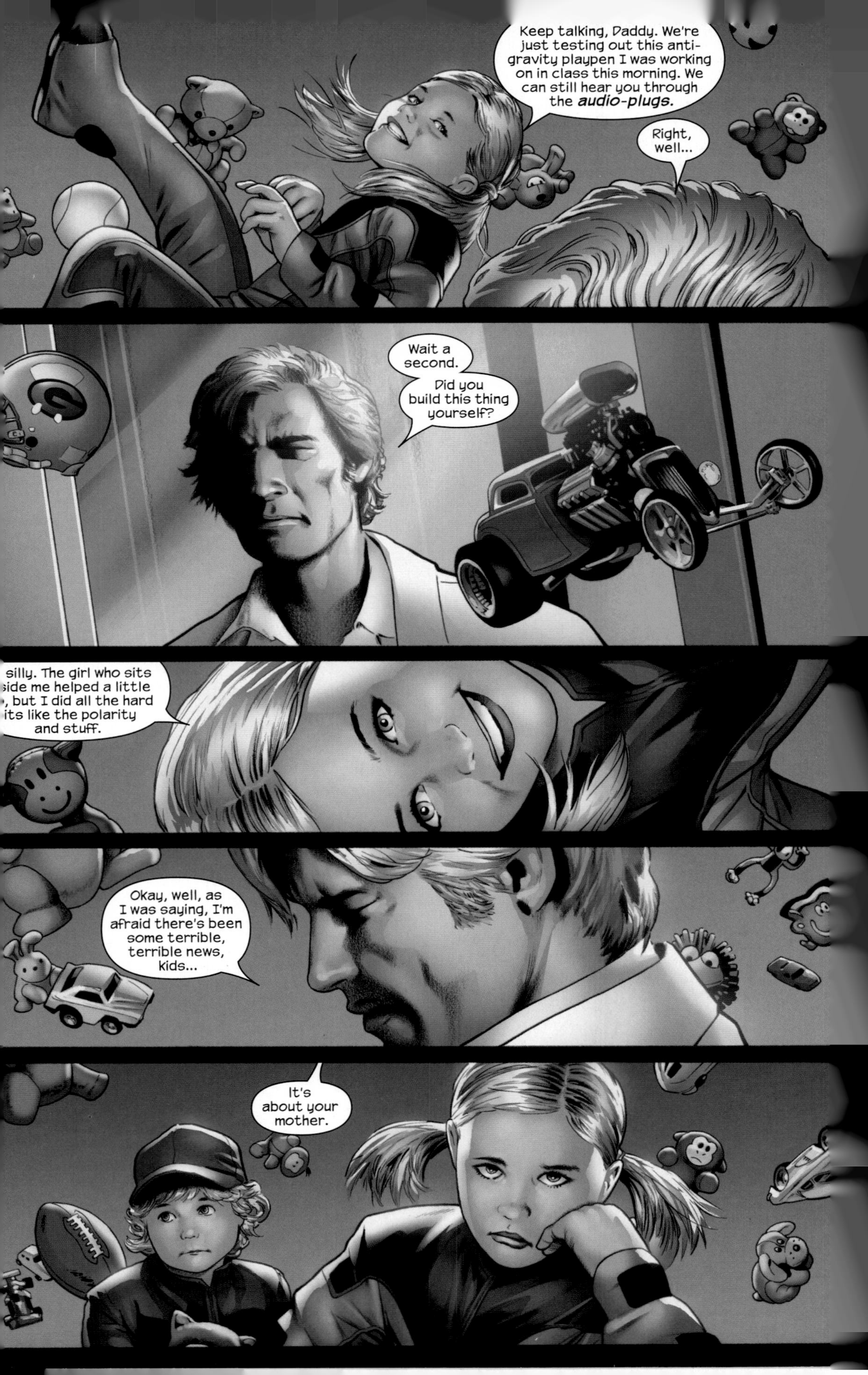
Keep talking, Daddy. We're just testing out this anti-gravity playpen I was working on in class this morning. We can still hear you through the audio-plugs.
Right, well...
Wait a second.
Did you build this thing yourself?
silly. The girl who sits side me helped a little , but I did all the hard its like the polarity and stuff.
Okay, well, as I was saying, I'm afraid there's been some terrible, terrible news, kids...
It's about your mother.

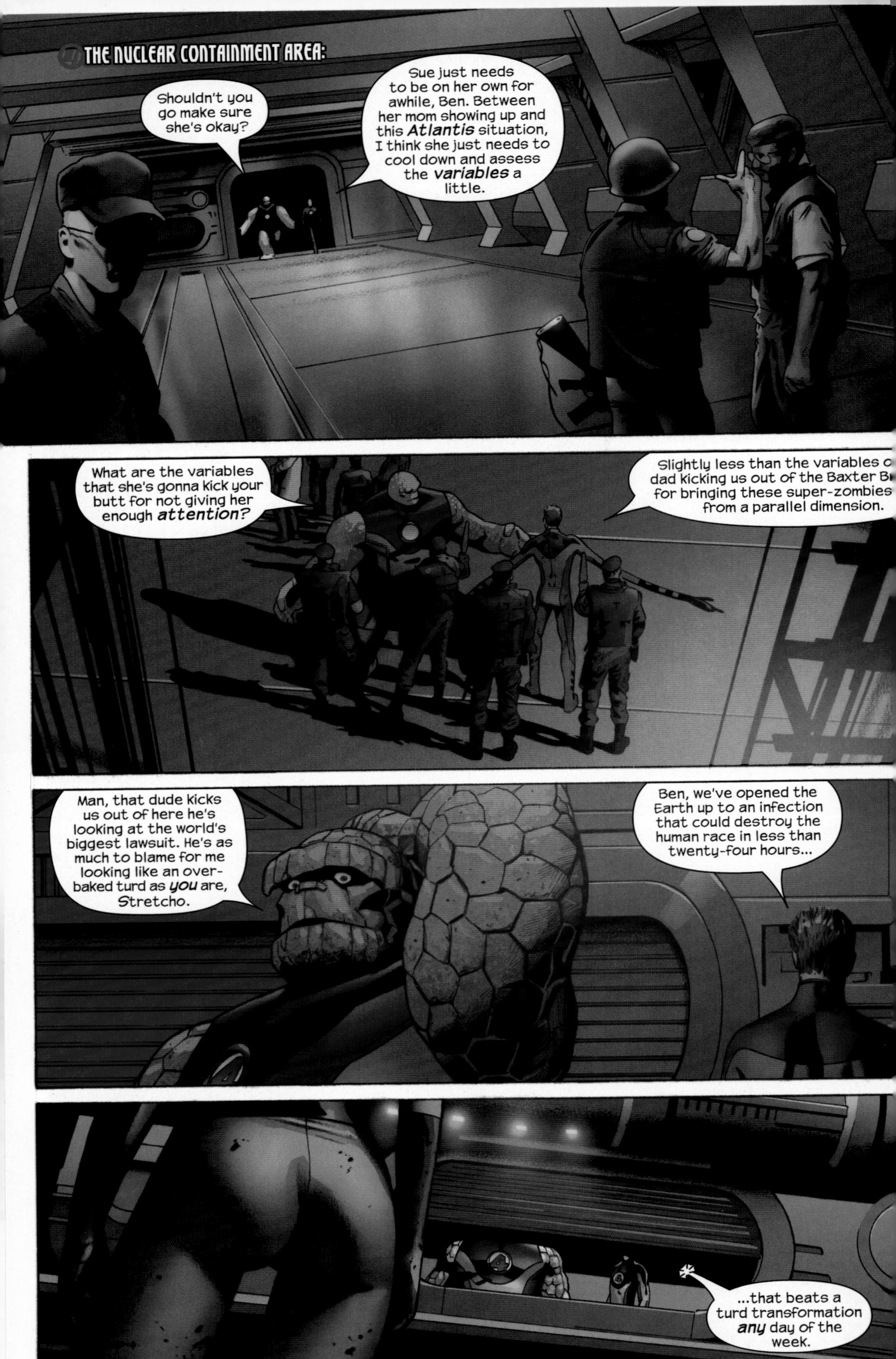
THE NUCLEAR CONTAINMENT AREA:
Shouldn't you go make sure she's okay?
Sue just needs to be on her own for awhile, Ben. Between her mom showing up and this Atlantis situation, I think she just needs to cool down and assess the variables a little.
What are the variables that she's gonna kick your butt for not giving her enough attention?
Slightly less than the variables dad kicking us out of the Baxter for bringing these super-zombies from a parallel dimension.
Man, that dude kicks us out of here he's looking at the world's biggest lawsuit. He's as much to blame for me looking like an over-baked turd as you are, Stretcho.
Ben, we've opened the Earth up to an infection that could destroy the human race in less than twenty-four hours...
...that beats a turd transformation any day of the week.

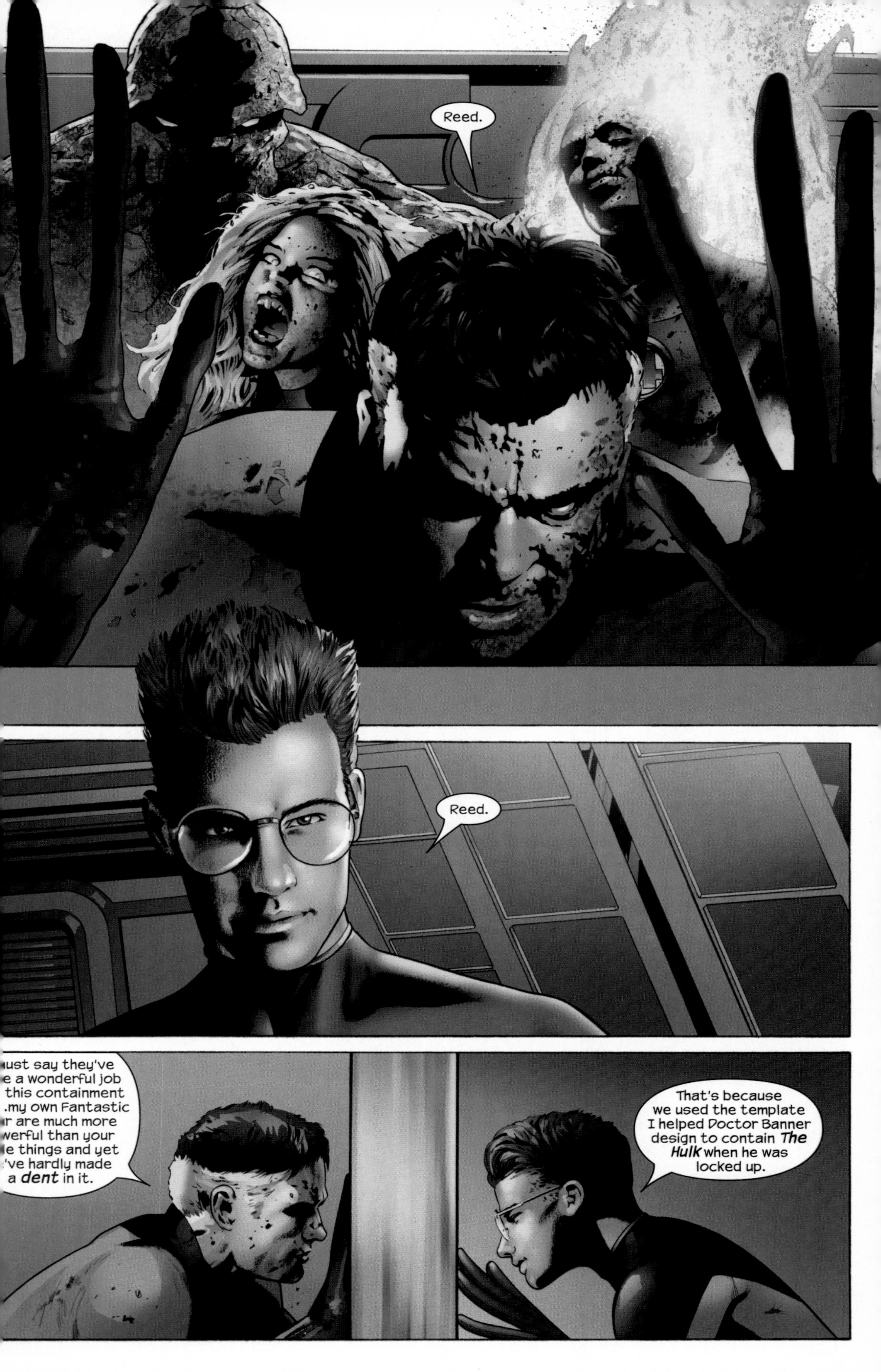

Reed.
Reed.
ust say they've e a wonderful job this containment .my own Fantastic r are much more werful than your e things and yet 've hardly made a *dent* in it.
That's because we used the template I helped Doctor Banner design to contain *The Hulk* when he was locked up.

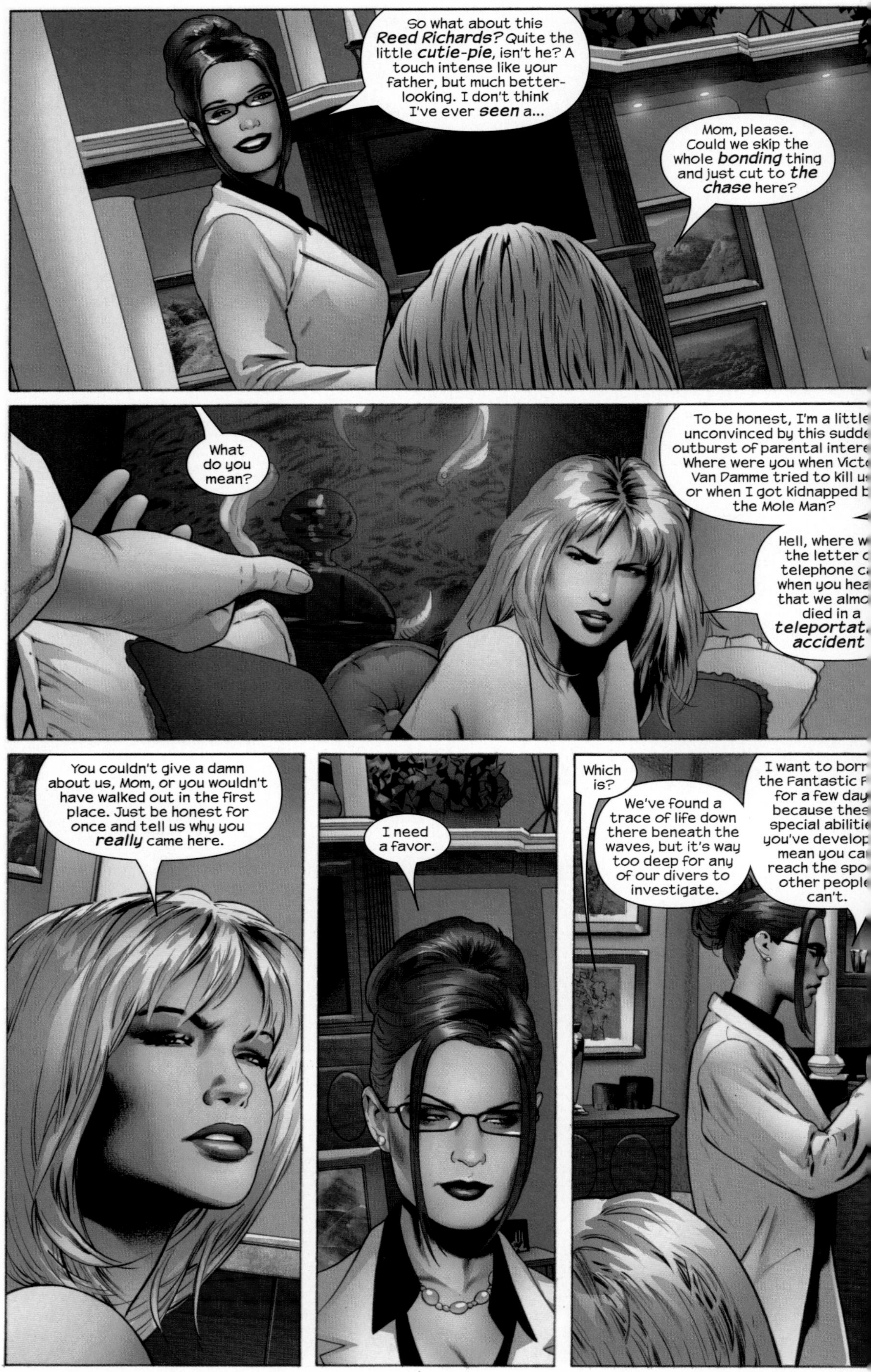
So what about this Reed Richards? Quite the little cutie-pie, isn't he? A touch intense like your father, but much better-looking. I don't think I've ever seen a...
Mom, please. Could we skip the whole bonding thing and just cut to the chase here?
What do you mean?
To be honest, I'm a little unconvinced by this sudde outburst of parental intere Where were you when Victo Van Damme tried to kill u or when I got kidnapped b the Mole Man?
Hell, where w the letter c telephone c when you hea that we almo died in a teleportat accident
You couldn't give a damn about us, Mom, or you wouldn't have walked out in the first place. Just be honest for once and tell us why you really came here.
I need a favor.
Which is?
We've found a trace of life down there beneath the waves, but it's way too deep for any of our divers to investigate.
I want to borr the Fantastic F for a few day because thes special abilitie you've develop mean you ca reach the spo other peopl can't.

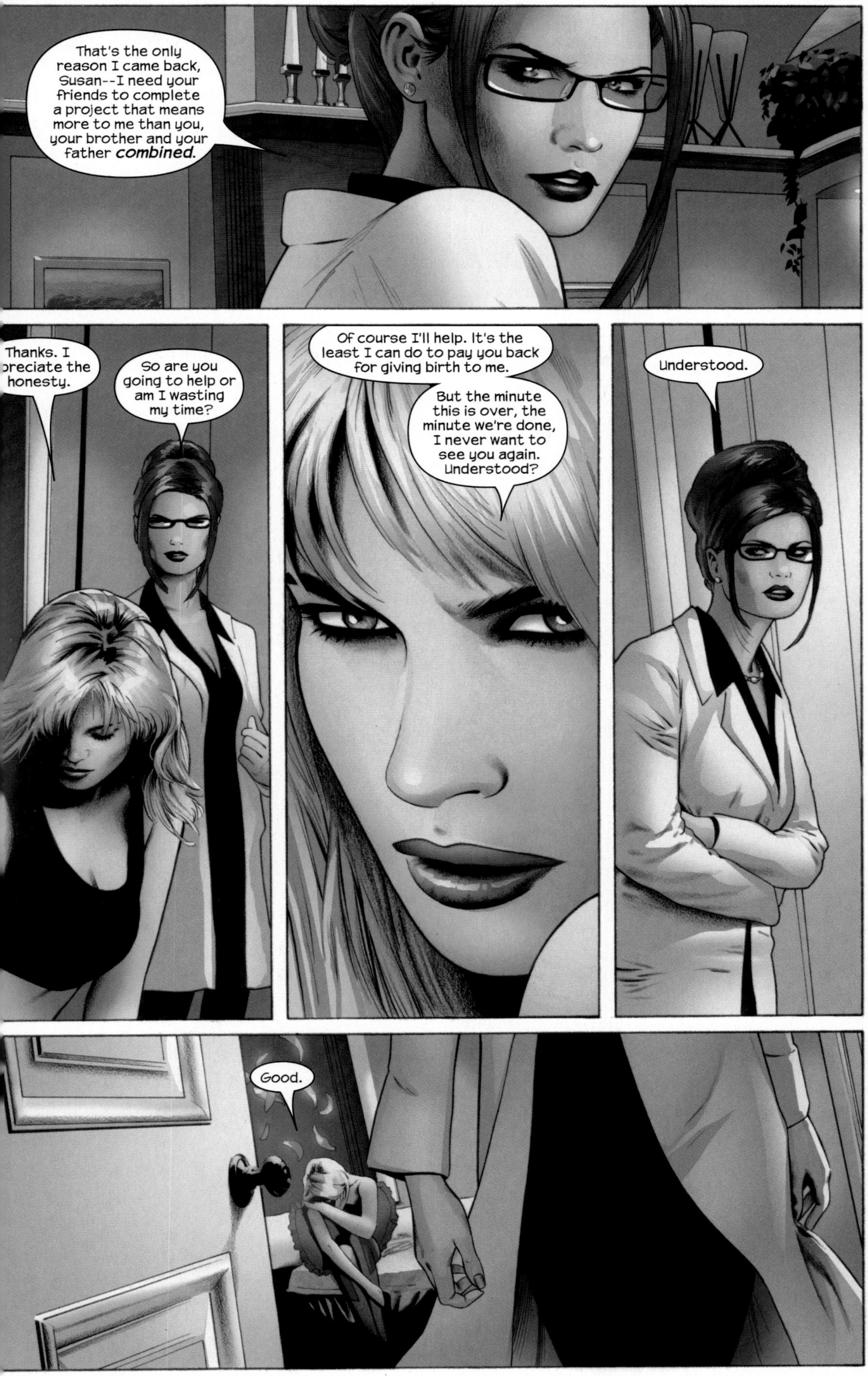
That's the only reason I came back, Susan--I need your friends to complete a project that means more to me than you, your brother and your father *combined*.
Thanks. I preciate the honesty.
So are you going to help or am I wasting my time?
Of course I'll help. It's the least I can do to pay you back for giving birth to me.
But the minute this is over, the minute we're done, I never want to see you again. Understood?
Understood.
Good.

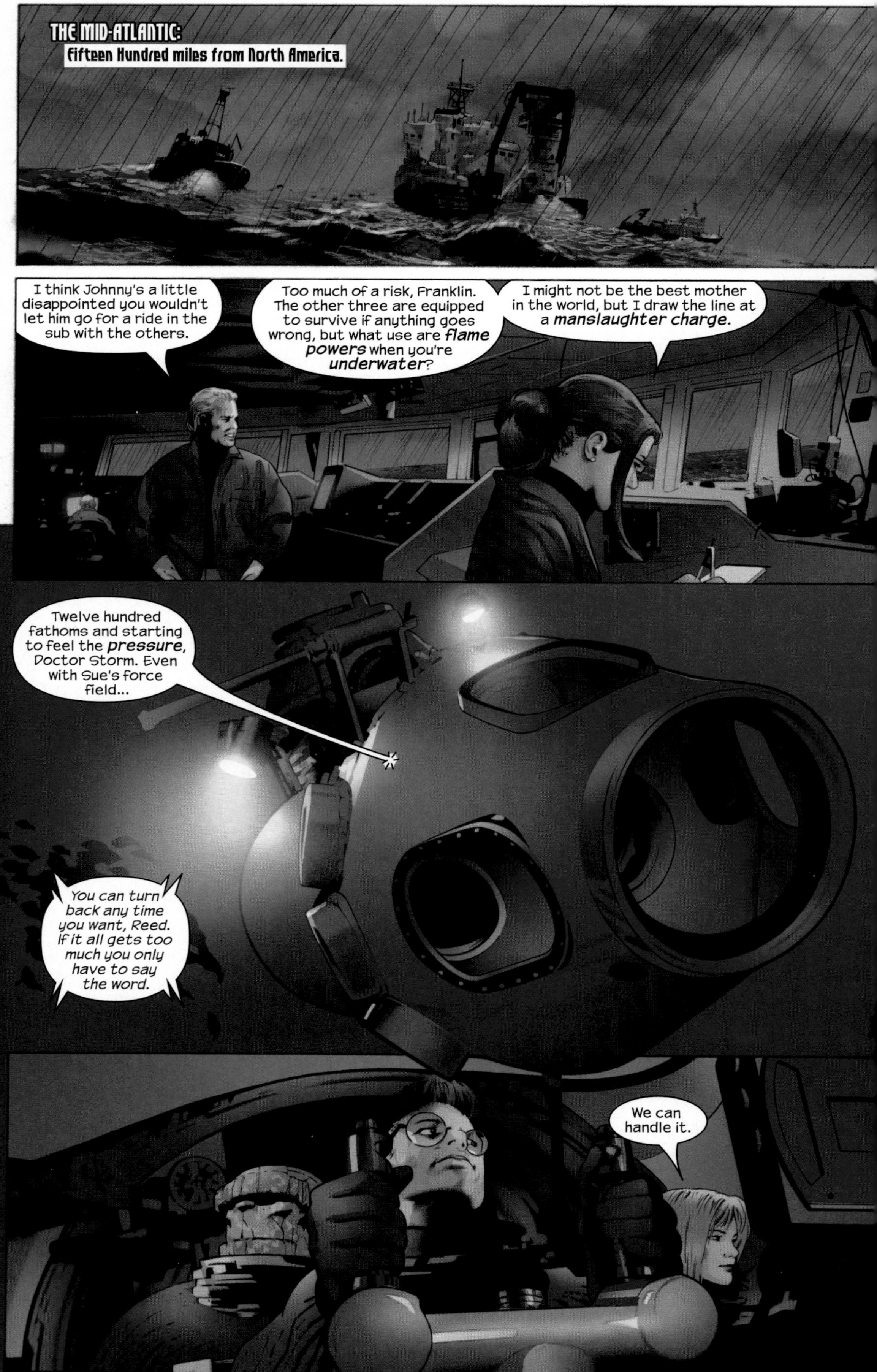
THE MID-ATLANTIC:
Fifteen Hundred miles from North America.
I think Johnny's a little disappointed you wouldn't let him go for a ride in the sub with the others.
Too much of a risk, Franklin. The other three are equipped to survive if anything goes wrong, but what use are *flame powers* when you're *underwater*?
I might not be the best mother in the world, but I draw the line at a *manslaughter charge.*
Twelve hundred fathoms and starting to feel the *pressure*, Doctor Storm. Even with Sue's force field...
You can turn back any time you want, Reed. If it all gets too much you only have to say the word.
We can handle it.

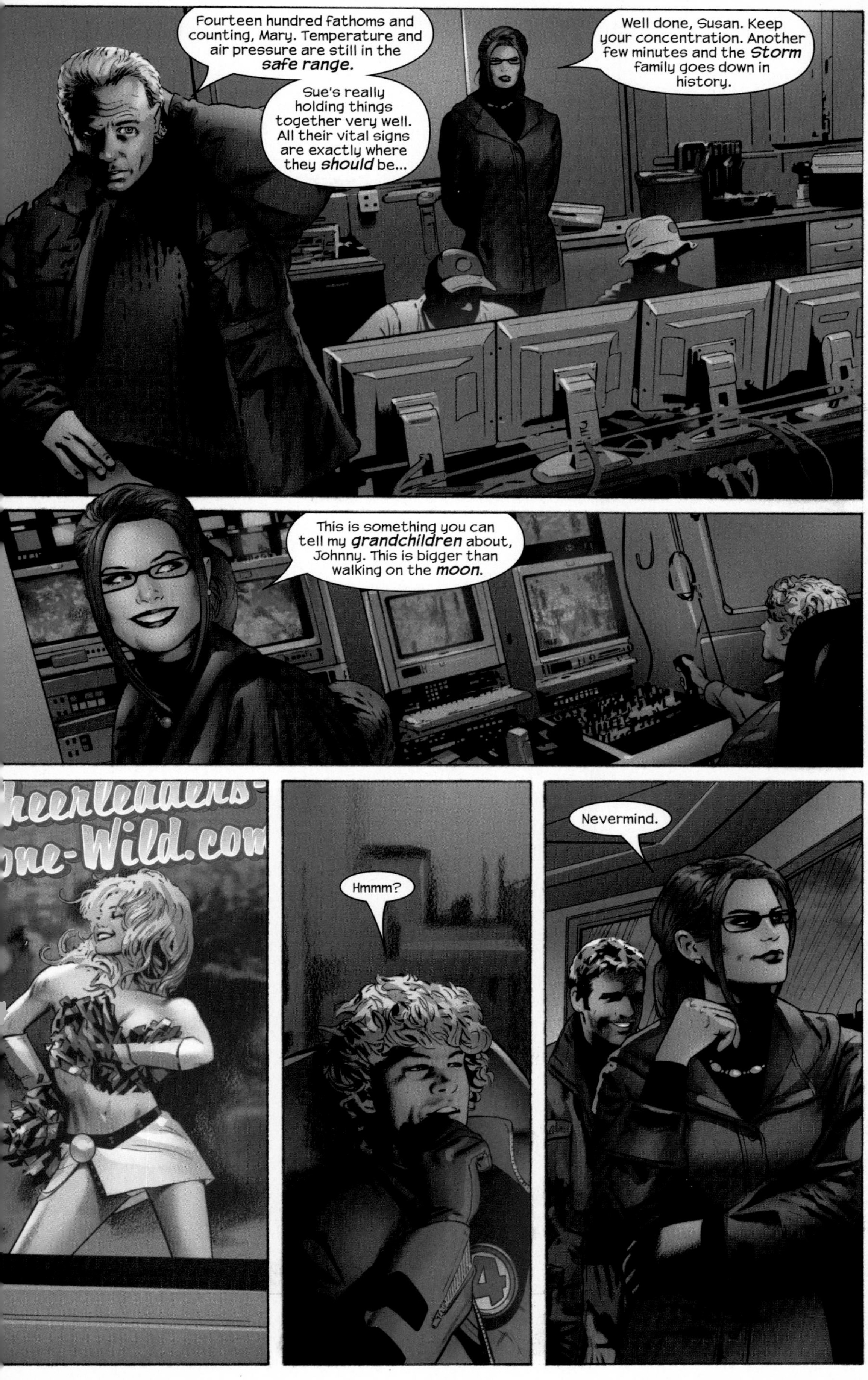

Fourteen hundred fathoms and counting, Mary. Temperature and air pressure are still in the safe range.
Sue's really holding things together very well. All their vital signs are exactly where they should be...
Well done, Susan. Keep your concentration. Another few minutes and the Storm family goes down in history.
This is something you can tell my grandchildren about, Johnny. This is bigger than walking on the moon.
heerleaders-
one-Wild.com
Hmmm?
Nevermind.

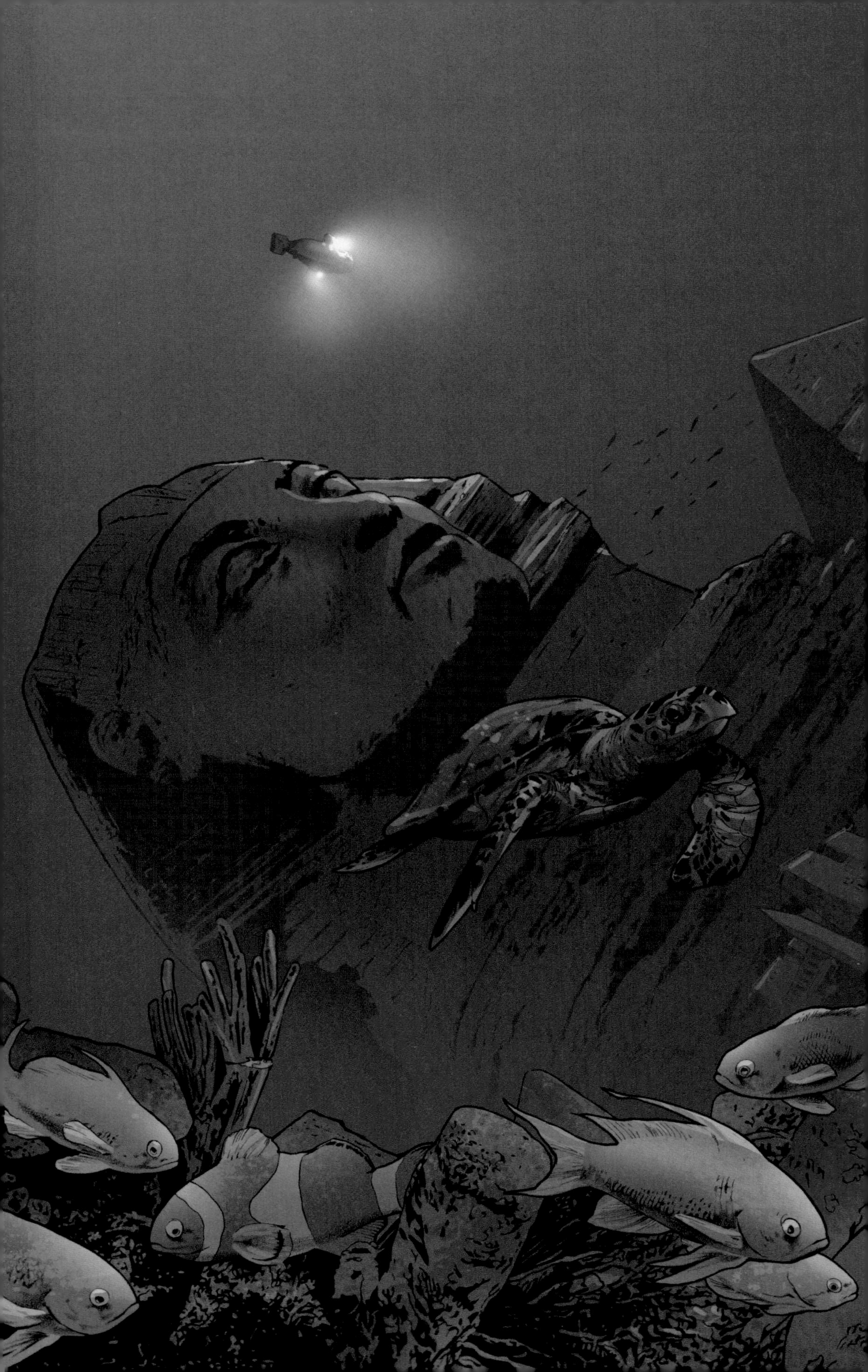

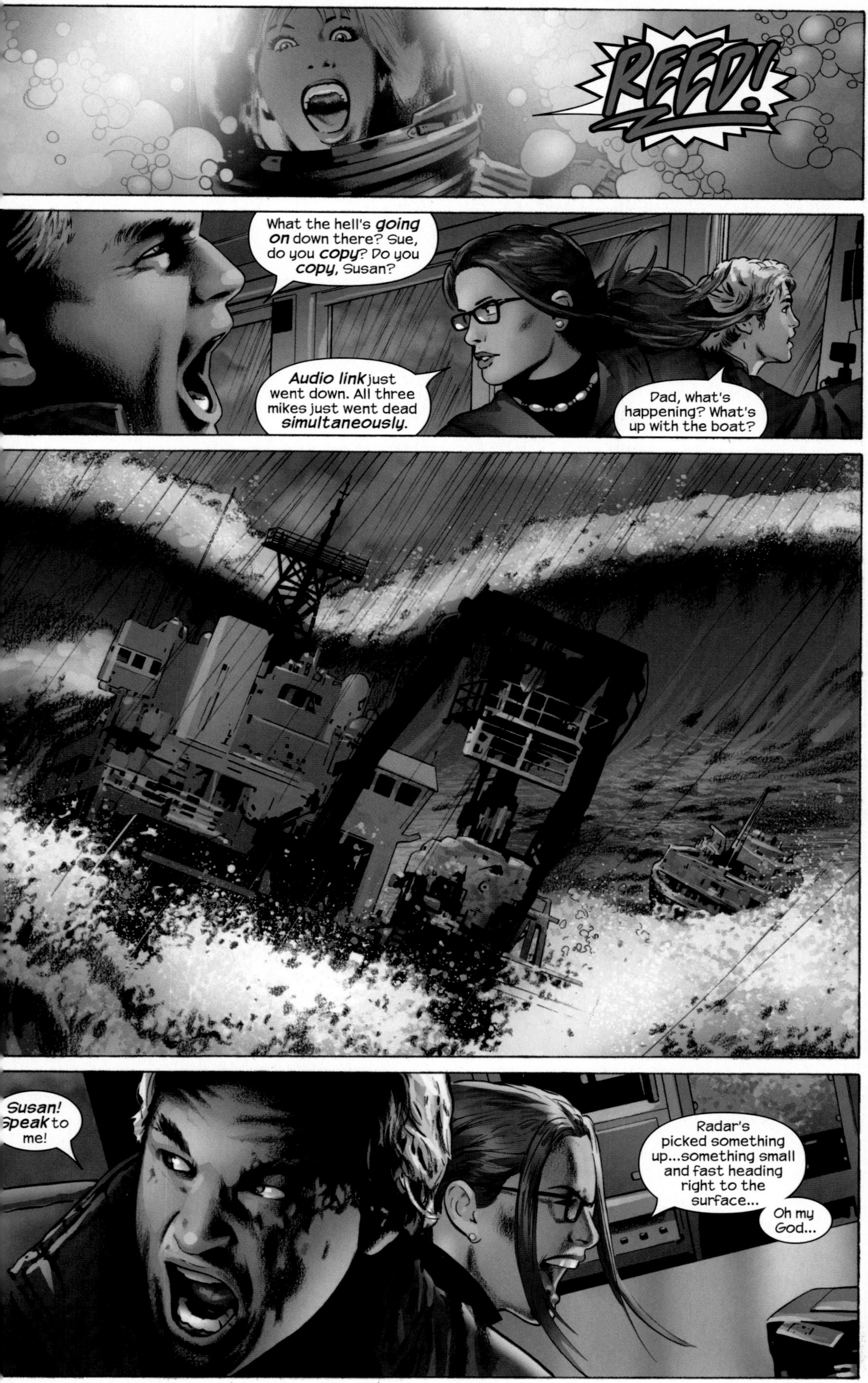
REED!
What the hell's going on down there? Sue, do you copy? Do you copy, Susan?
Audio link just went down. All three mikes just went dead simultaneously.
Dad, what's happening? What's up with the boat?
Susan! Speak to me!
Radar's picked something up...something small and fast heading right to the surface...
Oh my God...

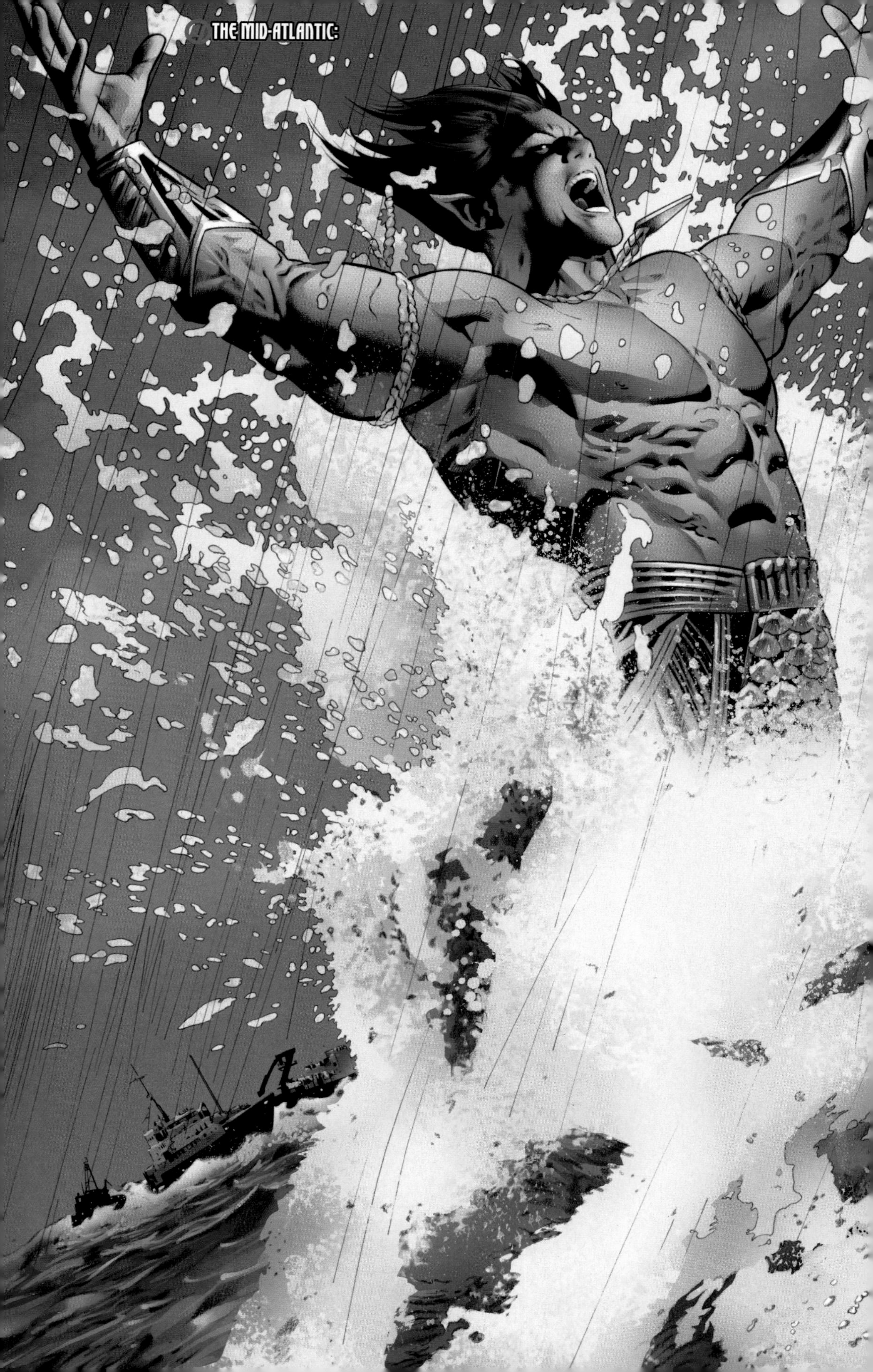
THE MID-ATLANTIC:

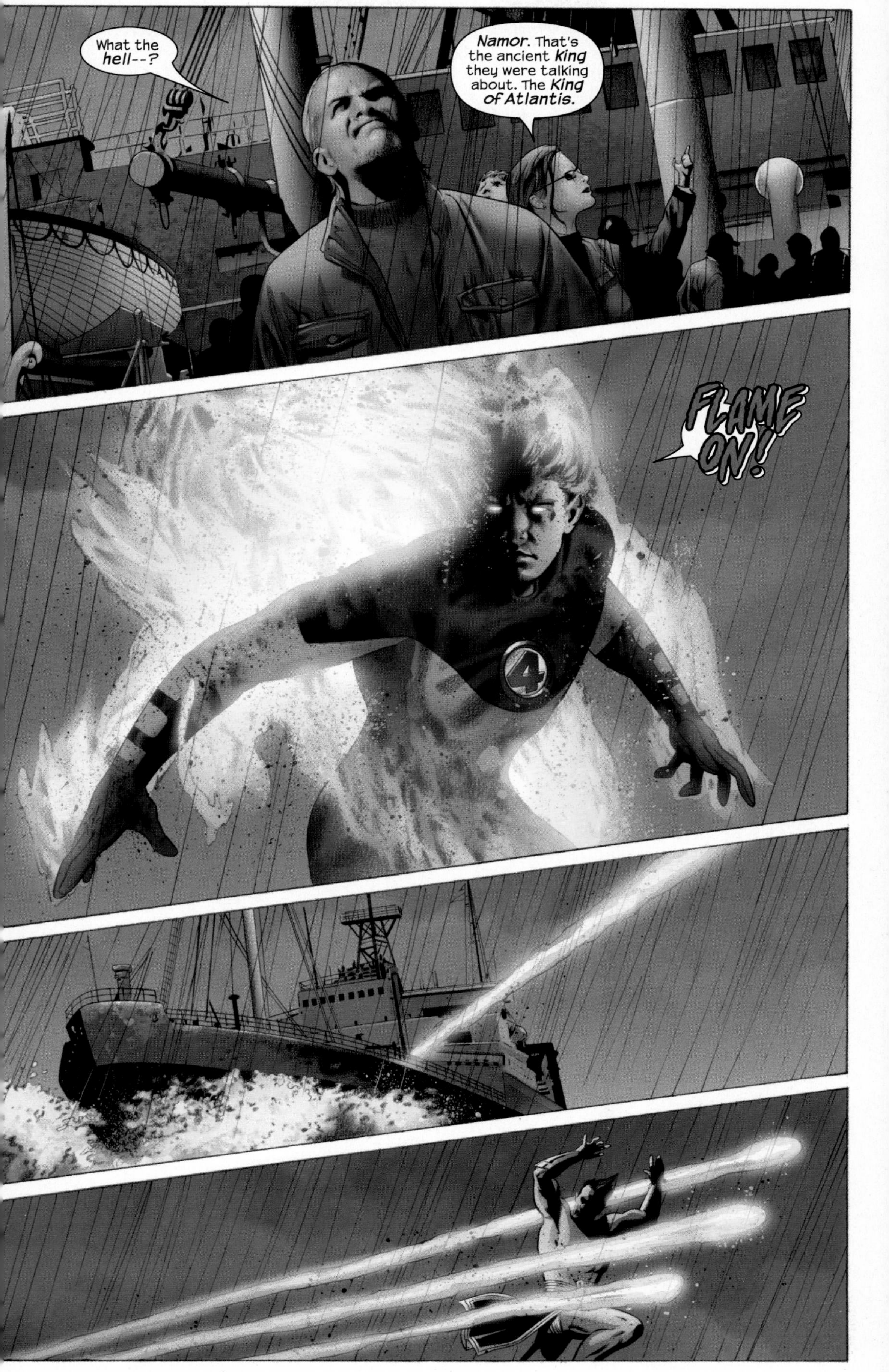

What the *hell*--?
Namor. That's the ancient *king* they were talking about. The *King of Atlantis*.
FLAME ON!

What are you doing standing around *gaping*? My daughter and her friends are *trapped* down there. *Do* something!

They're *five miles down*, Franklin--

What are they going to *do*?

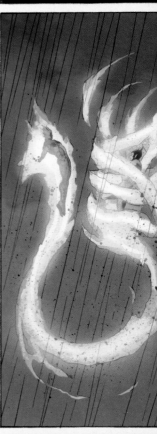

Burn, dog breath.

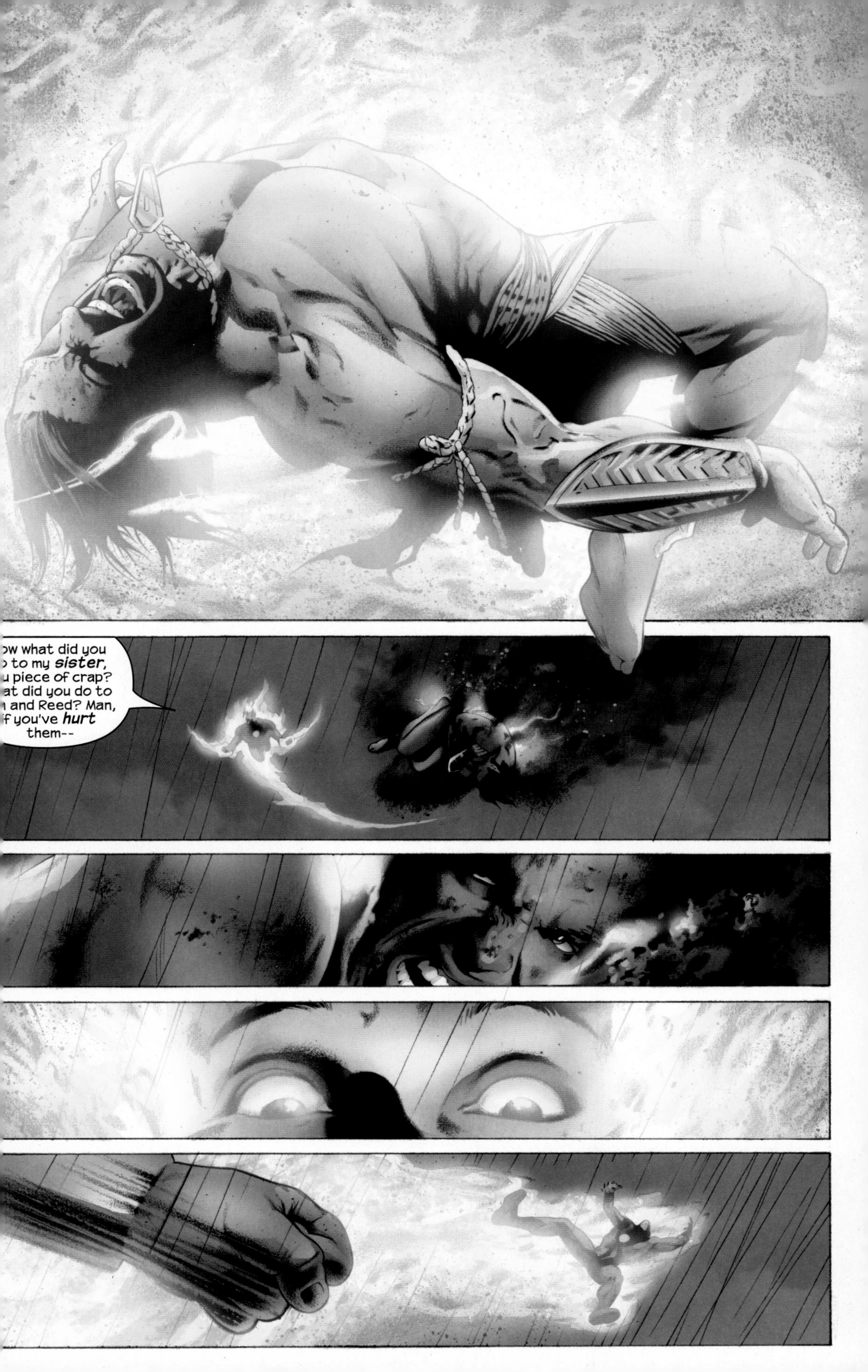
ow what did you
o to my *sister*,
u piece of crap?
at did you do to
n and Reed? Man,
f you've *hurt*
them--

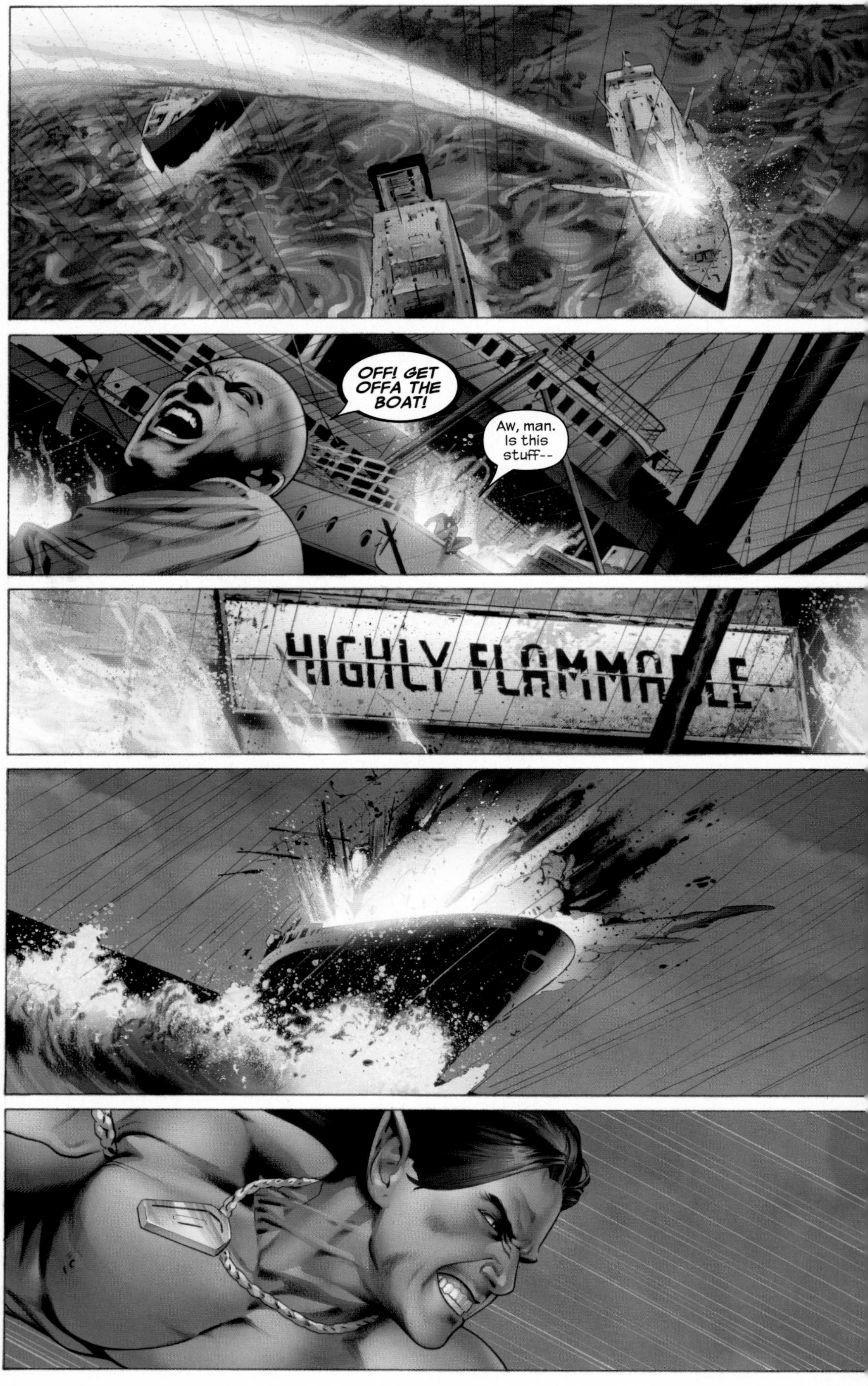
OFF! GET OFFA THE BOAT!
Aw, man. Is this stuff--
HIGHLY FLAMMABLE

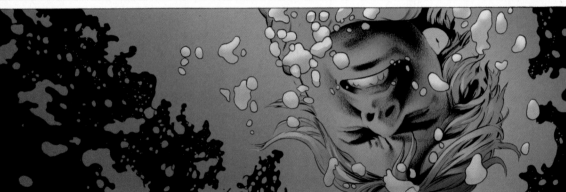

JOHNNY!!!

For God's sake-- Somebody *help* him! *Please!*

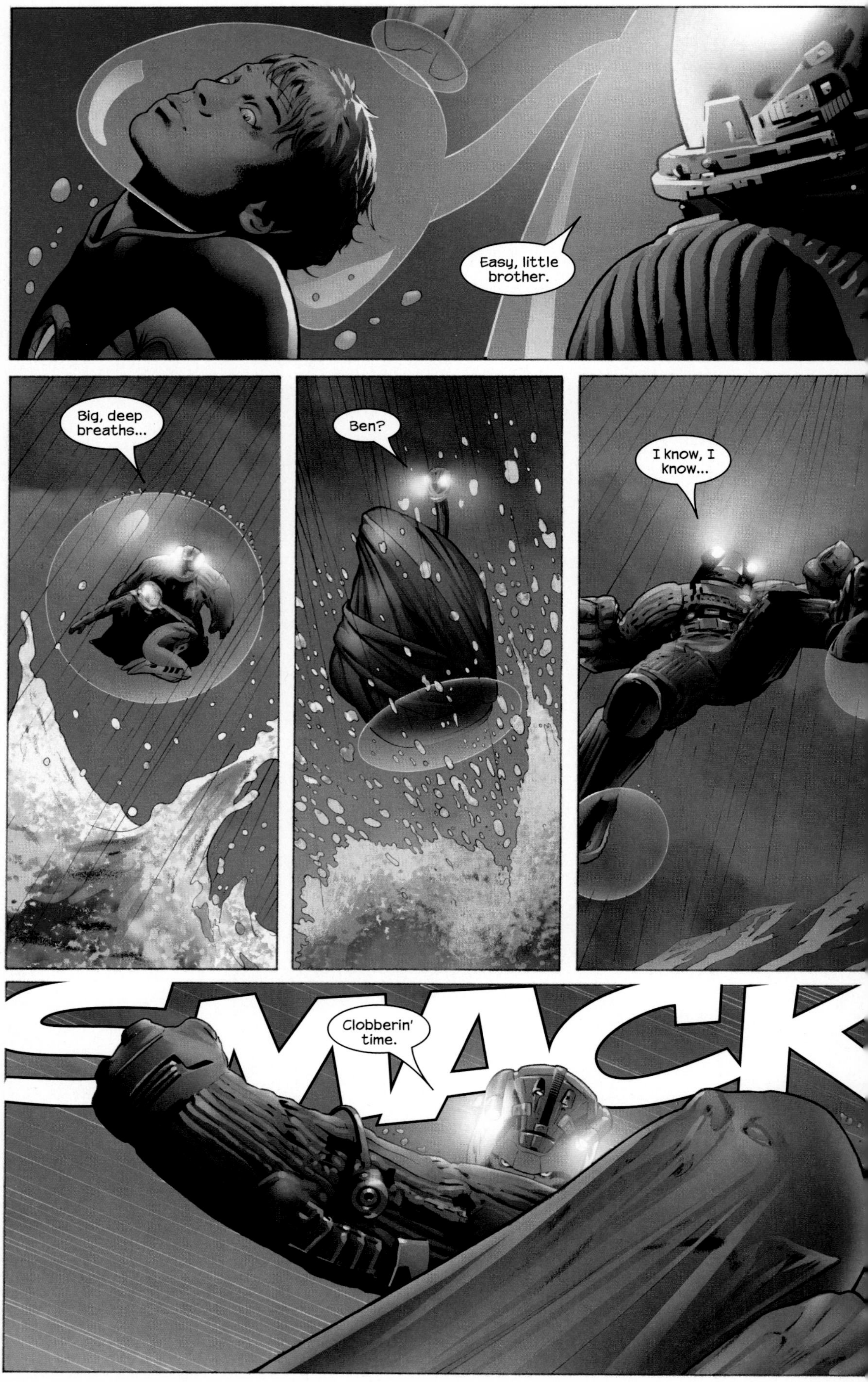
Easy, little brother.
Big, deep breaths...
Ben?
I know, I know...
SMACK
Clobberin' time.

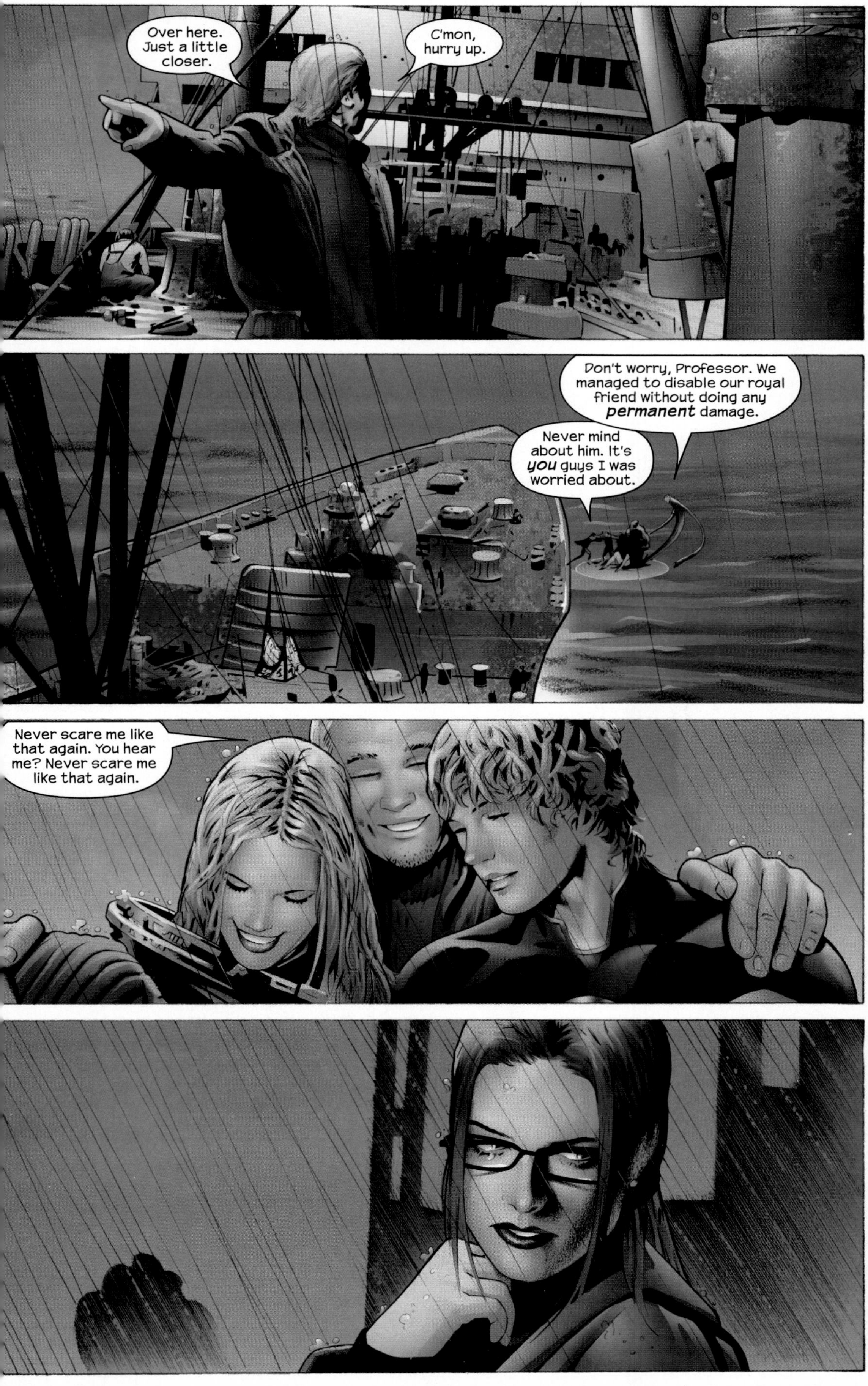
Over here. Just a little closer.
C'mon, hurry up.
Don't worry, Professor. We managed to disable our royal friend without doing any *permanent* damage.
Never mind about him. It's *you* guys I was worried about.
Never scare me like that again. You hear me? Never scare me like that again.

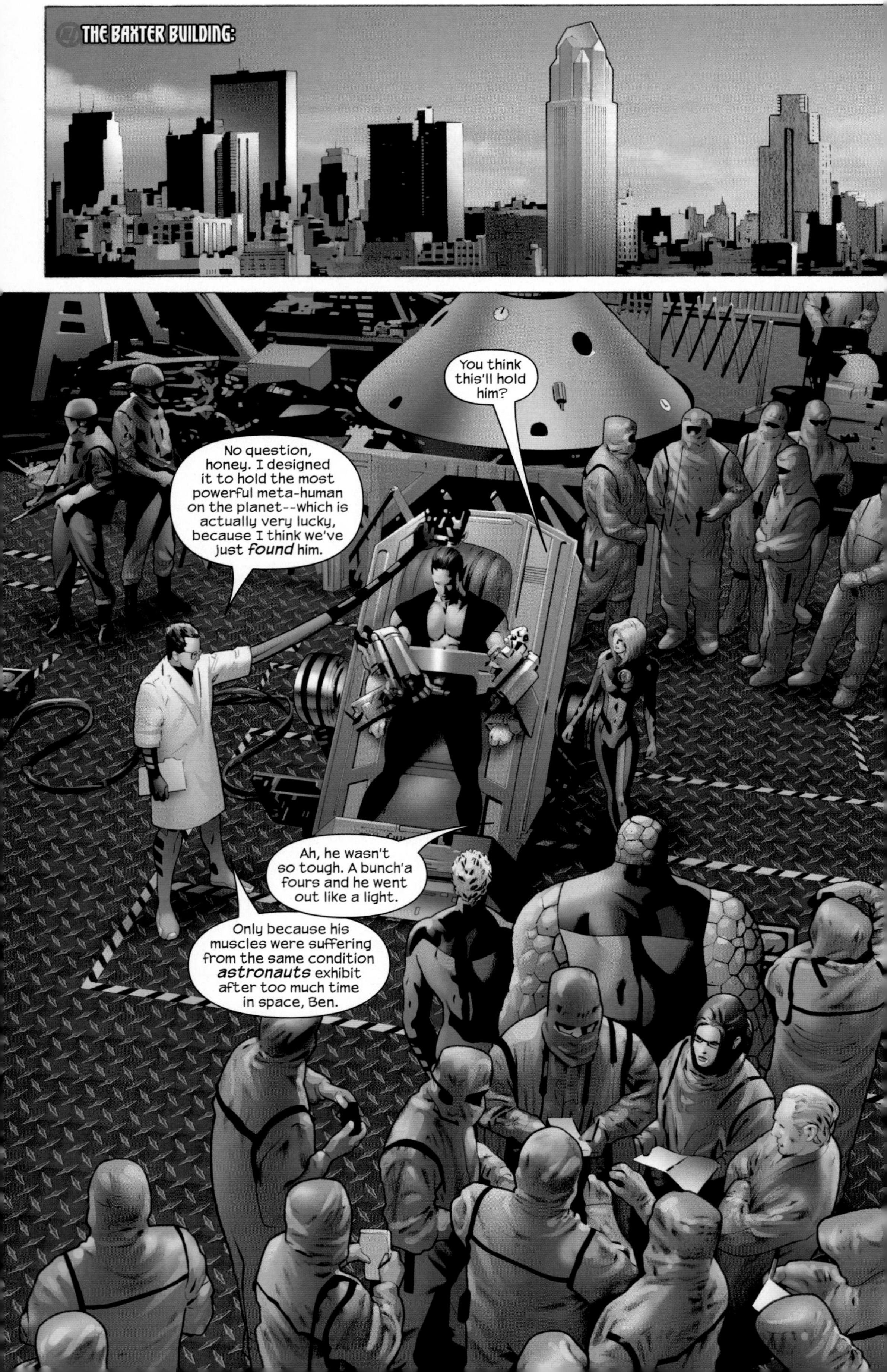
THE BAXTER BUILDING:
You think this'll hold him?
No question, honey. I designed it to hold the most powerful meta-human on the planet--which is actually very lucky, because I think we've just *found* him.
Ah, he wasn't so tough. A bunch'a fours and he went out like a light.
Only because his muscles were suffering from the same condition *astronauts* exhibit after too much time in space, Ben.

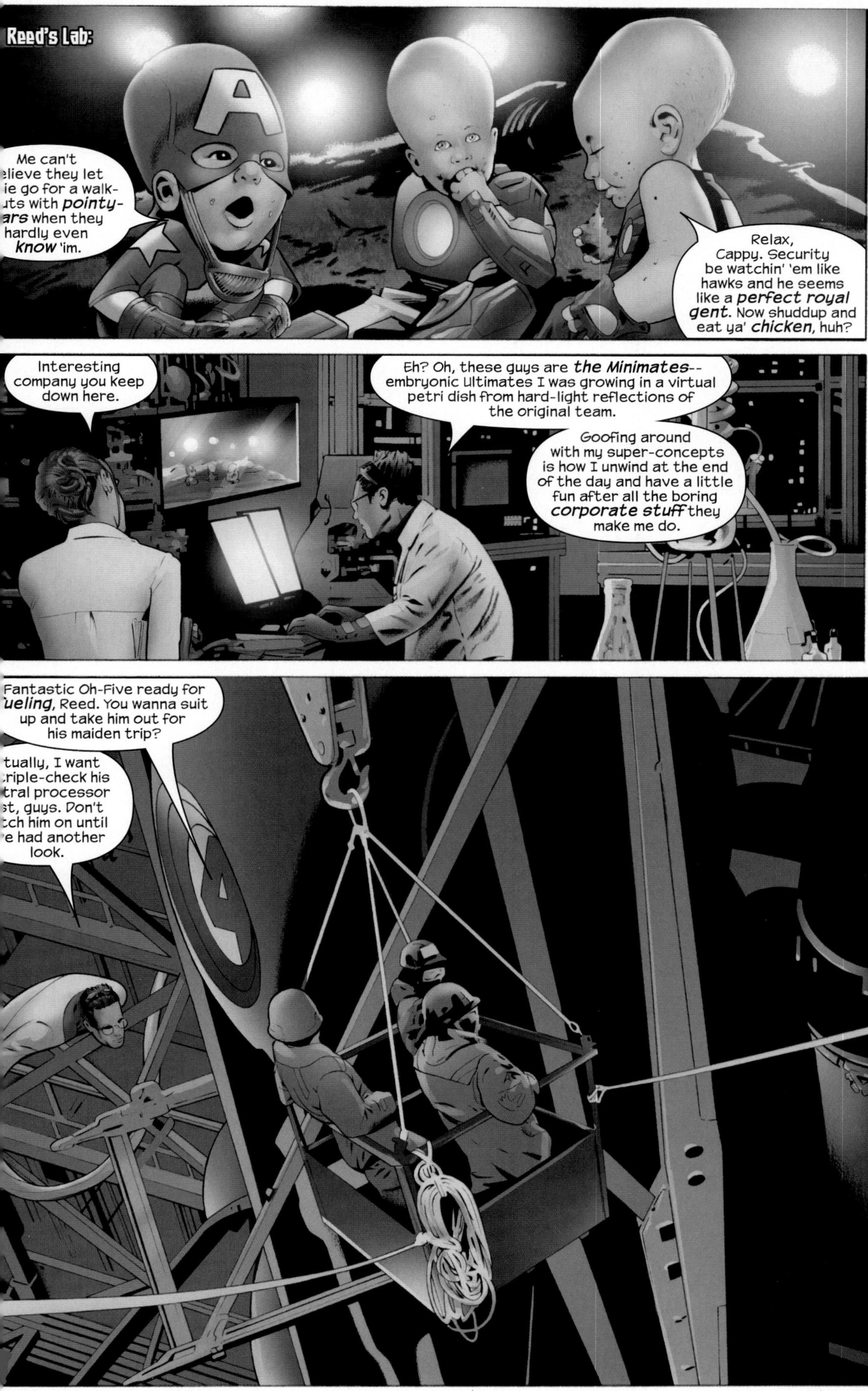
Reed's Lab:
Me can't elieve they let ie go for a walk- uts with pointy- ars when they hardly even know 'im.
Relax, Cappy. Security be watchin' 'em like hawks and he seems like a perfect royal gent. Now shuddup and eat ya' chicken, huh?
Interesting company you keep down here.
Eh? Oh, these guys are the Minimates-- embryonic Ultimates I was growing in a virtual petri dish from hard-light reflections of the original team.
Goofing around with my super-concepts is how I unwind at the end of the day and have a little fun after all the boring corporate stuff they make me do.
Fantastic Oh-Five ready for ueling, Reed. You wanna suit up and take him out for his maiden trip?
tually, I want riple-check his tral processor st, guys. Don't tch him on until e had another look.

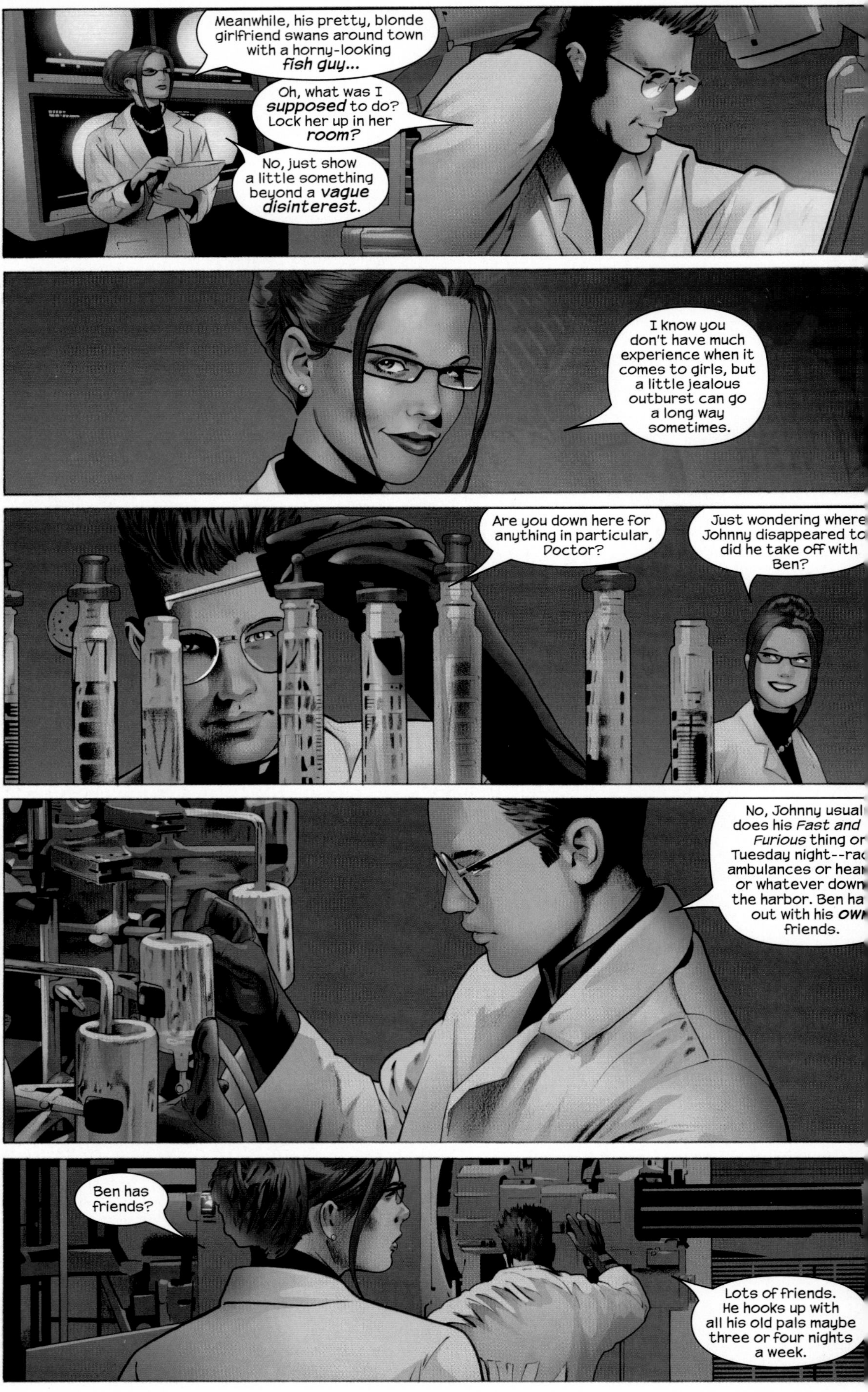

Meanwhile, his pretty, blonde girlfriend swans around town with a horny-looking *fish guy...*
Oh, what was I *supposed* to do? Lock her up in her *room?*
No, just show a little something beyond a *vague disinterest.*
I know you don't have much experience when it comes to girls, but a little jealous outburst can go a long way sometimes.
Are you down here for anything in particular, Doctor?
Just wondering where Johnny disappeared to did he take off with Ben?
No, Johnny usual does his *Fast and Furious* thing or Tuesday night--ra ambulances or hea or whatever down the harbor. Ben ha out with his *OW* friends.
Ben has friends?
Lots of friends. He hooks up with all his old pals maybe three or four nights a week.

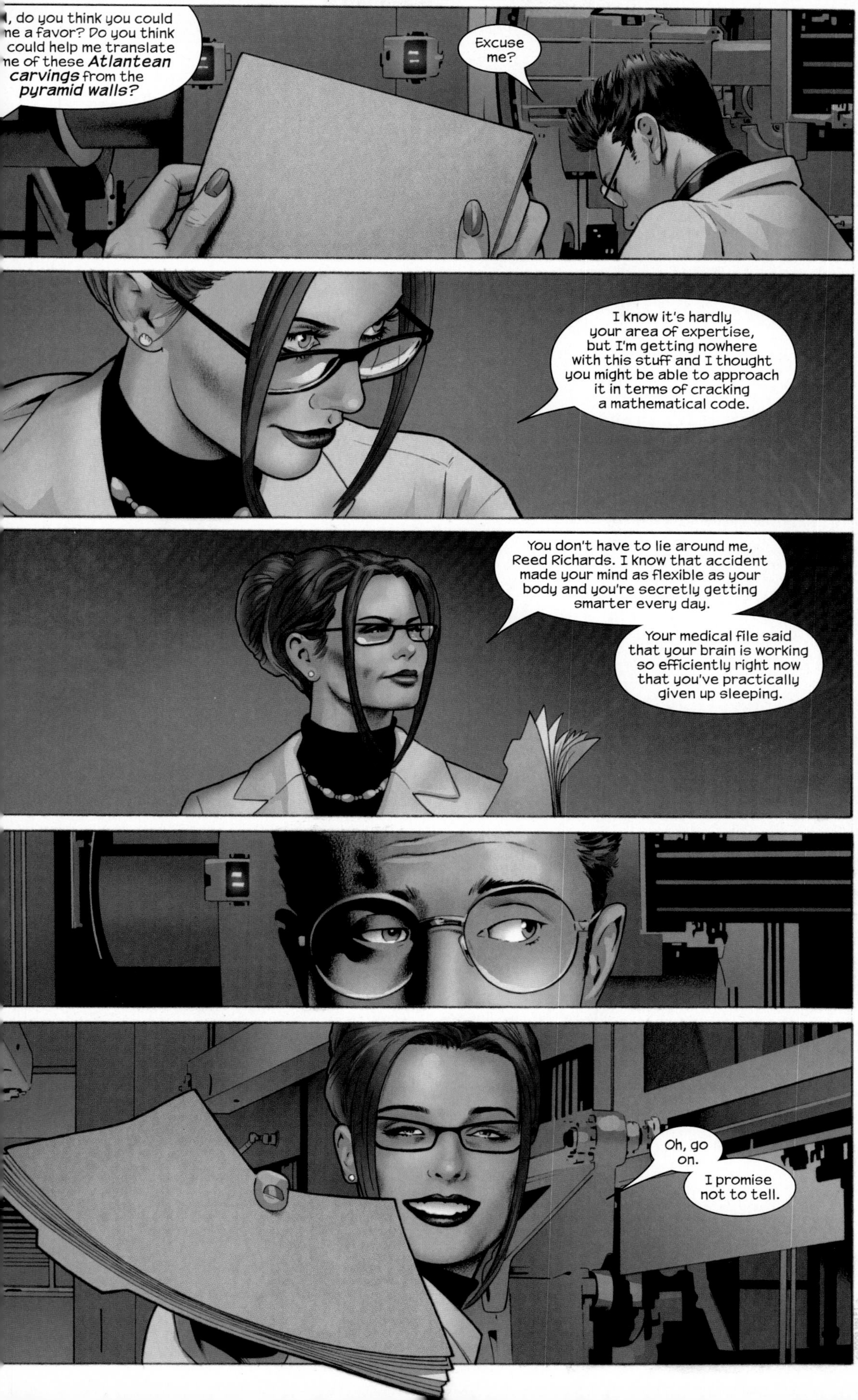
, do you think you could
me a favor? Do you think
could help me translate
me of these *Atlantean carvings* from the *pyramid walls*?
Excuse me?
I know it's hardly your area of expertise, but I'm getting nowhere with this stuff and I thought you might be able to approach it in terms of cracking a mathematical code.
You don't have to lie around me, Reed Richards. I know that accident made your mind as flexible as your body and you're secretly getting smarter every day.
Your medical file said that your brain is working so efficiently right now that you've practically given up sleeping.
Oh, go on.
I promise not to tell.

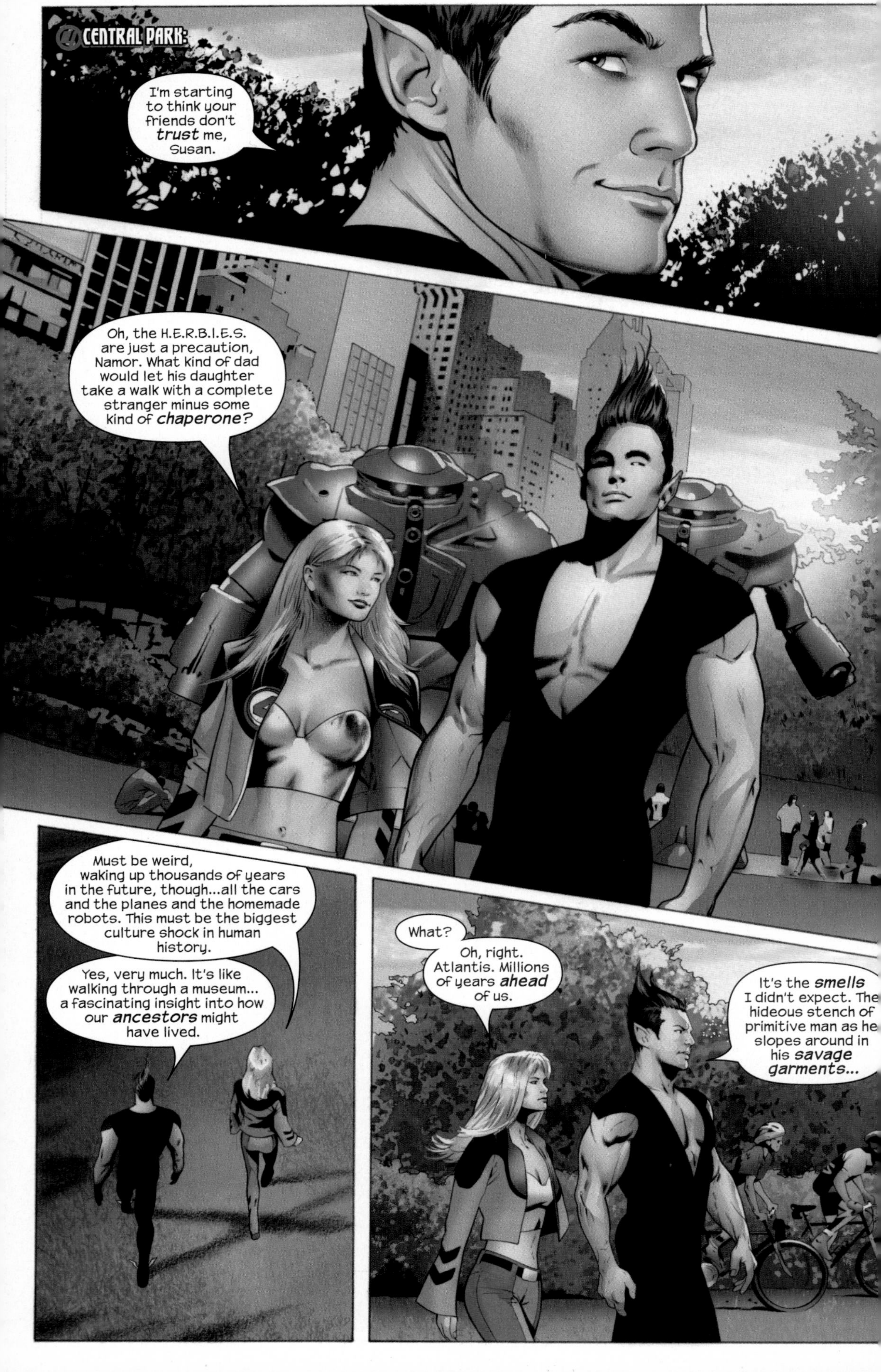
CENTRAL PARK:
I'm starting to think your friends don't trust me, Susan.
Oh, the H.E.R.B.I.E.S. are just a precaution, Namor. What kind of dad would let his daughter take a walk with a complete stranger minus some kind of chaperone?
Must be weird, waking up thousands of years in the future, though...all the cars and the planes and the homemade robots. This must be the biggest culture shock in human history.
Yes, very much. It's like walking through a museum... a fascinating insight into how our ancestors might have lived.
What?
Oh, right. Atlantis. Millions of years ahead of us.
It's the smells I didn't expect. The hideous stench of primitive man as he slopes around in his savage garments...

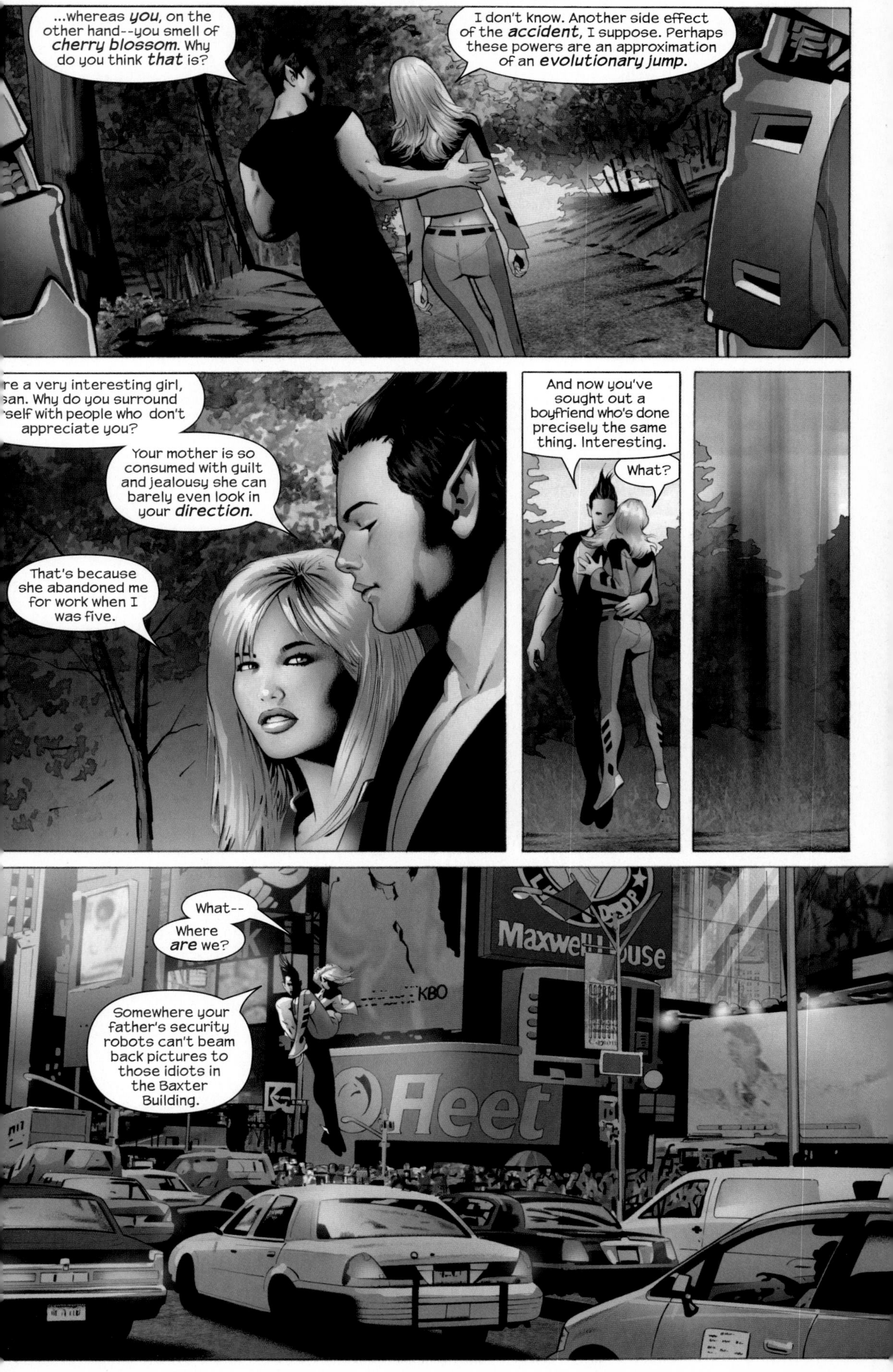
...whereas you, on the other hand--you smell of cherry blossom. Why do you think that is?
I don't know. Another side effect of the accident, I suppose. Perhaps these powers are an approximation of an evolutionary jump.
re a very interesting girl, san. Why do you surround rself with people who don't appreciate you?
Your mother is so consumed with guilt and jealousy she can barely even look in your direction.
That's because she abandoned me for work when I was five.
And now you've sought out a boyfriend who's done precisely the same thing. Interesting.
What?
What--
Where are we?
Somewhere your father's security robots can't beam back pictures to those idiots in the Baxter Building.
Maxwell House
Fleet
KBO

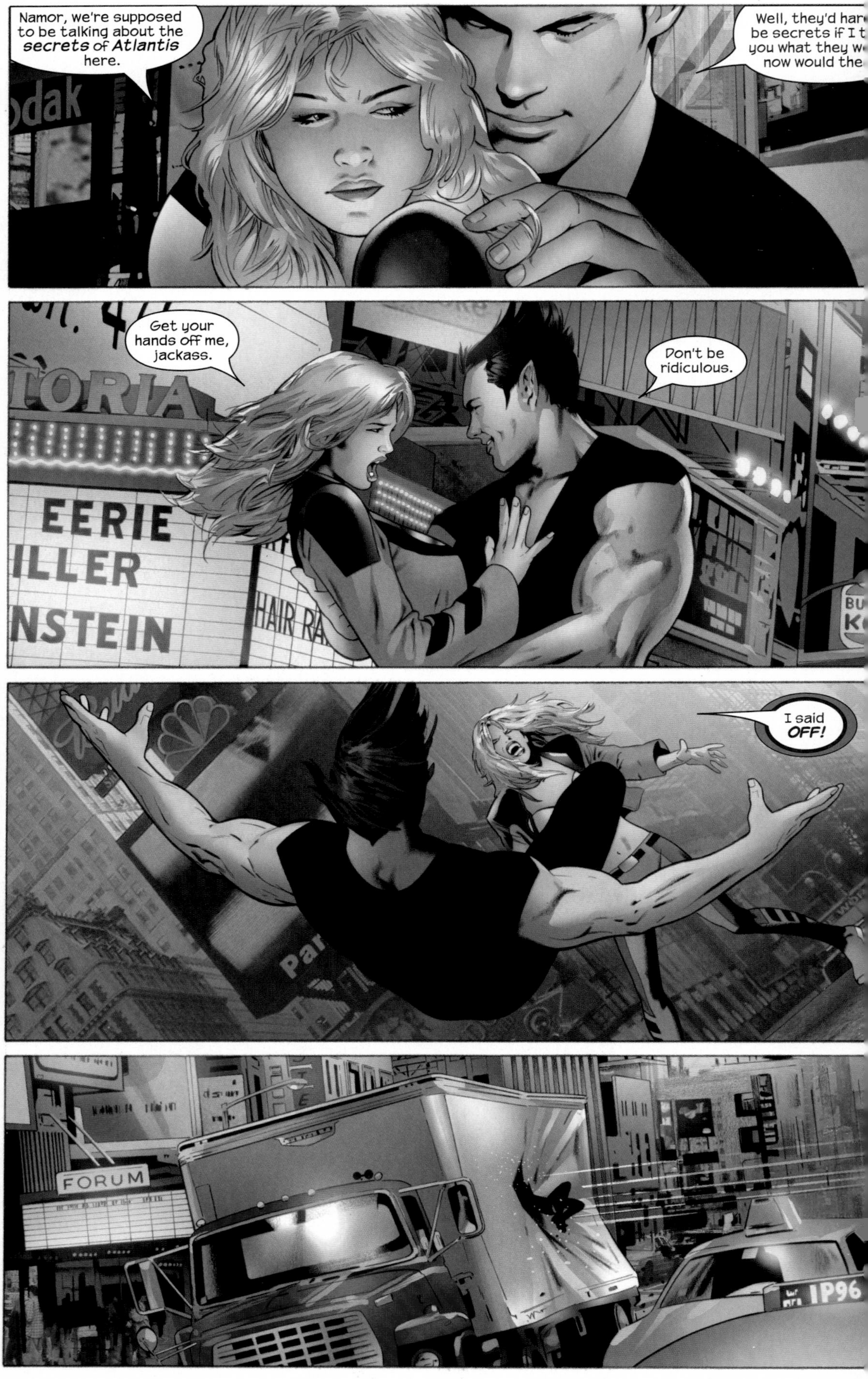

Namor, we're supposed to be talking about the *secrets* of *Atlantis* here.
Well, they'd har
be secrets if I t
you what they w
now would the
odak
Get your hands off me, jackass.
Don't be ridiculous.
TORIA
EERIE
ILLER
NSTEIN
HAIR RA
I said *OFF!*
FORUM
IP96

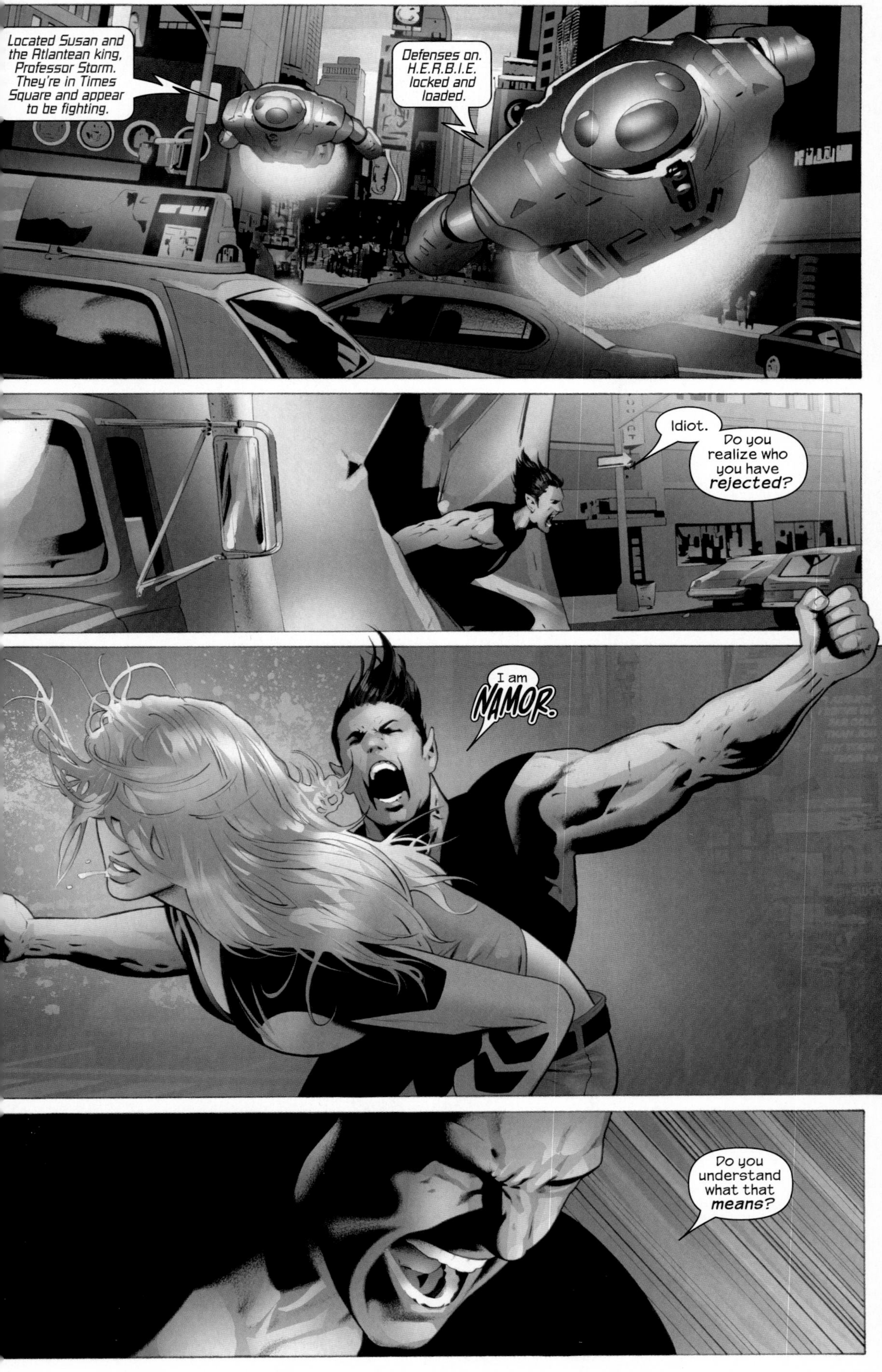
Located Susan and the Atlantean king, Professor Storm. They're in Times Square and appear to be fighting.
Defenses on. H.E.R.B.I.E. locked and loaded.
Idiot.
Do you realize who you have rejected?
I am NAMOR.
Do you understand what that means?

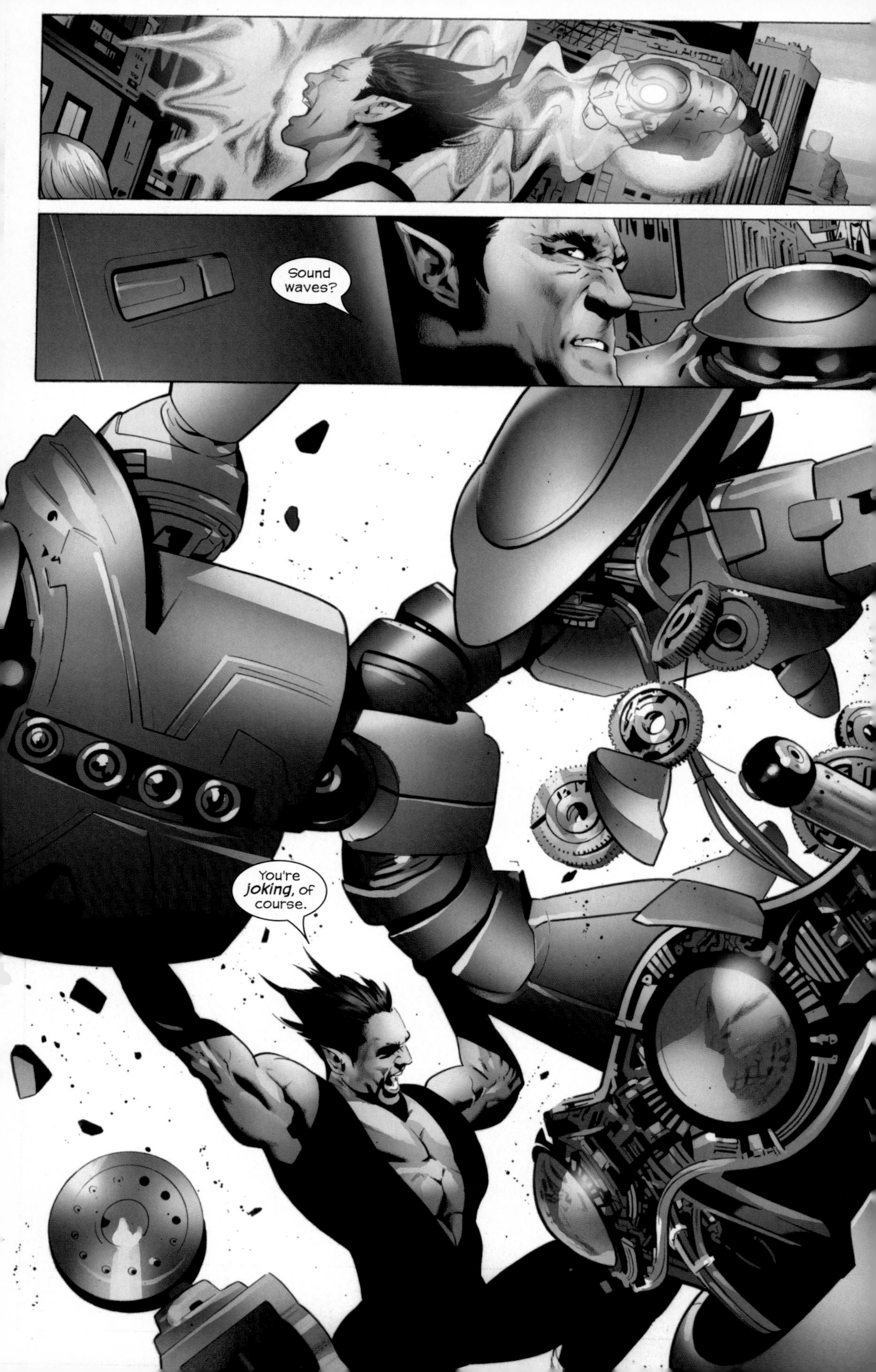
Sound waves?
You're *joking*, of course.

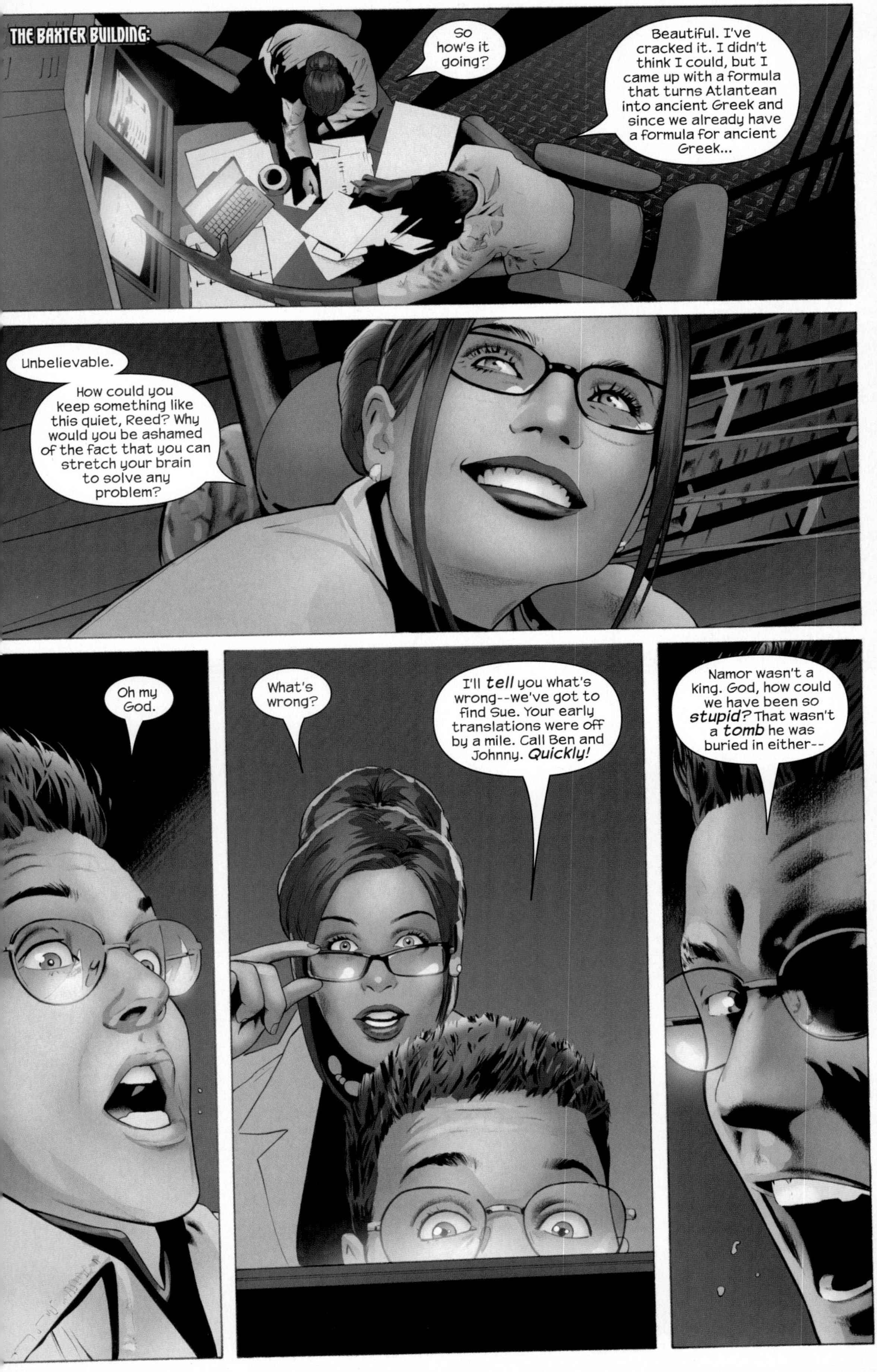
THE BAXTER BUILDING:
So how's it going?
Beautiful. I've cracked it. I didn't think I could, but I came up with a formula that turns Atlantean into ancient Greek and since we already have a formula for ancient Greek...
Unbelievable.
How could you keep something like this quiet, Reed? Why would you be ashamed of the fact that you can stretch your brain to solve any problem?
Oh my God.
What's wrong?
I'll *tell* you what's wrong--we've got to find Sue. Your early translations were off by a mile. Call Ben and Johnny. *Quickly!*
Namor wasn't a king. God, how could we have been so *stupid?* That wasn't a *tomb* he was buried in either--

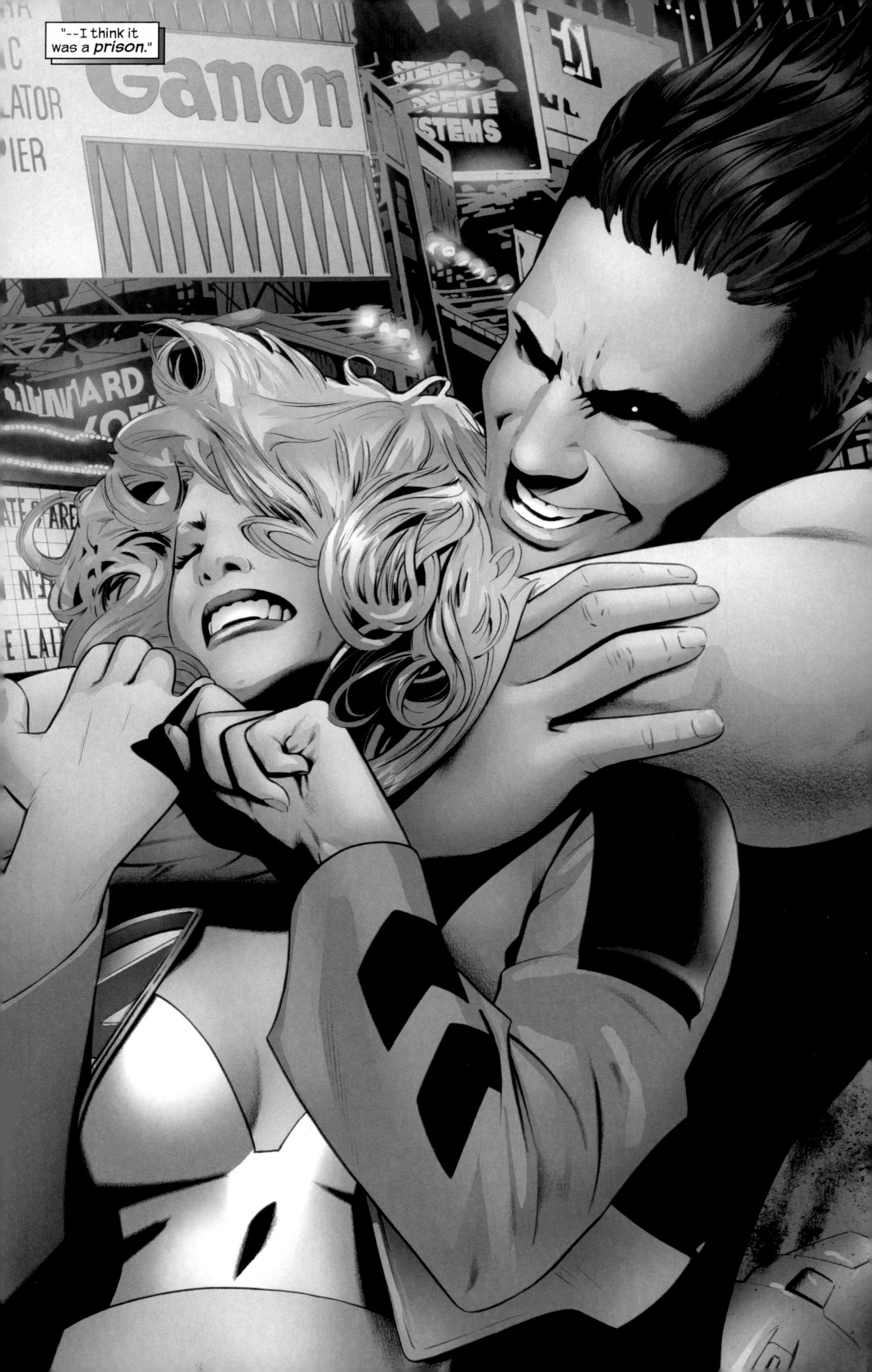
"--I think it was a *prison*."
Ganon

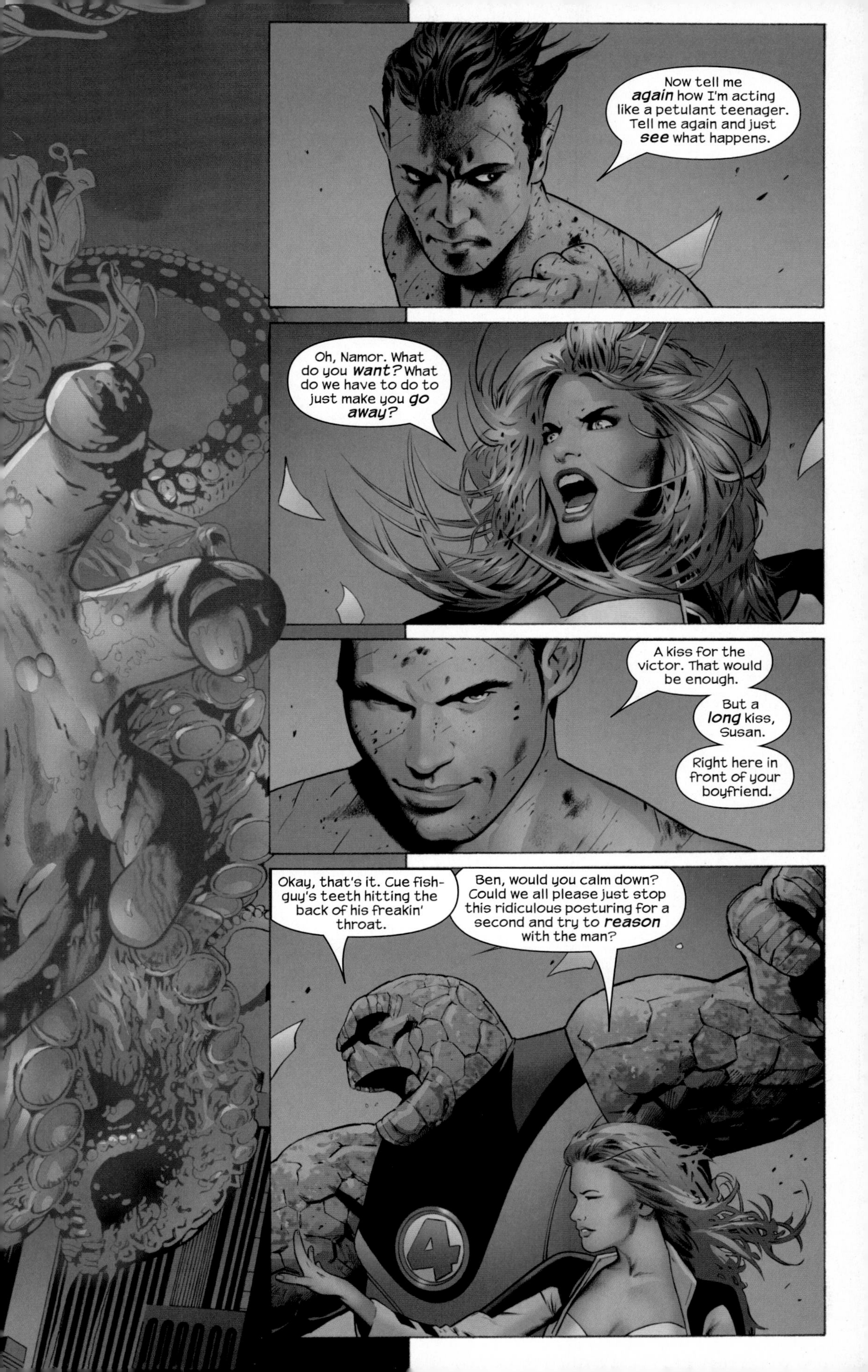
Now tell me again how I'm acting like a petulant teenager. Tell me again and just see what happens.
Oh, Namor. What do you want? What do we have to do to just make you go away?
A kiss for the victor. That would be enough.
But a long kiss, Susan.
Right here in front of your boyfriend.
Okay, that's it. Cue fish-guy's teeth hitting the back of his freakin' throat.
Ben, would you calm down? Could we all please just stop this ridiculous posturing for a second and try to reason with the man?

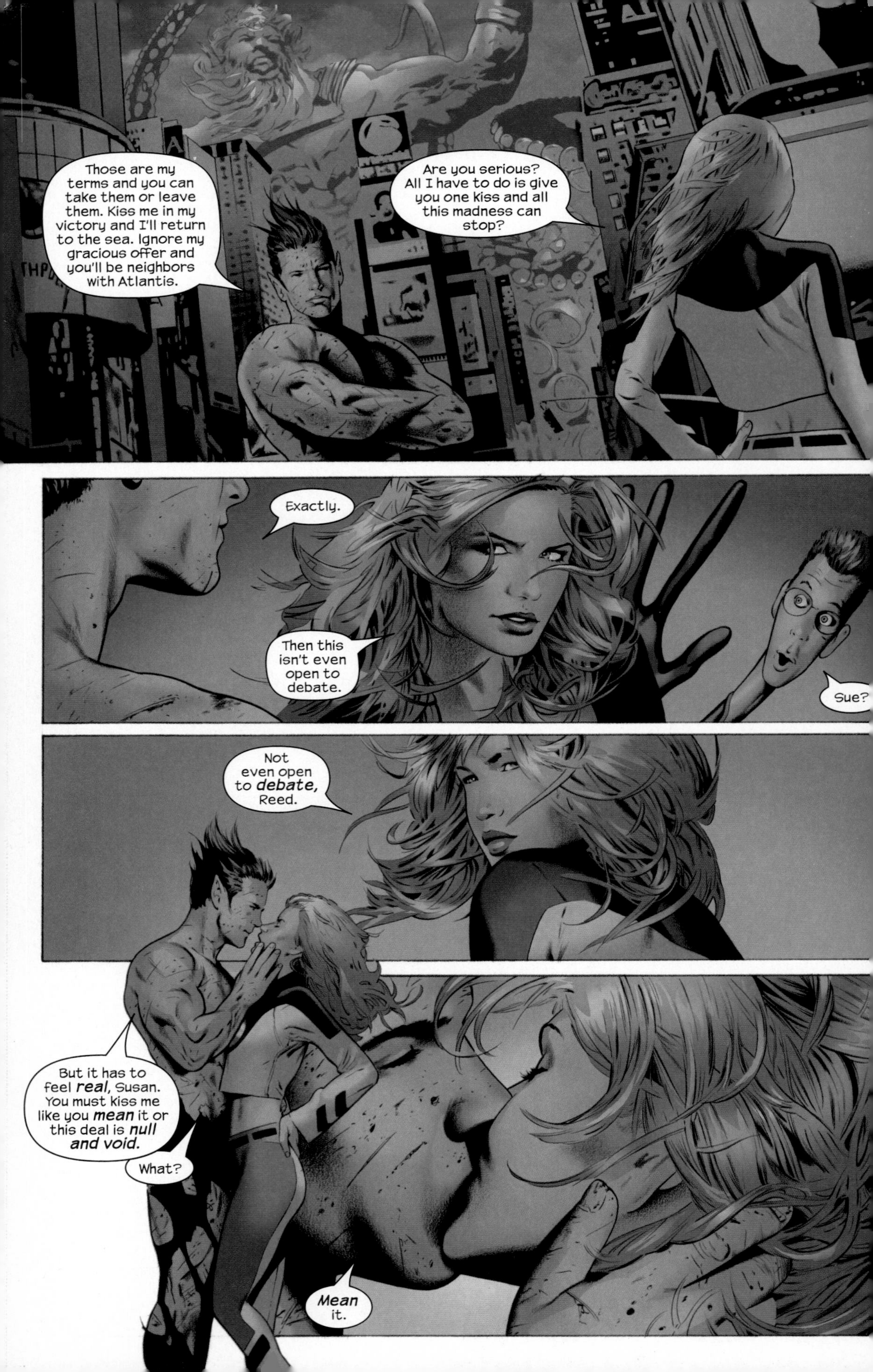
Those are my terms and you can take them or leave them. Kiss me in my victory and I'll return to the sea. Ignore my gracious offer and you'll be neighbors with Atlantis.
Are you serious? All I have to do is give you one kiss and all this madness can stop?
Exactly.
Then this isn't even open to debate.
Sue?
Not even open to *debate,* Reed.
But it has to feel *real,* Susan. You must kiss me like you *mean* it or this deal is *null and void.*
What?
Mean it.

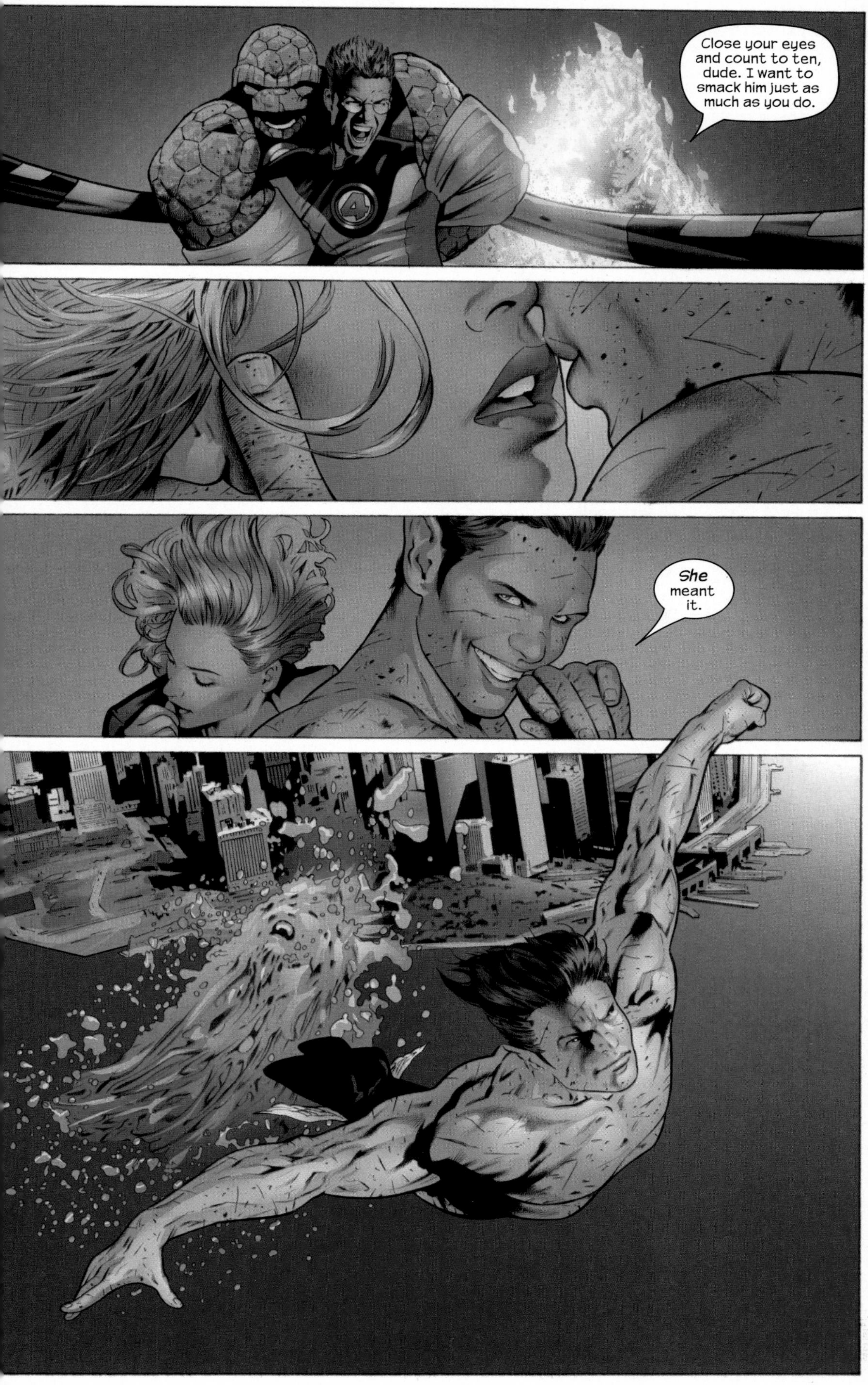
Close your eyes and count to ten, dude. I want to smack him just as much as you do.
She meant it.

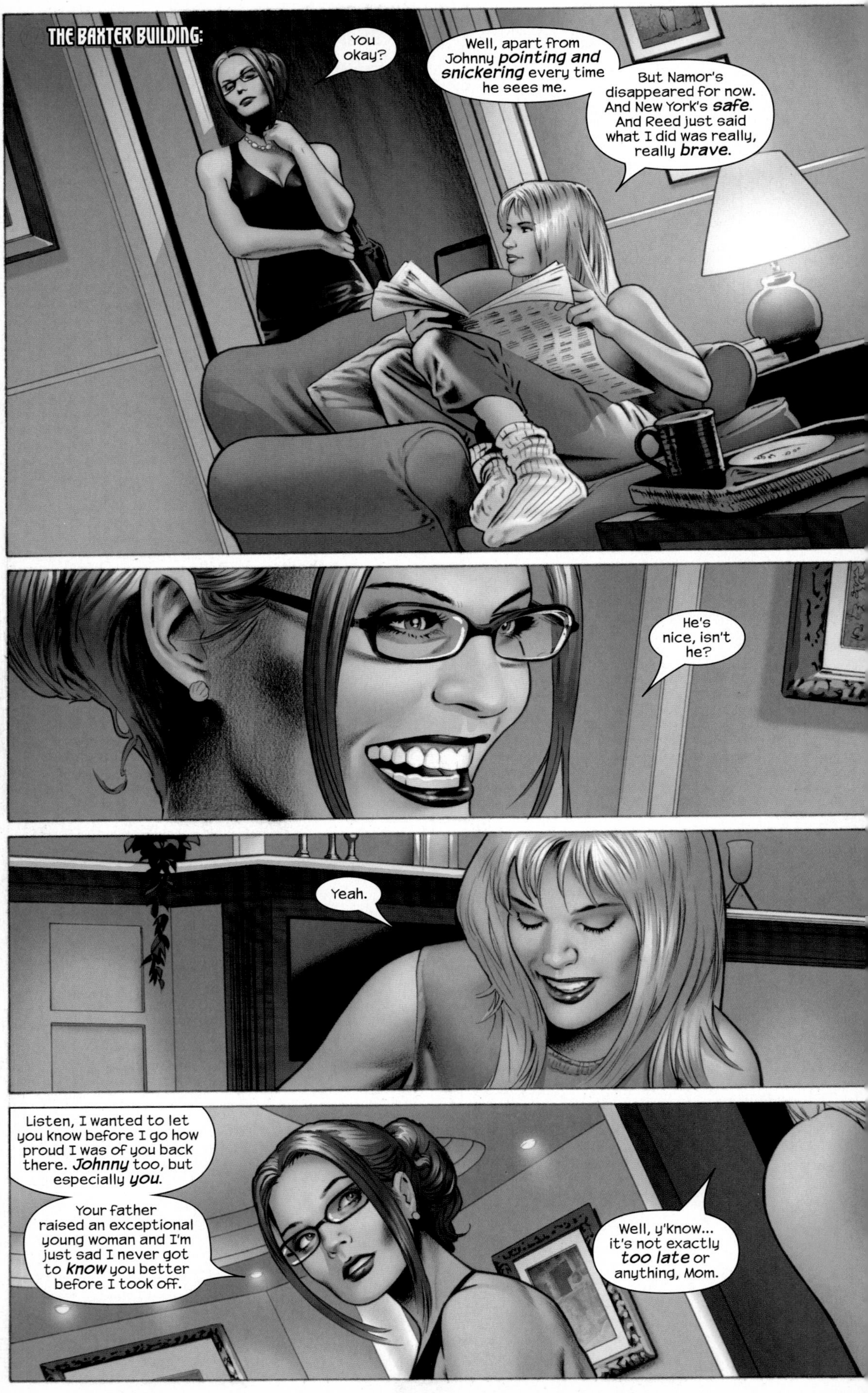
THE BAXTER BUILDING:
You okay?
Well, apart from Johnny pointing and snickering every time he sees me.
But Namor's disappeared for now. And New York's safe. And Reed just said what I did was really, really brave.
He's nice, isn't he?
Yeah.
Listen, I wanted to let you know before I go how proud I was of you back there. Johnny too, but especially you.
Your father raised an exceptional young woman and I'm just sad I never got to know you better before I took off.
Well, y'know... it's not exactly too late or anything, Mom.

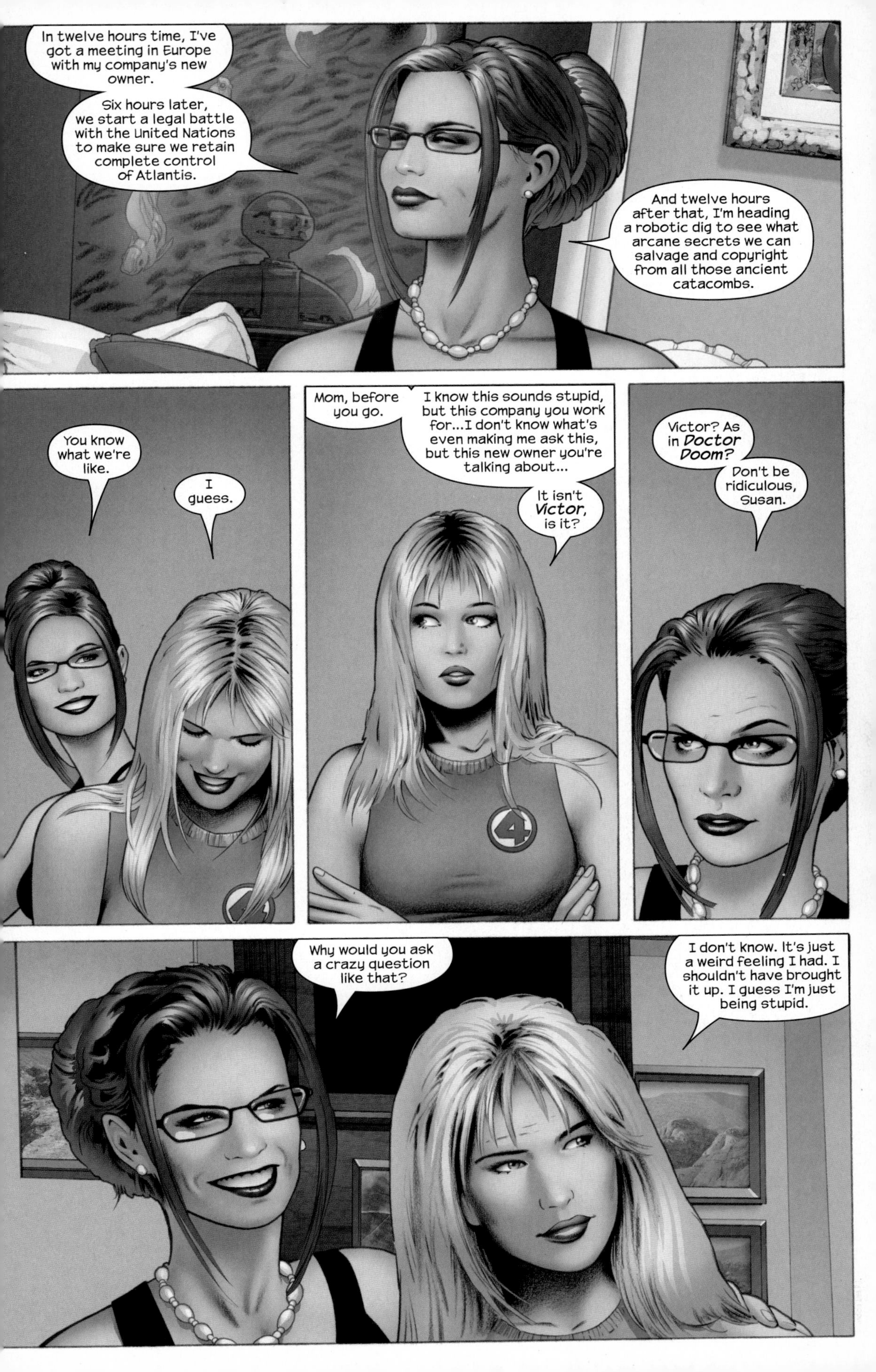
In twelve hours time, I've got a meeting in Europe with my company's new owner.
Six hours later, we start a legal battle with the United Nations to make sure we retain complete control of Atlantis.
And twelve hours after that, I'm heading a robotic dig to see what arcane secrets we can salvage and copyright from all those ancient catacombs.
You know what we're like.
I guess.
Mom, before you go.
I know this sounds stupid, but this company you work for...I don't know what's even making me ask this, but this new owner you're talking about...
It isn't *Victor*, is it?
Victor? As in *Doctor Doom?*
Don't be ridiculous, Susan.
Why would you ask a crazy question like that?
I don't know. It's just a weird feeling I had. I shouldn't have brought it up. I guess I'm just being stupid.

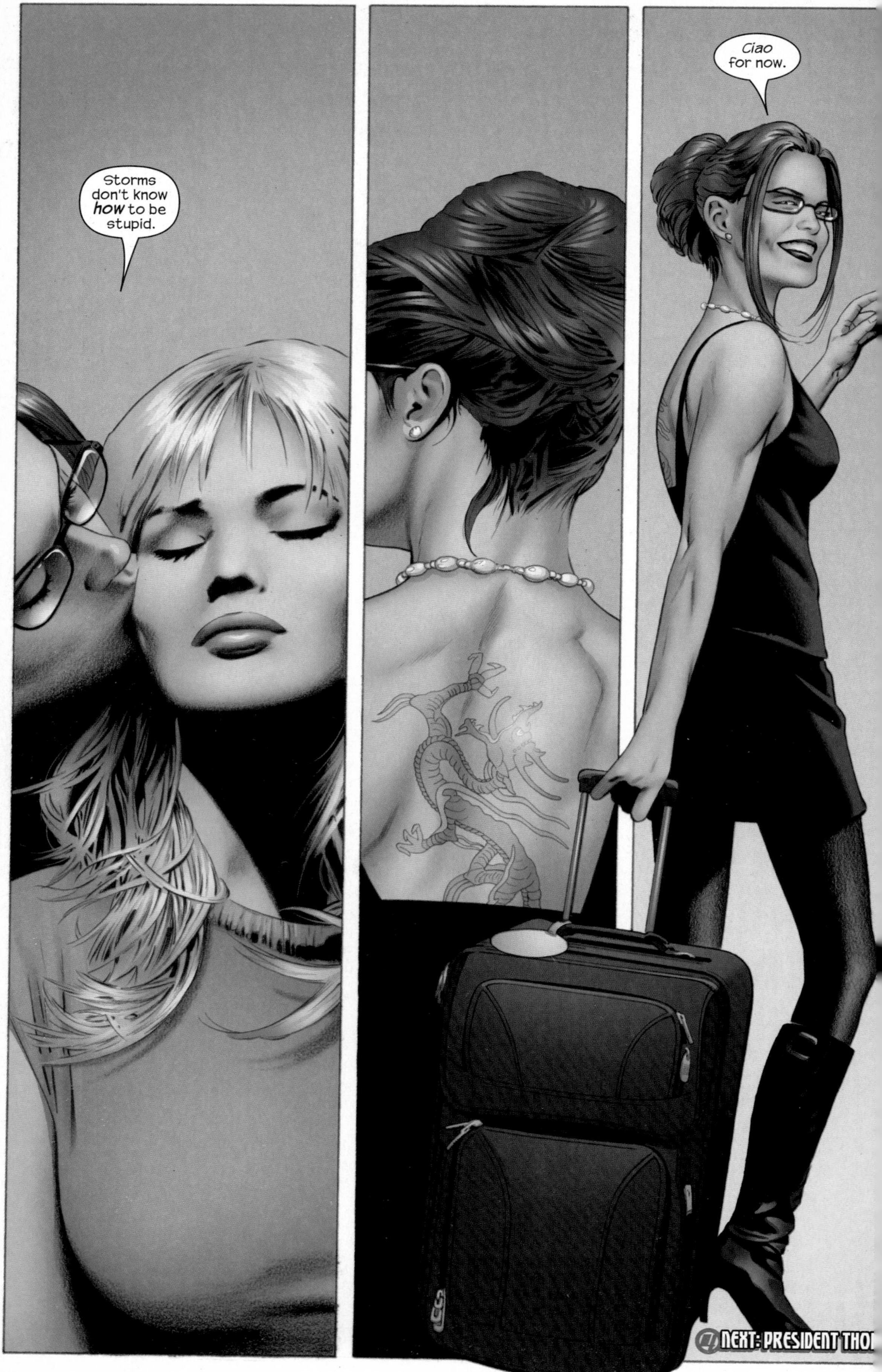
Storms don't know *how* to be stupid.
Ciao for now.
NEXT: PRESIDENT THO

THE ULTIMATE MARVEL LIBRARY

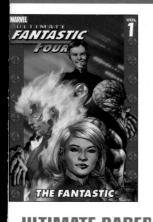

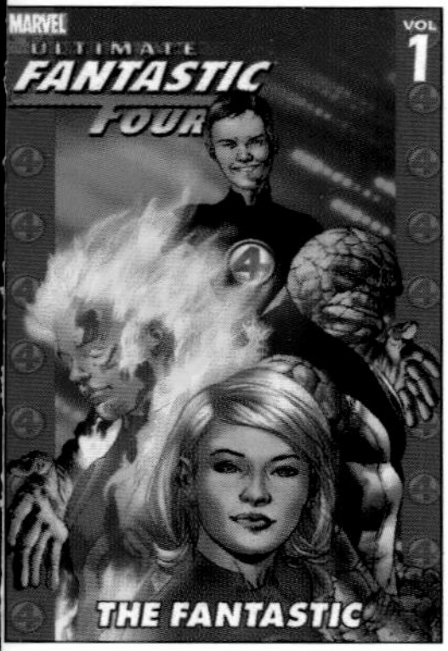
MARVEL
ULTIMATE
FANTASTIC FOUR
VOL 1
THE FANTASTIC

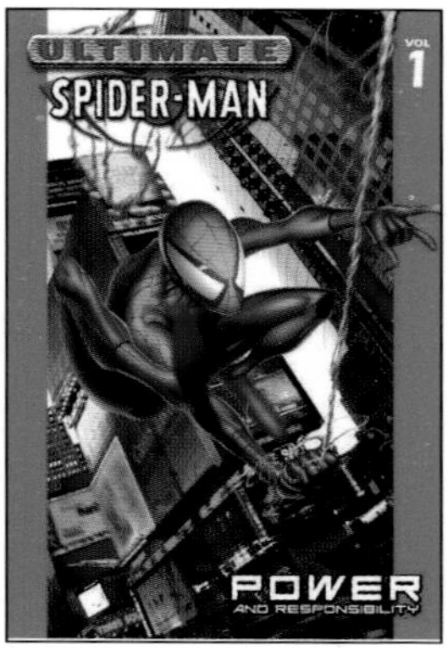
ULTIMATE
SPIDER-MAN
VOL 1
POWER
AND RESPONSIBILITY

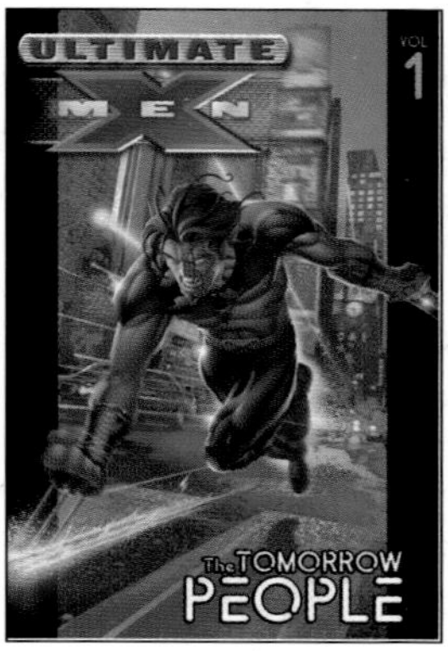
ULTIMATE
X-MEN
VOL 1
The TOMORROW PEOPLE

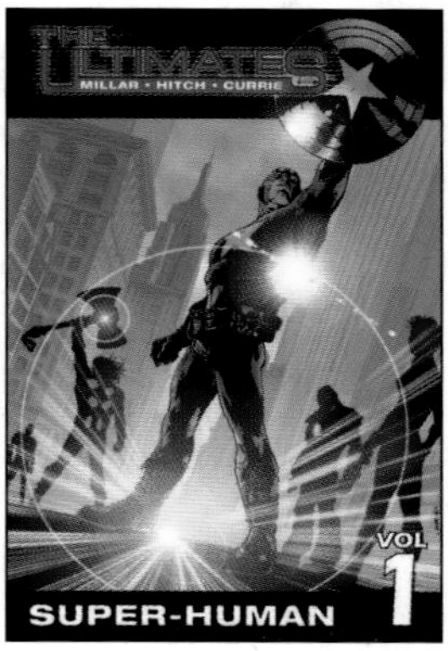
THE ULTIMATES
MILLAR • HITCH • CURRIE
VOL 1
SUPER-HUMAN

ULTIMATE DAREDEVIL AND ELEKTRA

ULTIMATE DAREDEVIL AND
(ISBN: 0-7851-1076-3)

ULTIMATE ELEKTRA: DEVIL'S DUE TPB...$11.99
(ISBN: 0-7851-1504-8)

THE ULTIMATES

VOL. 1: SUPER-HUMAN TPB...$12.99
(ISBN: 0-7851-0960-9)

VOL. 2: HOMELAND SECURITY TPB...
(ISBN: 0-7851-1078-X)

THE ULTIMATES 2

VOL. 1: GODS AND MONSTERS TPB...$14.99
(ISBN: 0-7851-1093-3)

ULTIMATE FANTASTIC FOUR

VOL. 1: THE FANTASTIC TPB...$12.99
(ISBN: 0-7851-1393-2)

VOL. 2: DOOM TPB...$12.99
(ISBN: 0-7851-1457-2)

VOL. 3: N-ZONE TPB...$12.99
(ISBN: 0-7851-1495-5)

VOL. 4: INHUMAN TPB...$12.99
(ISBN: 0-7851-1667-2)

ULTIMATE GALACTUS

VOL. 1: NIGHTMARE TPB...$12.99
(ISBN: 0-7851-1497-1)

VOL. 2: SECRET...$12.99
(ISBN: 0-7851-1660-5)

ULTIMATE SPIDER-MAN

VOL. 1: POWER & RESPONSIBILITY TPB...$14.99
(ISBN: 0-7851-0786-X)

VOL. 2: LEARNING CURVE TPB...$12.99
(ISBN: 0-7851-0820-3)

VOL. 3: DOUBLE TROUBLE TPB...$17.99
(ISBN: 0-7851-0879-3)

VOL. 4: LEGACY TPB...$14.99
(ISBN: 0-7851-0968-4)

VOL. 5: PUBLIC SCRUTINY TPB...$11.99
(ISBN: 0-7851-1087-9)

VOL. 6: VENOM TPB...$15.99
(ISBN: 0-7851-1094-1)

VOL. 7: IRRESPONSIBLE TPB...$12.99
(ISBN: ...5)

VOL. 8: CATS & KINGS TPB...$17.99
(ISBN: 0-7851-1250-2)

VOL. 9: ULTIMATE SIX TPB...$17.99
(ISBN: ...6)

VOL. 10: HOLLYWOOD TPB...$12.99
(ISBN: 0-7851-1402-5)

VOL. 11: CARNAGE TPB...$12.99
(ISBN: ...3)

VOL. 12: SUPERSTARS TPB...$12.99
(ISBN: ...X)

VOL. 13: HOBGOBLIN TPB...$12.99
(ISBN: 0-7851-1...8)

VOL. 14: WARRIORS TPB...$17.99
(ISBN: 0-7851-...X)

ULTIMATE X-MEN

VOL. 1: THE TOMORROW PEOPLE TPB...$14.95
(ISBN: 0-7851-...6)

VOL. 2: RETURN TO WEAPON X TPB...$14.95
(ISBN: ...8)

VOL. 3: WORLD TOUR TPB...$17.99
(ISBN: 0-7851-...7)

VOL. 4: HELLFIRE & BRIMSTONE TPB...$12.99
(ISBN: 0-7851-...5)

VOL. 5: ULTIMATE WAR TPB...$10.99
(ISBN: 0-7851-1...8)

VOL. 6: RETURN OF THE KING TPB...$16.99
(ISBN: ...-7)

VOL. 7: BLOCKBUSTER TPB...$12.99
(ISBN: 0-7851-...7)

VOL. 8: NEW MUTANTS TPB...$12.99
(ISBN: ...1-1)

VOL. 9: THE TEMPEST TPB...$10.99
(ISBN: 0-7851-1404-1)

VOL. 10: CRY WOLF TPB...$8.99
(ISBN: 0-7851-1405-X)

VOL. 11: THE MOST DANGEROUS GAME TPB...$12.99
(ISBN: 0-7851-1659-1)

VOL. 12: HARD LESSONS TPB...$12.99
(ISBN: 0-7851-1801-2)

VOL. 13: MAGNETIC NORTH TPB...$12.99
(ISBN: 0-7851-1906-X)

For a comic store near you, call 1-888-comicbook.

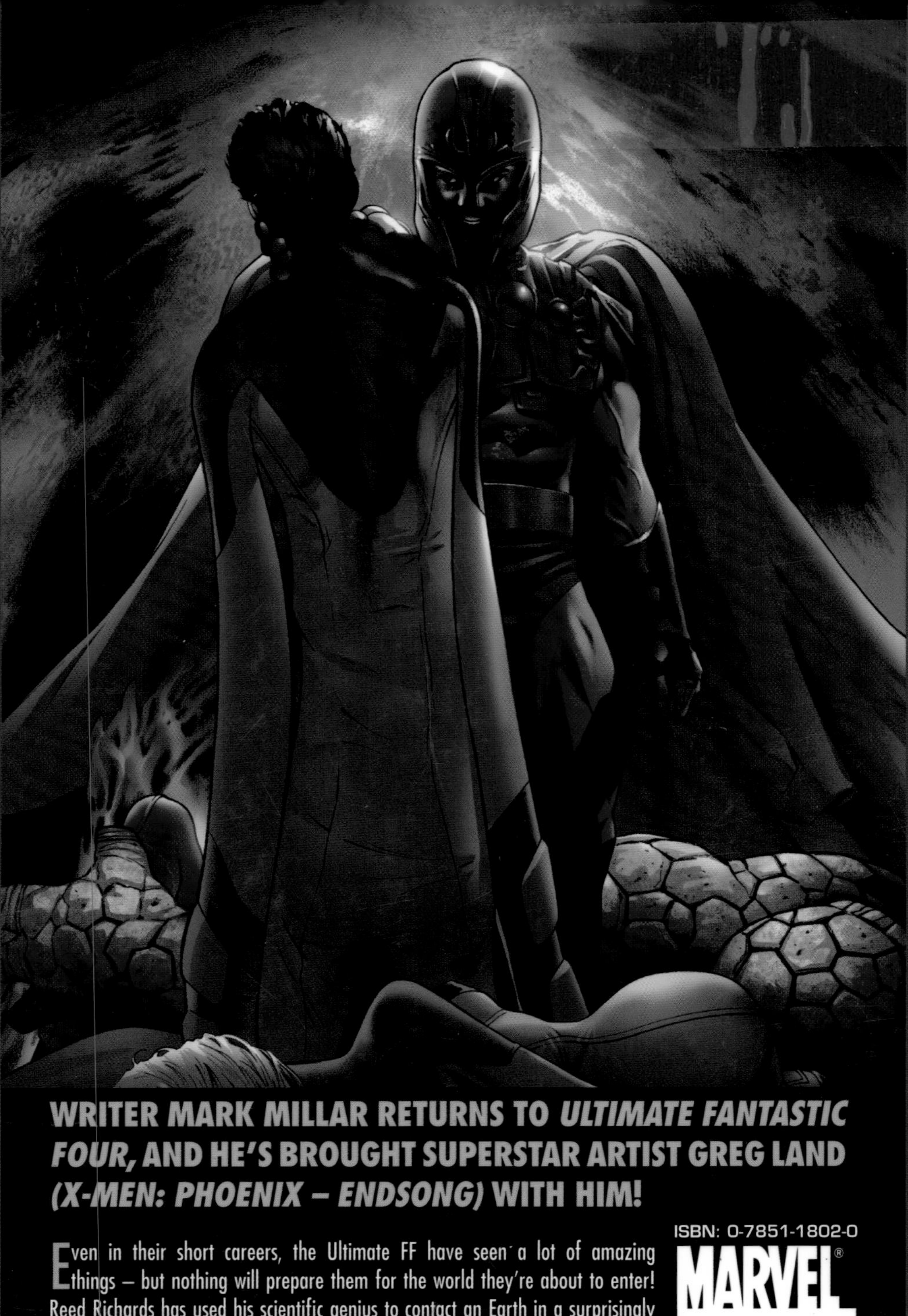

WRITER MARK MILLAR RETURNS TO *ULTIMATE FANTASTIC FOUR*, AND HE'S BROUGHT SUPERSTAR ARTIST GREG LAND *(X-MEN: PHOENIX – ENDSONG)* WITH HIM!

Even in their short careers, the Ultimate FF have seen a lot of amazing things – but nothing will prepare them for the world they're about to enter! Reed Richards has used his scientific genius to contact an Earth in a surprisingly familiar parallel dimension, and he's ready to visit!

Plus: Locked away at the bottom of the ocean for 5,000 years, Namor the Sub-Mariner's Atlantean tomb has been breached; now, he's back to rule a planet. This is a Namor you've never seen before with a vastly different agenda. This is Ultimate Namor! Learn about the ties between Atlantis, the Ultimate Inhumans and the super-races that existed before man ruled the Earth! All this, and the shocking secret of the Storm family is finally revealed!

Collecting *Ultimate Fantastic Four* #21-26.

ISBN: 0-7851-1802-0

MARVEL®

$12.99 US $21.00 CAN

A

CANADIAN ROCKIES

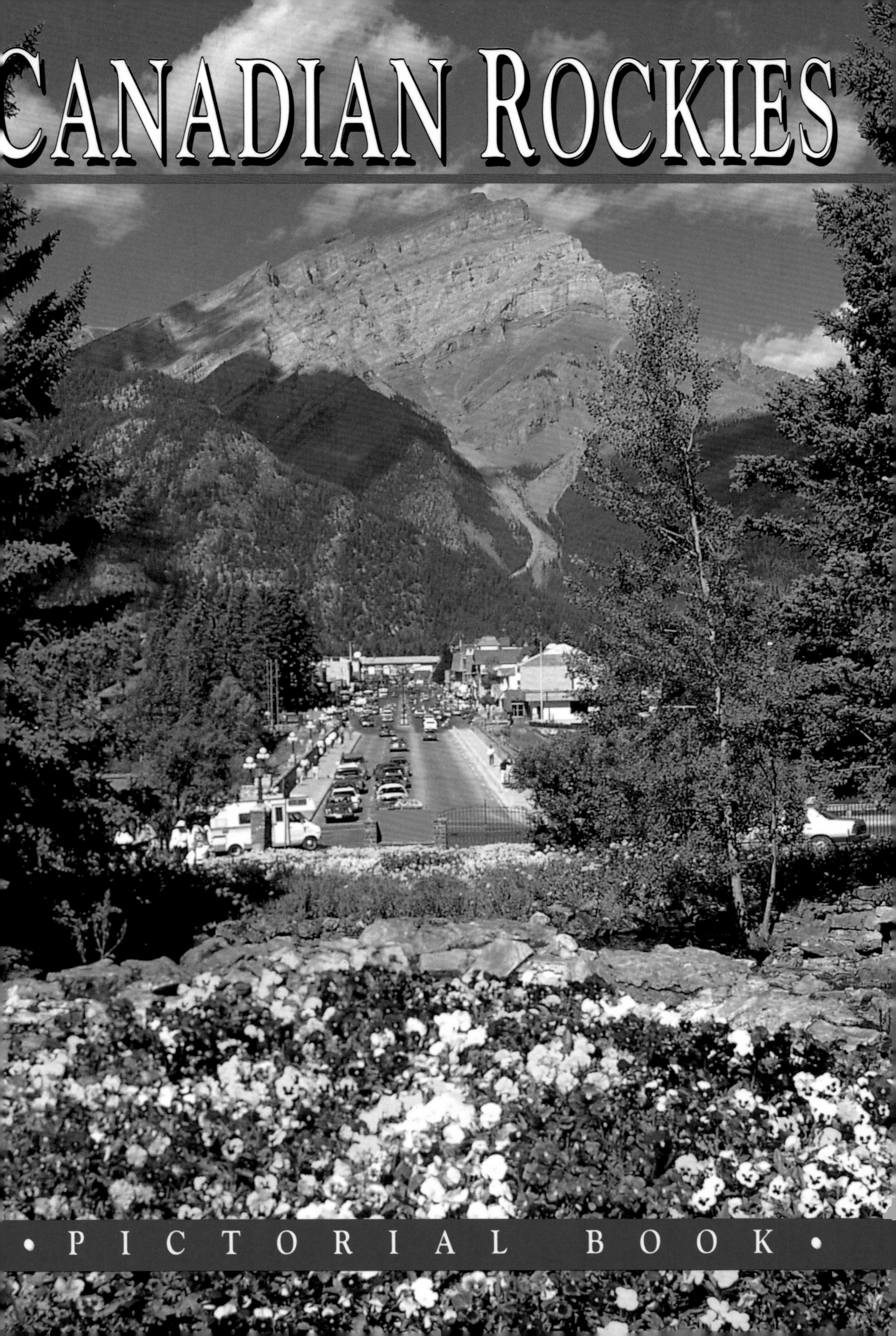

• PICTORIAL BOOK •

PLACE NAMES IN THE CANADIAN ROCKIES

BANFF: Named for the birthplace of George Stephen (1829-1921) who was born in Dufftown, Banffshire (now Grampian), Scotland.

BOW RIVER: This river rises at the Bow Glacier and flows into Bow Lake, through the Rockies, into Calgary and then becomes a part of the South Saskatchewan River system. It gets its name from the Cree *"ma-na-cha-ban"* meaning "bow". Wood, which was used by the Natives to make bows, grew plentifully along the river.

CANMORE: The Gaelic meaning is *ceann mòr* "big head" or "height"; after Malcolm III (a Scottish king). Malcolm III was known as Canmore, the large-headed son of Duncan I. In 1054, he became king after overthrowing Macbeth.

CASCADE MOUNTAIN: This well-known mountain that overlooks the Town of Banff, and gets it name from an Indian translation meaning, "mountain where the water falls."

JASPER: Jasper Hawes was in charge of the North West Company's trading post on Brûlé Lake in 1817. Between 1827 and 1829, Jasper House was rebuilt about 12 miles east of the townsite now known as Jasper. In early 1900, Lewis Swift arrived and became the first resident of Jasper House, whose name had by then been changed to Fithugh. It was changed back to Jasper in 1911.

LAKE LOUISE: The town of Lake Louise has had several names. The first was Holt City which was then changed to Laggan between 1883 - 1914 (this was named after Laggan, Iverness in Scotland by Lord Strathcona). In 1916 it was changed to Lake Louise after Princess Caroline Louise. The lake itself was discovered in 1882 by Tom Wilson who called it Emerald Lake. The original Native name for the lake was "Lake of Little Fishes".

MALIGNE LAKE: Referred to as "Maline" meaning "bad" (in French) by Father de Smet, it was known as this in 1846. In 1875, H.A.F. McLeod explored the lake while doing some CPR surveys and called it Sorefoot Lake. In 1911 it was named "Maligne".

(continued on inside back cover)

The Canadian Rockies Pictorial Book
© 1994, 1999 Altitude Publishing Canada Ltd.

Altitude Publishing
The Canadian Rockies
1500 Railway Avenue
Canmore, Alberta Canada T1W 1P6

10 9

ISBN 1-55153-145-3

Text and photo editing: Steven Flagler
Design and page layout: Stephen Hutchings

Photo credits:
Doug Leighton: 4
Carole Harmon: Front cover, 1, 7A, 9A, 9D, 13B, 15A, 23A, 26A, 29A, 29B, 30B, 31B, 32B
Don Harmon: 5A, 5B, 7B, 9B, 12, 15B, 16/17, 18, 19B, 20, 21B, 22A, 22B, 24/25, 27A, 27B, 31A, 32A
Stephen Hutchings: 6, 8A, 8B, 9C, 10, 11A, 11B, 13A, 14, 19A, 23B, 26B, 28, 30A, Back cover A, Back cover B
Joe Scanlon: 3

Made in Western Canada
Printed and bound by Friesen Printers in Altona, Manitoba using Canadian made paper and vegetable inks.

Altitude GreenTree Program
Altitude will plant in Western Canada twice as many trees as were used in the manufacturing of this book.